A Witch's Love at the End of the World

I

KUJIRA

contents

A Witch's Love at the End of the World

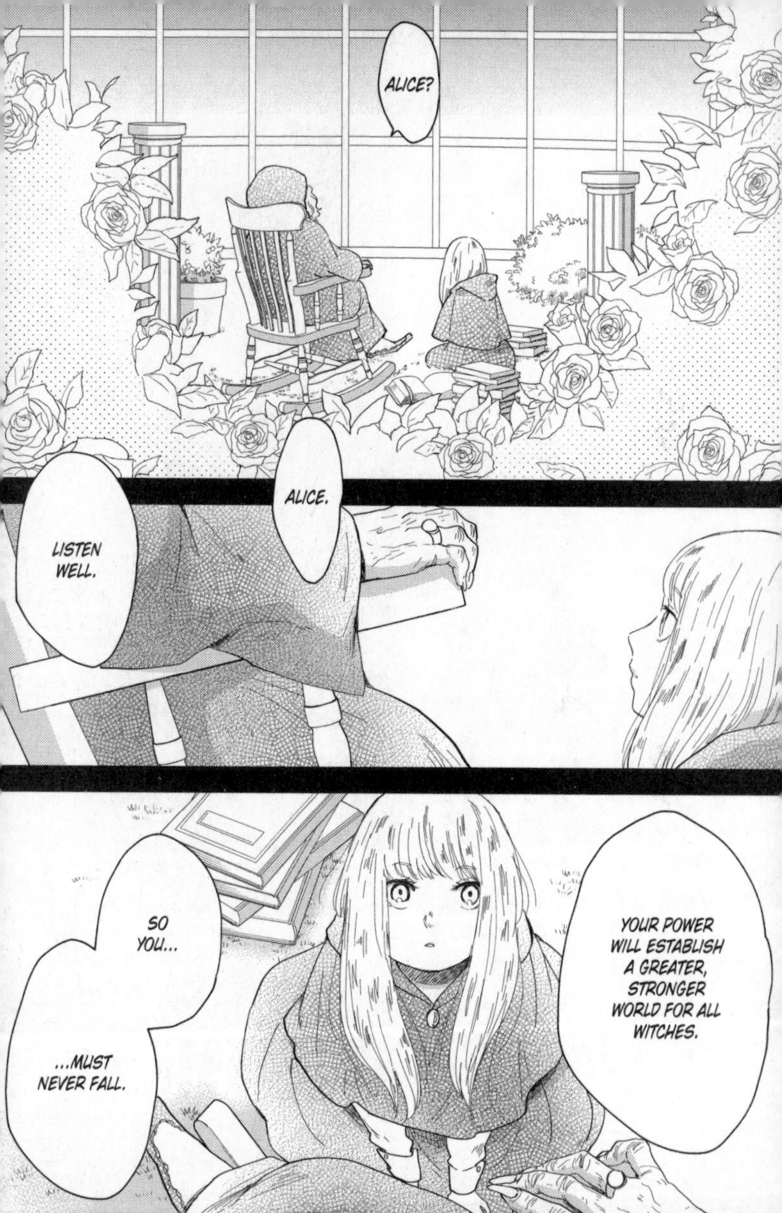
ALICE?
ALICE.
LISTEN WELL.
YOUR POWER WILL ESTABLISH A GREATER, STRONGER WORLD FOR ALL WITCHES.
SO YOU...
...MUST NEVER FALL.

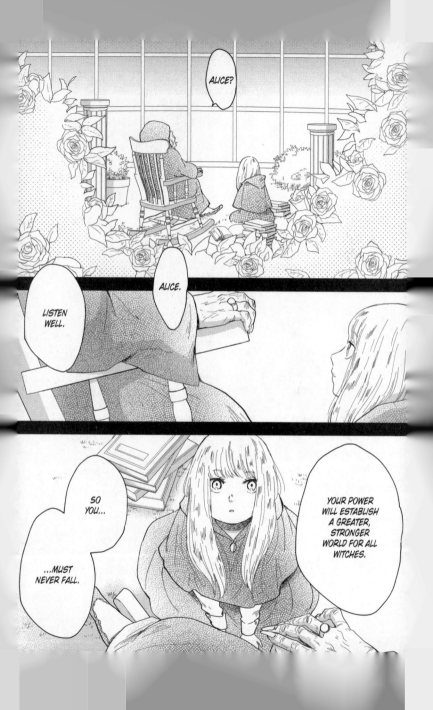

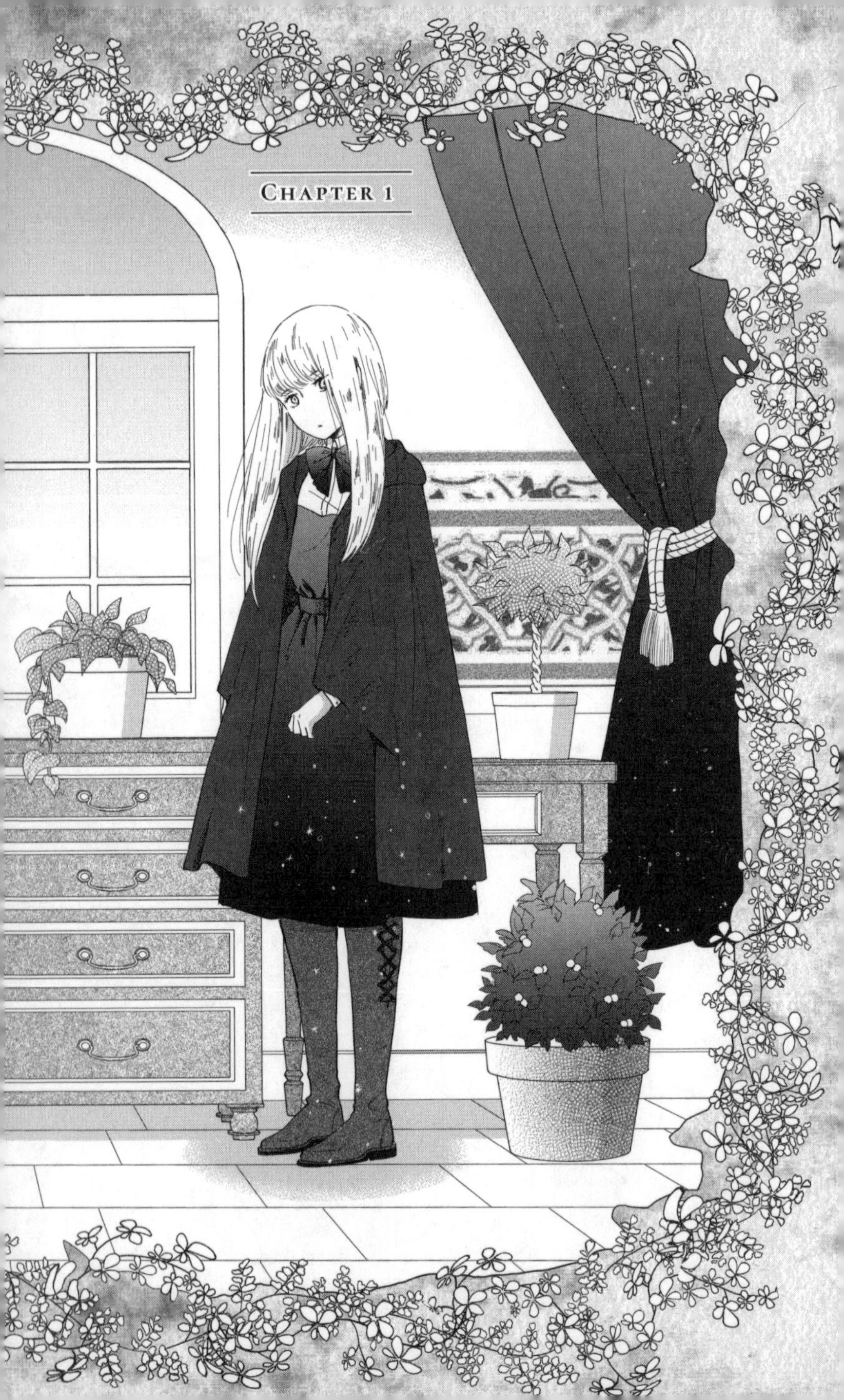
CHAPTER 1

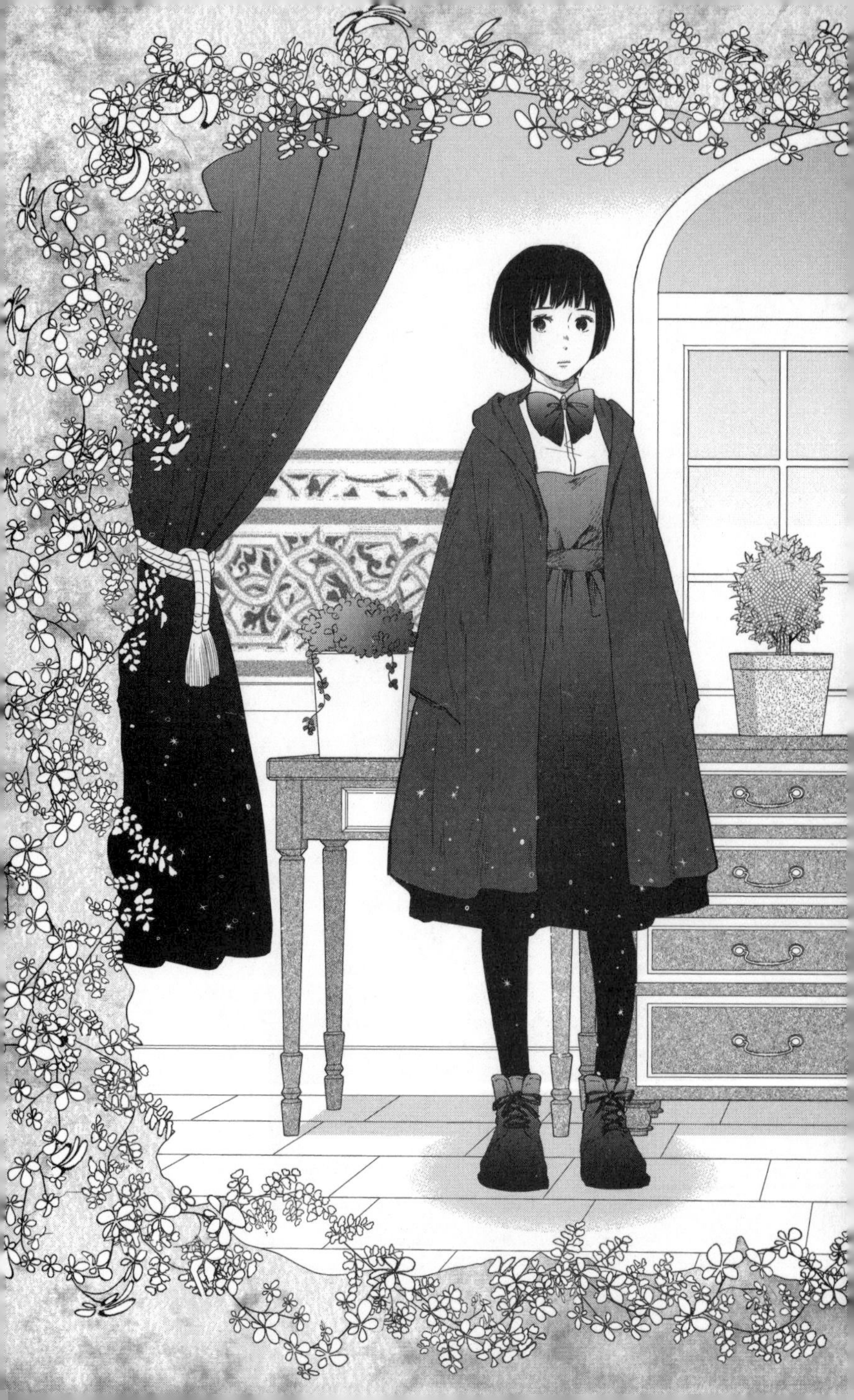

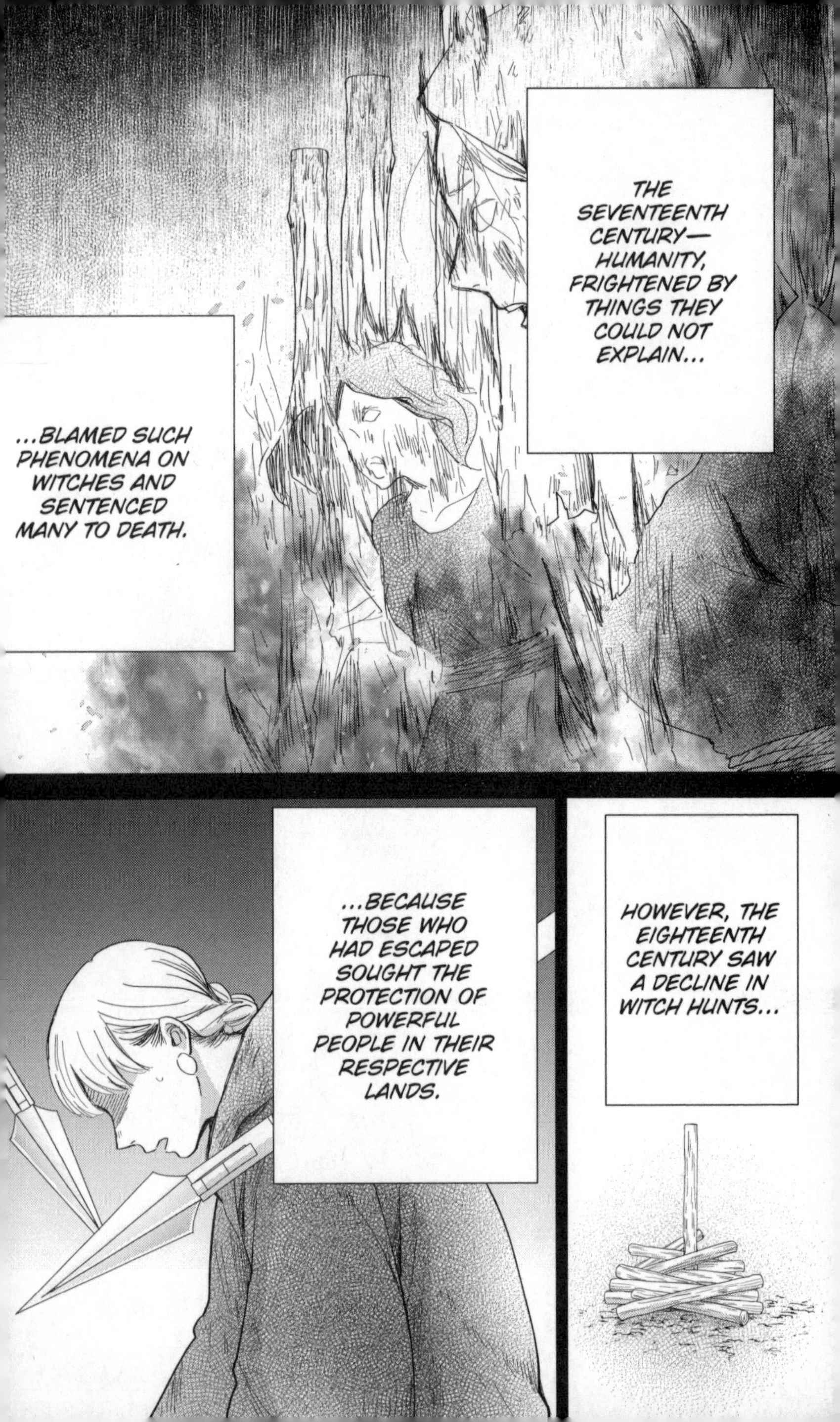
THE SEVENTEENTH CENTURY— HUMANITY, FRIGHTENED BY THINGS THEY COULD NOT EXPLAIN...
...BLAMED SUCH PHENOMENA ON WITCHES AND SENTENCED MANY TO DEATH.
HOWEVER, THE EIGHTEENTH CENTURY SAW A DECLINE IN WITCH HUNTS...
...BECAUSE THOSE WHO HAD ESCAPED SOUGHT THE PROTECTION OF POWERFUL PEOPLE IN THEIR RESPECTIVE LANDS.

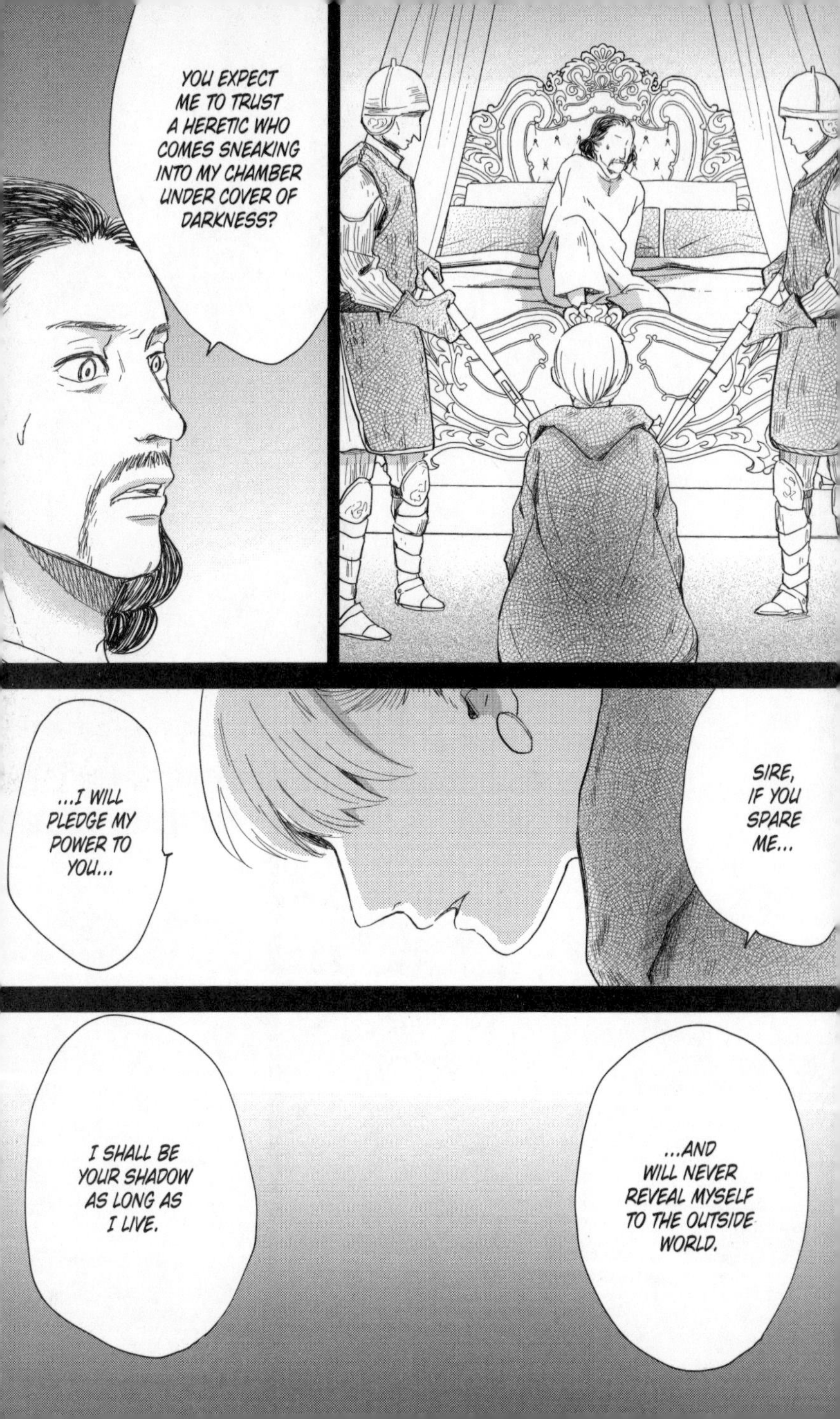
YOU EXPECT ME TO TRUST A HERETIC WHO COMES SNEAKING INTO MY CHAMBER UNDER COVER OF DARKNESS?
SIRE, IF YOU SPARE ME...
...I WILL PLEDGE MY POWER TO YOU...
...AND WILL NEVER REVEAL MYSELF TO THE OUTSIDE WORLD.
I SHALL BE YOUR SHADOW AS LONG AS I LIVE.

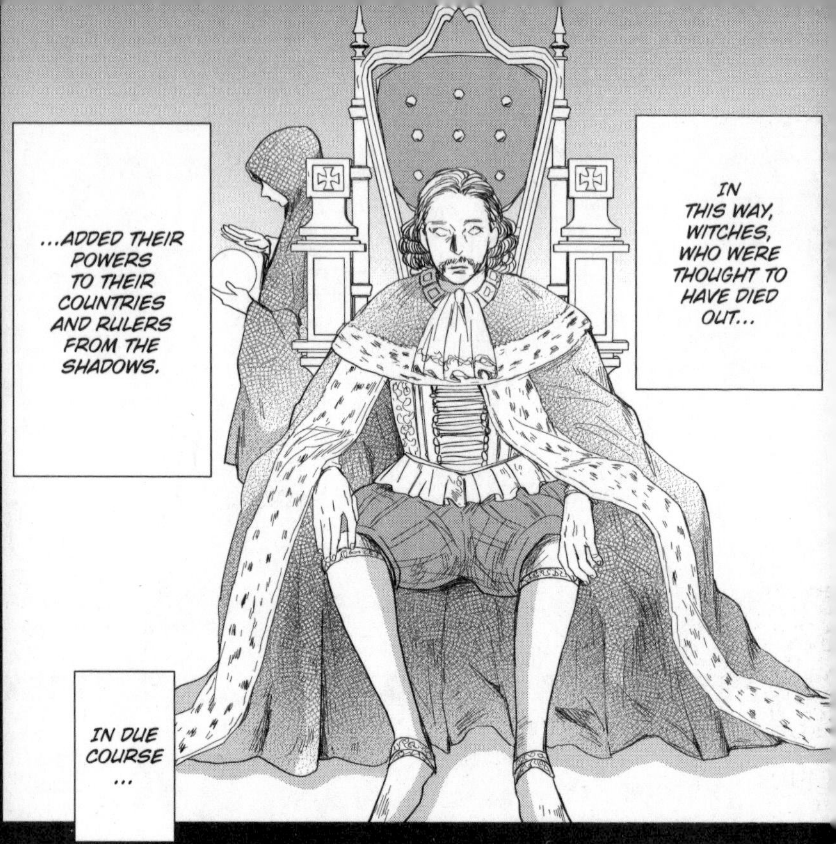
IN THIS WAY, WITCHES, WHO WERE THOUGHT TO HAVE DIED OUT...
...ADDED THEIR POWERS TO THEIR COUNTRIES AND RULERS FROM THE SHADOWS.
IN DUE COURSE...

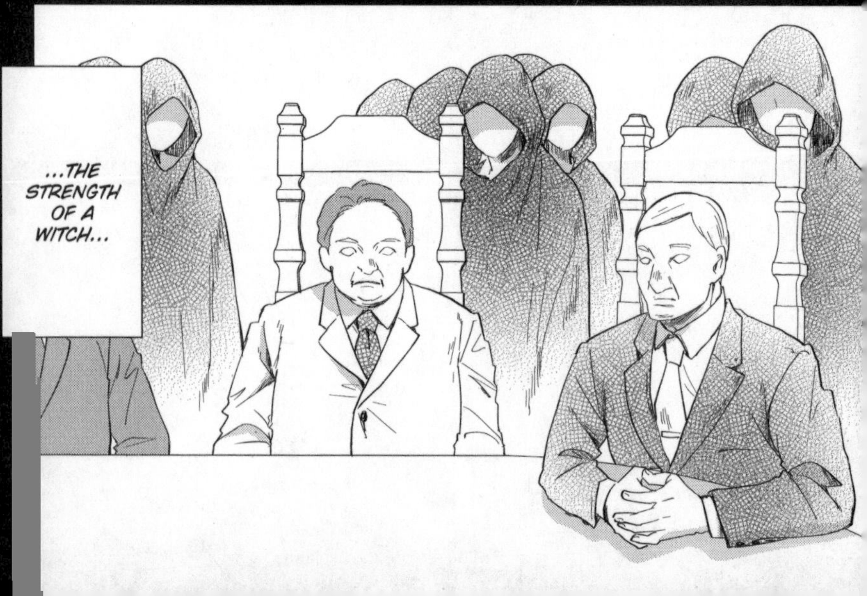
...THE STRENGTH OF A WITCH...

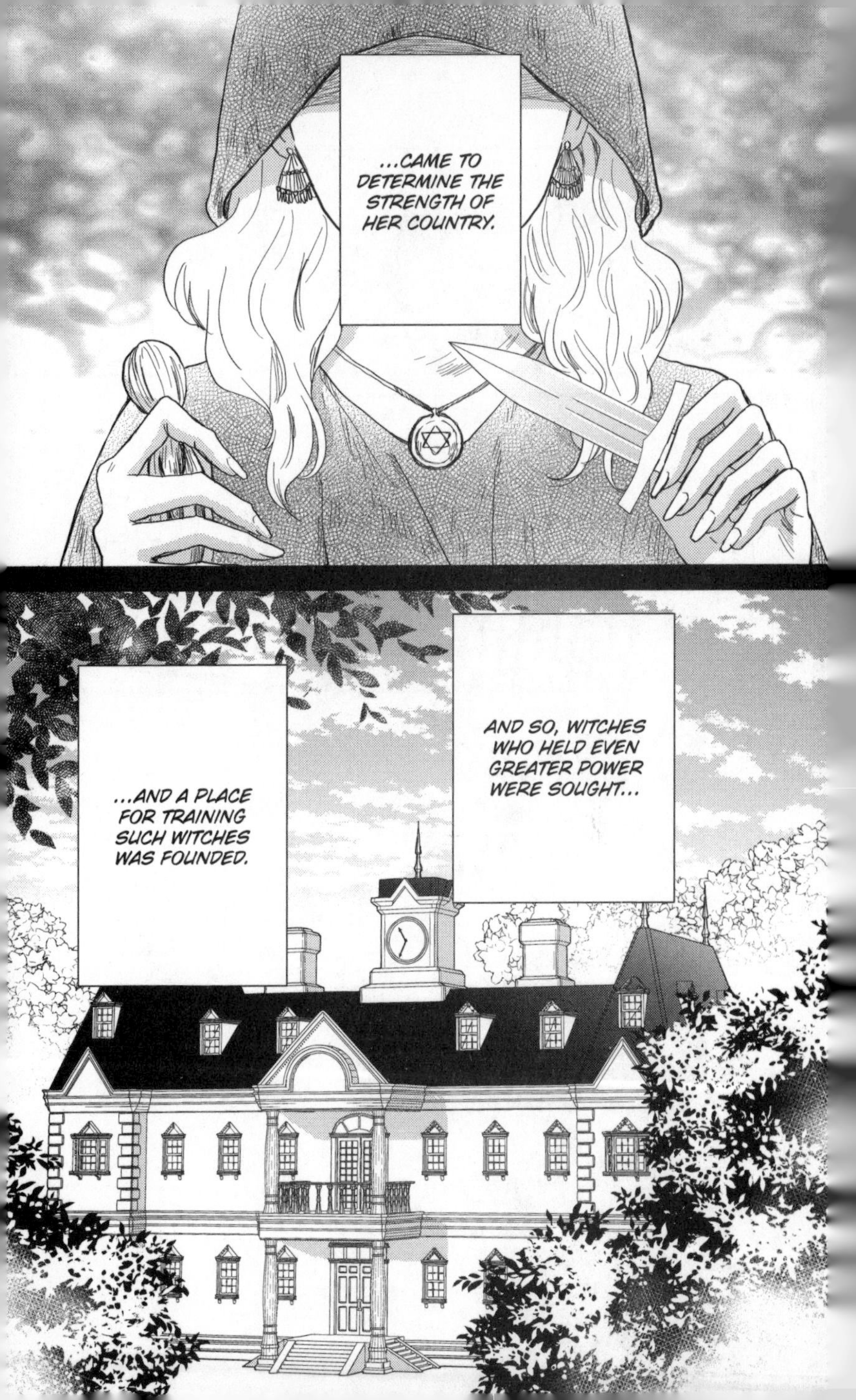
...CAME TO DETERMINE THE STRENGTH OF HER COUNTRY.
AND SO, WITCHES WHO HELD EVEN GREATER POWER WERE SOUGHT...
...AND A PLACE FOR TRAINING SUCH WITCHES WAS FOUNDED.

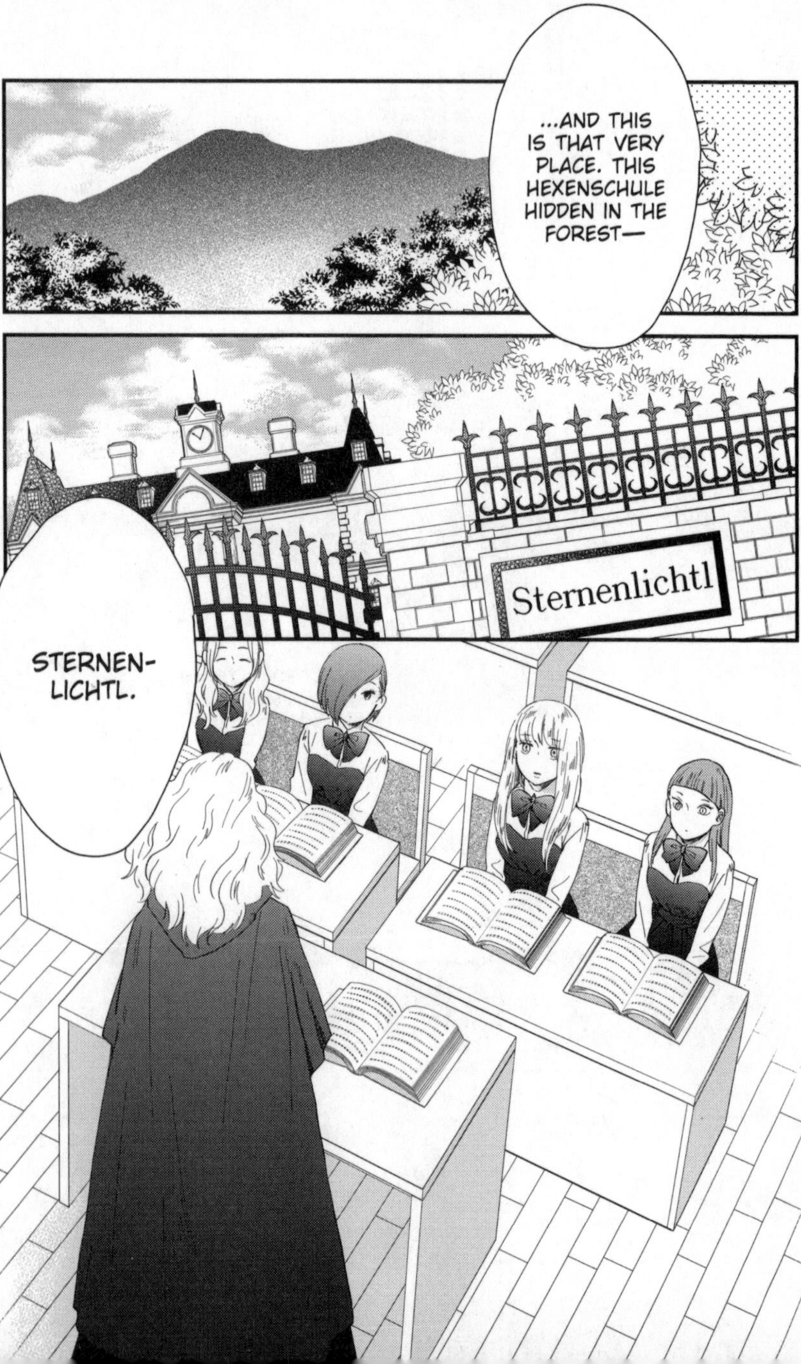
...AND THIS IS THAT VERY PLACE. THIS HEXENSCHULE HIDDEN IN THE FOREST—
Sternenlichtl
STERNEN-LICHTL.

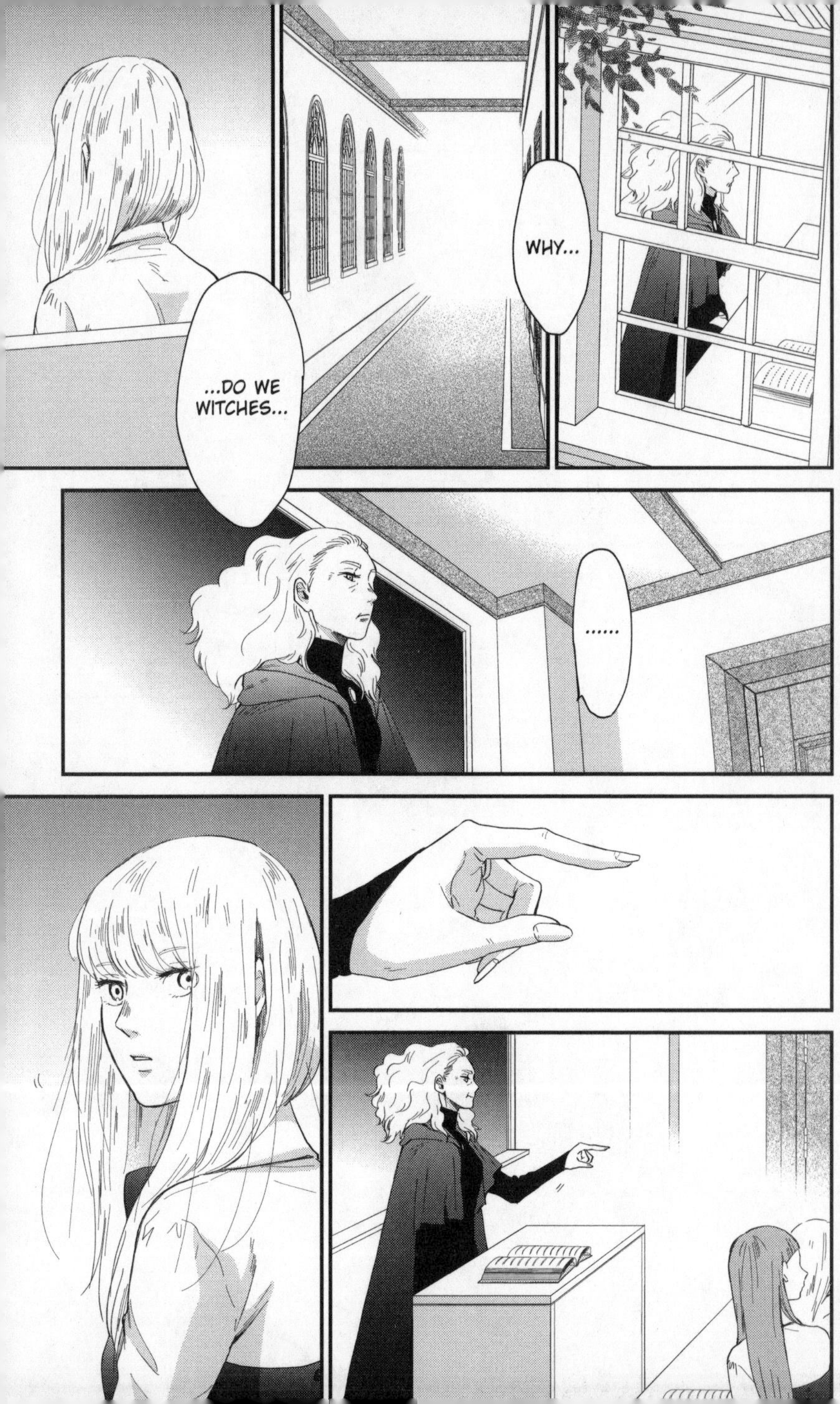
WHY...
...DO WE WITCHES...
......

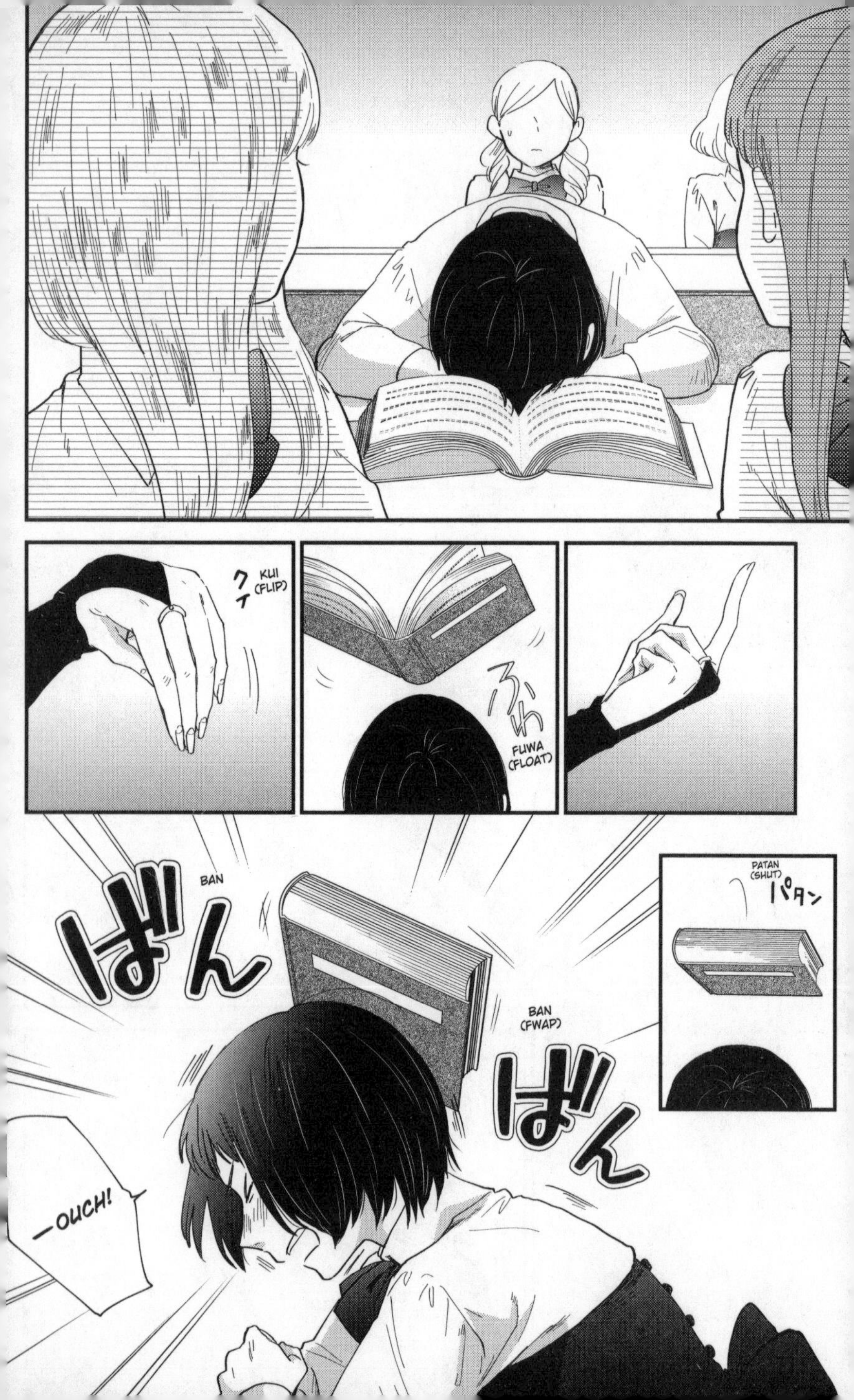
ふわ
FUWA (FLOAT)
クイ
KUI (FLIP)
パタン
PATAN (SHUT)
ばん
BAN
ばん
BAN (FWAP)
—OUCH!

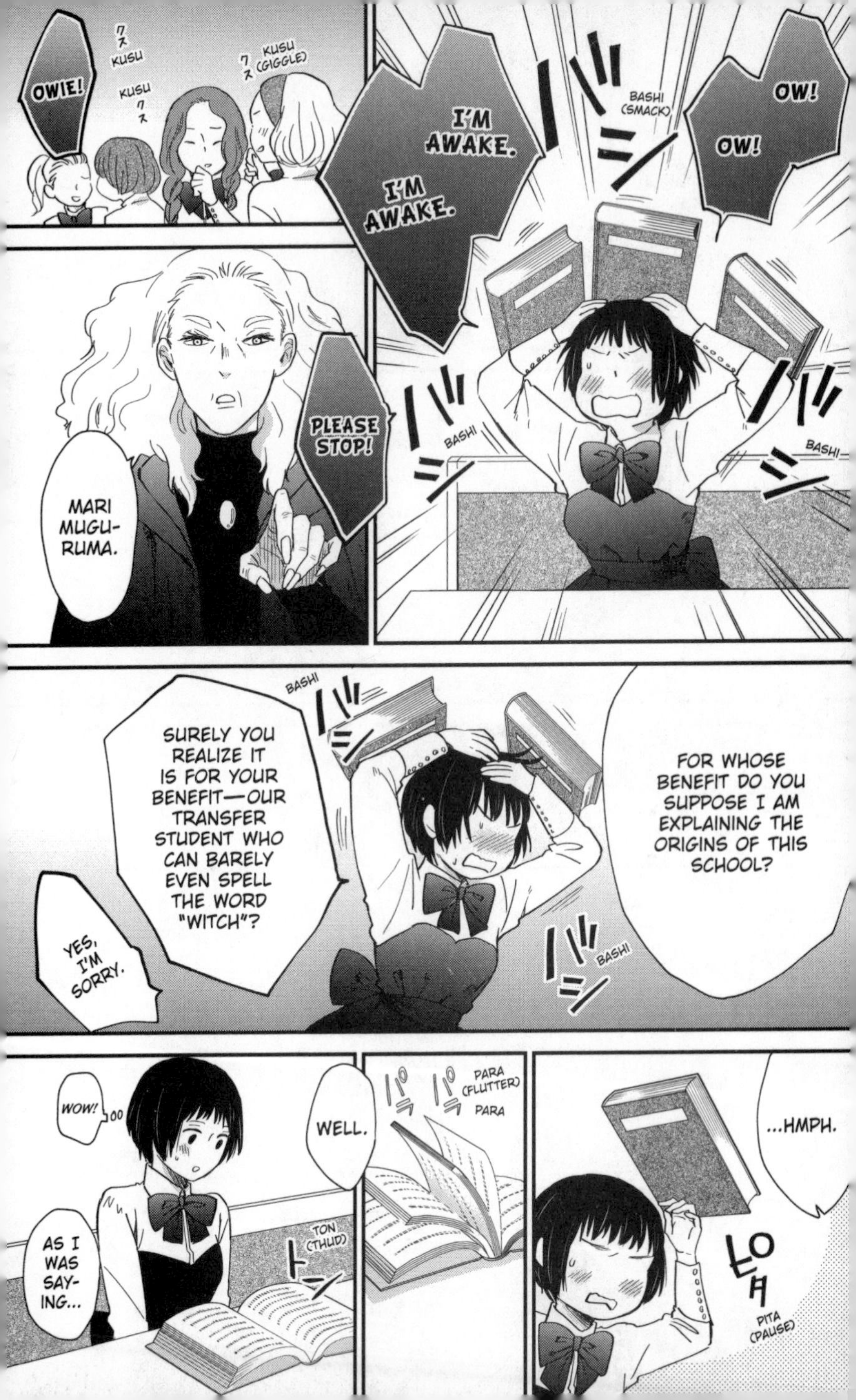
OW!
OW!
バシ
BASHI (SMACK)
I'M AWAKE.
I'M AWAKE.
バシ
BASHI
バシ
BASHI
PLEASE STOP!
クス
KUSU (GIGGLE)
クス
KUSU
クス
KUSU
OWIE!
MARI MUGU-RUMA.
FOR WHOSE BENEFIT DO YOU SUPPOSE I AM EXPLAINING THE ORIGINS OF THIS SCHOOL?
バシ
BASHI
バシ
BASHI
SURELY YOU REALIZE IT IS FOR YOUR BENEFIT—OUR TRANSFER STUDENT WHO CAN BARELY EVEN SPELL THE WORD "WITCH"?
YES, I'M SORRY.
...HMPH.
ピタ
PITA (PAUSE)
パラ
PARA (FLUTTER)
パラ
PARA
WELL.
WOW!
TON (THUD)
AS I WAS SAY-ING...

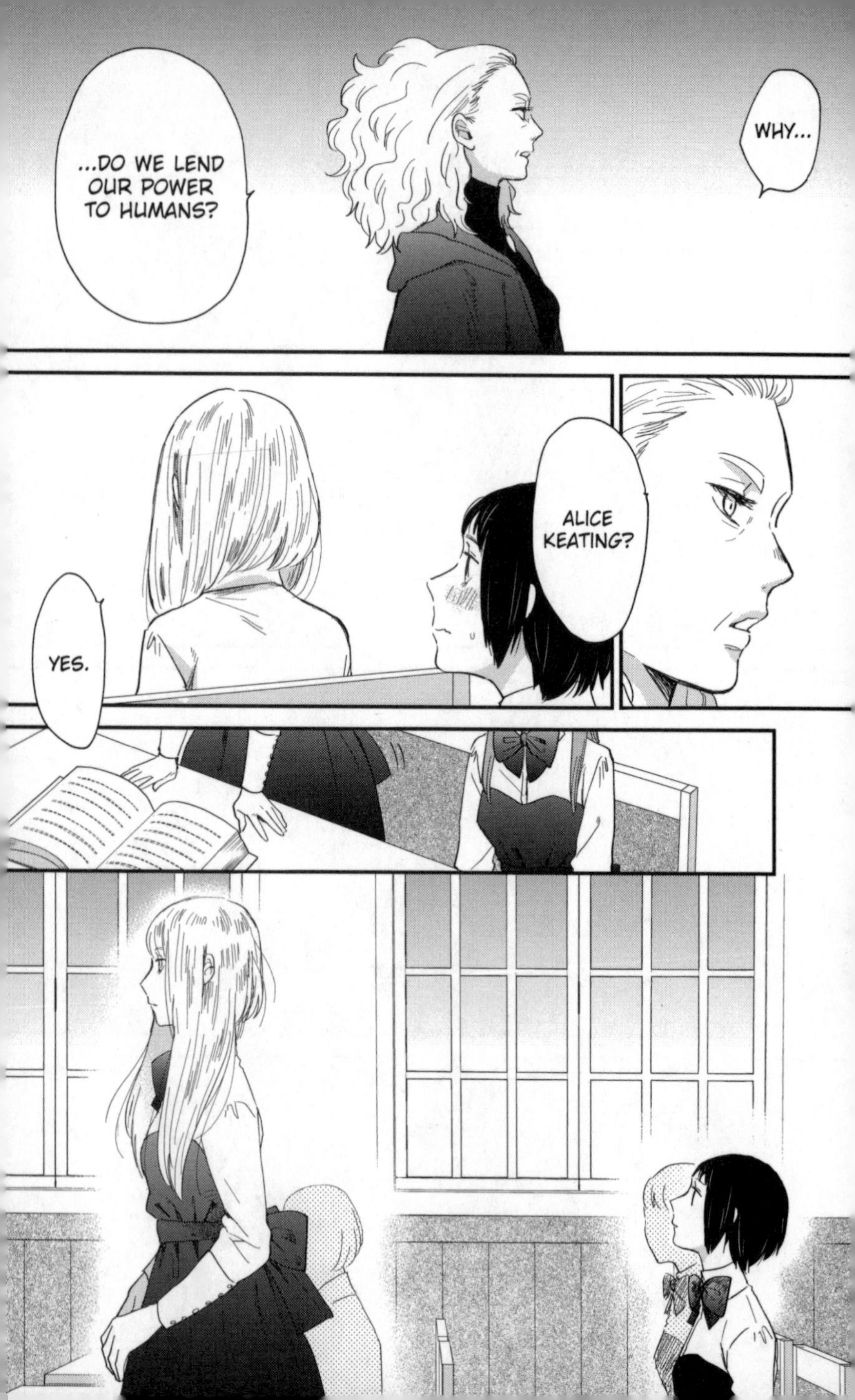
WHY...
...DO WE LEND OUR POWER TO HUMANS?
ALICE KEATING?
YES.

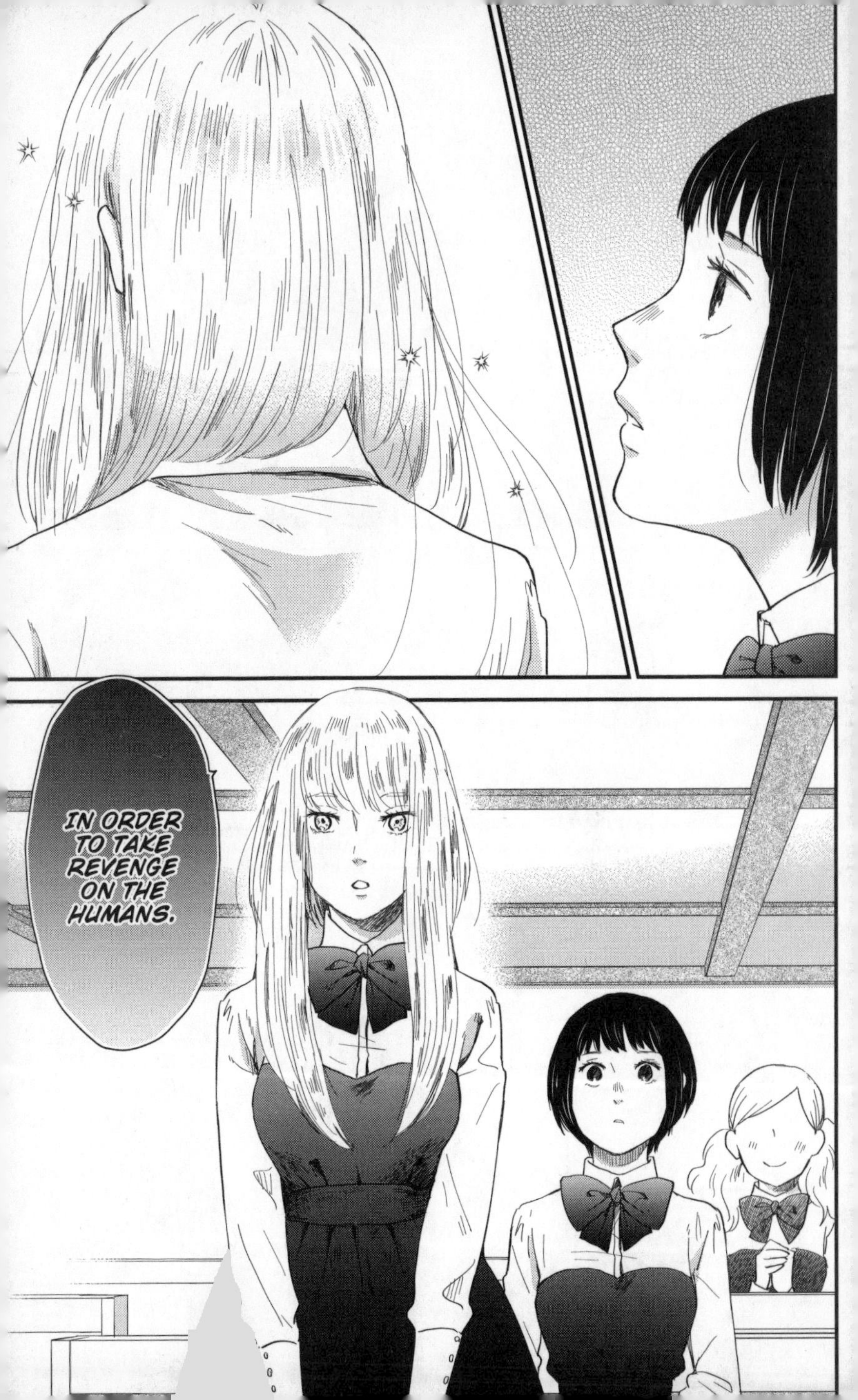
IN ORDER TO TAKE REVENGE ON THE HUMANS.

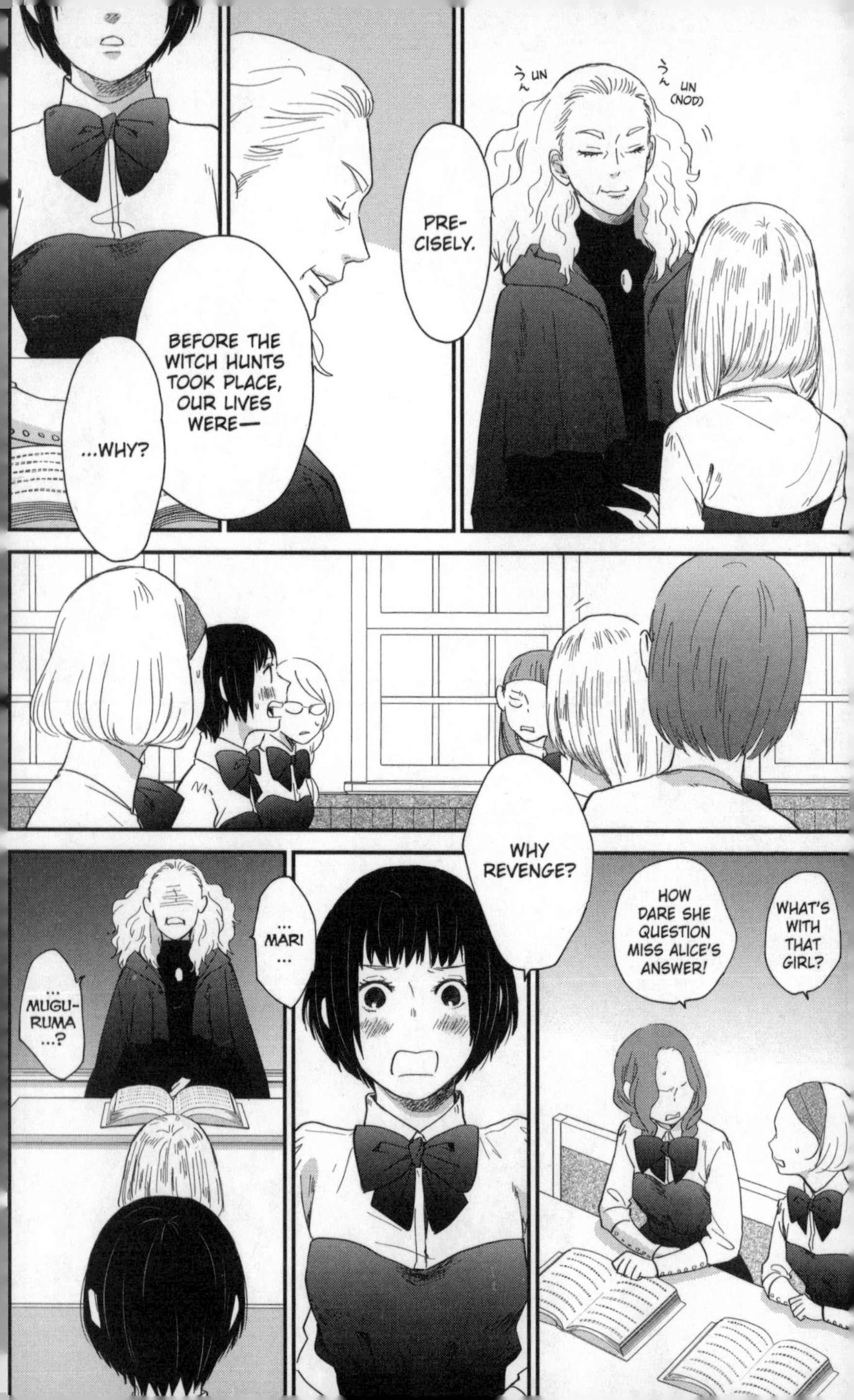
うん UN
うん UN (NOD)
PRE-CISELY.
BEFORE THE WITCH HUNTS TOOK PLACE, OUR LIVES WERE—
...WHY?
WHY REVENGE?
WHAT'S WITH THAT GIRL?
HOW DARE SHE QUESTION MISS ALICE'S ANSWER!
... MARI ...
... MUGURUMA ...?

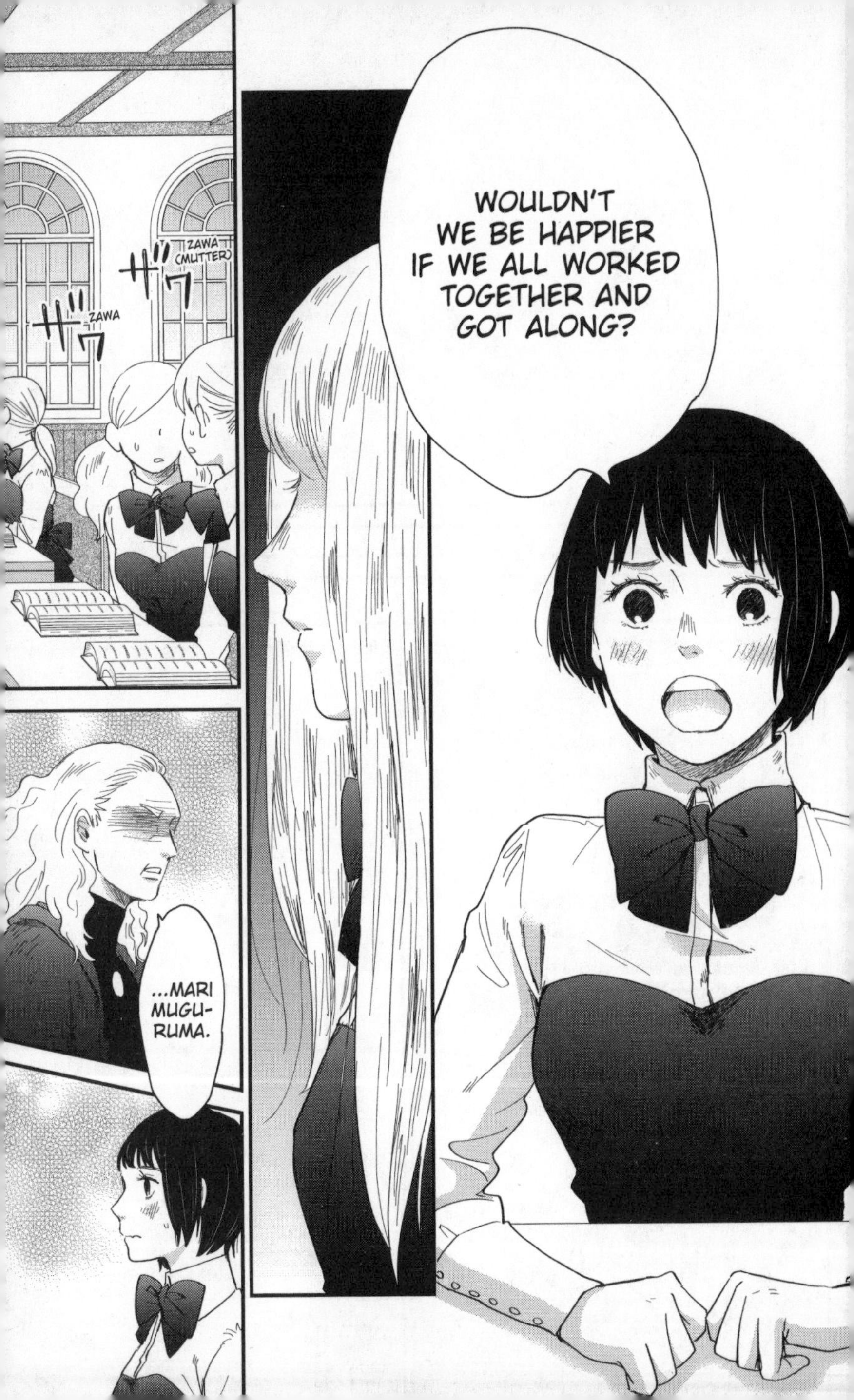
WOULDN'T WE BE HAPPIER IF WE ALL WORKED TOGETHER AND GOT ALONG?
ザワ ZAWA (MUTTER)
ザワ ZAWA
...MARI MUGURUMA.

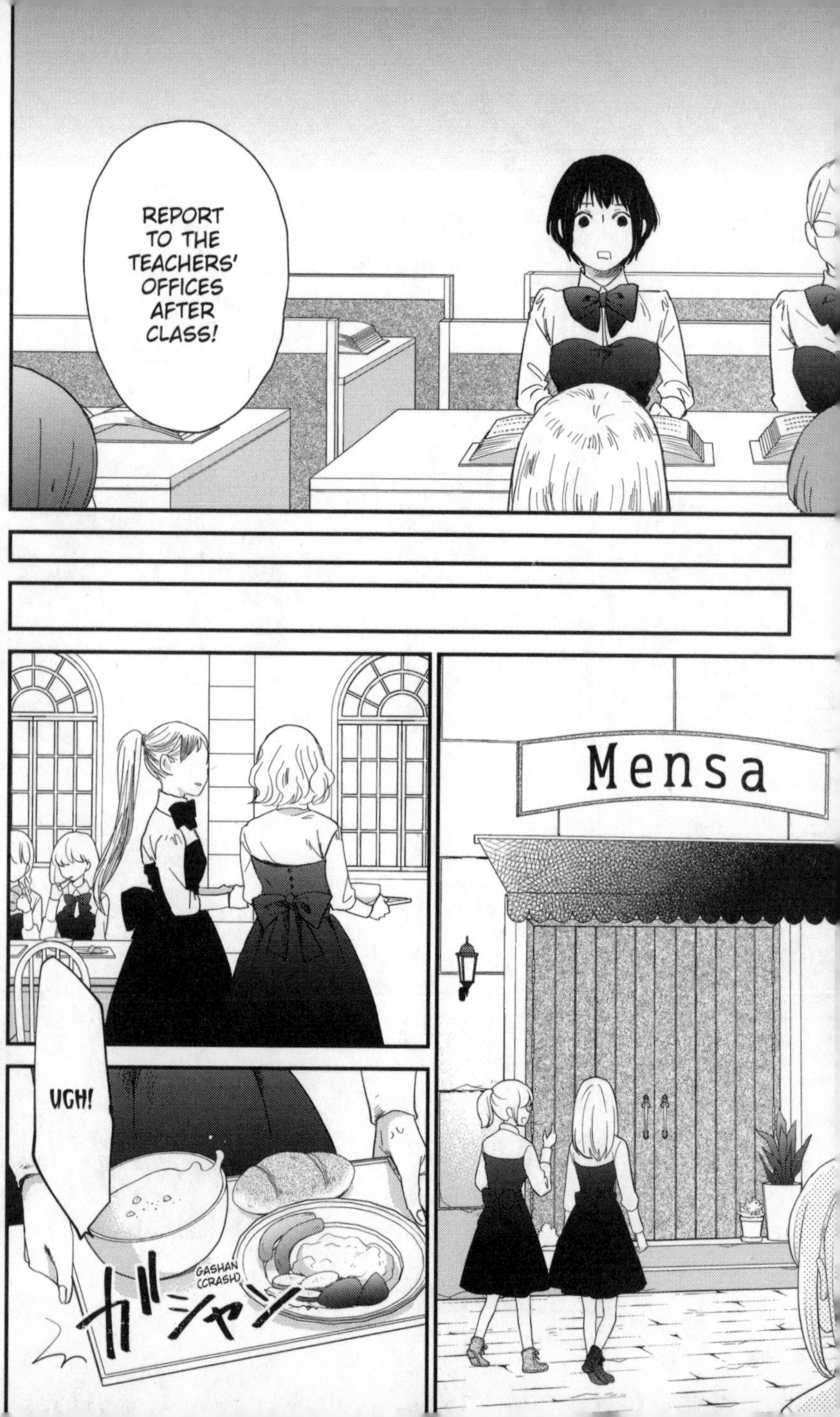
REPORT TO THE TEACHERS' OFFICES AFTER CLASS!
Mensa
UGH!
GASHAN (CRASH)
ガシャン

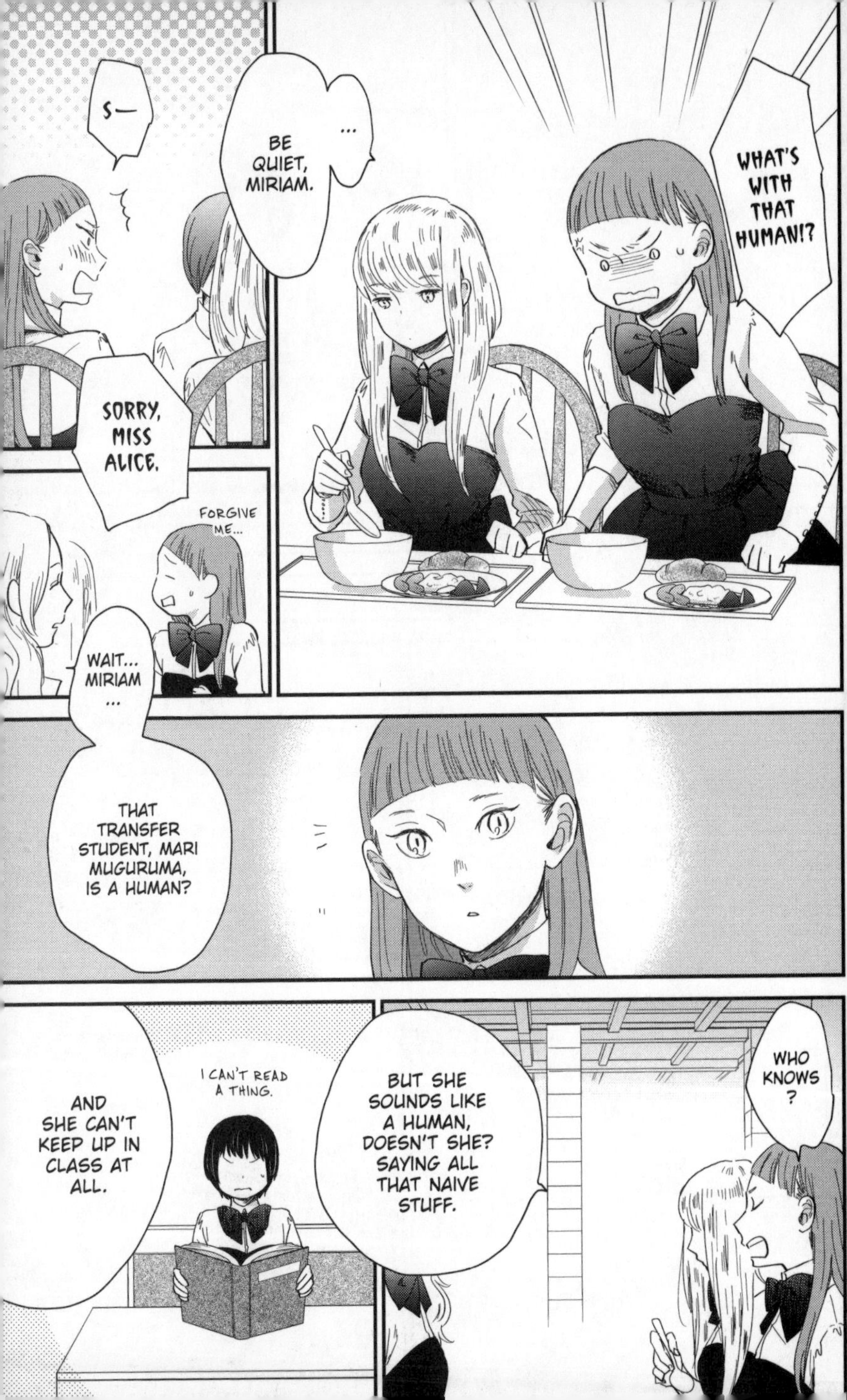
WHAT'S WITH THAT HUMAN!?
...
BE QUIET, MIRIAM.
S—
SORRY, MISS ALICE.
FORGIVE ME...
WAIT... MIRIAM ...
THAT TRANSFER STUDENT, MARI MUGURUMA, IS A HUMAN?
WHO KNOWS?
BUT SHE SOUNDS LIKE A HUMAN, DOESN'T SHE? SAYING ALL THAT NAIVE STUFF.
I CAN'T READ A THING.
AND SHE CAN'T KEEP UP IN CLASS AT ALL.

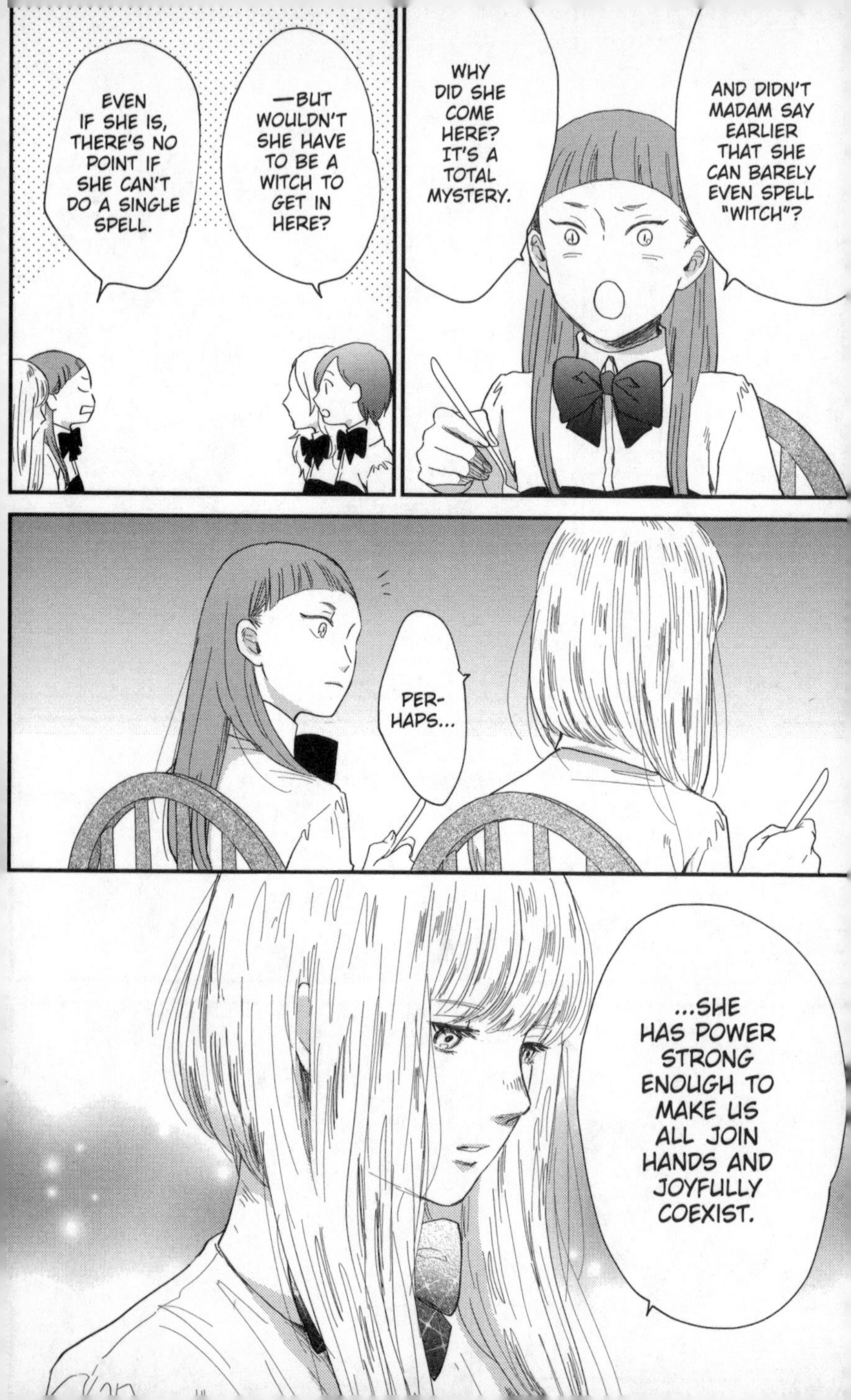
AND DIDN'T MADAM SAY EARLIER THAT SHE CAN BARELY EVEN SPELL "WITCH"?
WHY DID SHE COME HERE? IT'S A TOTAL MYSTERY.
—BUT WOULDN'T SHE HAVE TO BE A WITCH TO GET IN HERE?
EVEN IF SHE IS, THERE'S NO POINT IF SHE CAN'T DO A SINGLE SPELL.
PER-HAPS...
...SHE HAS POWER STRONG ENOUGH TO MAKE US ALL JOIN HANDS AND JOYFULLY COEXIST.

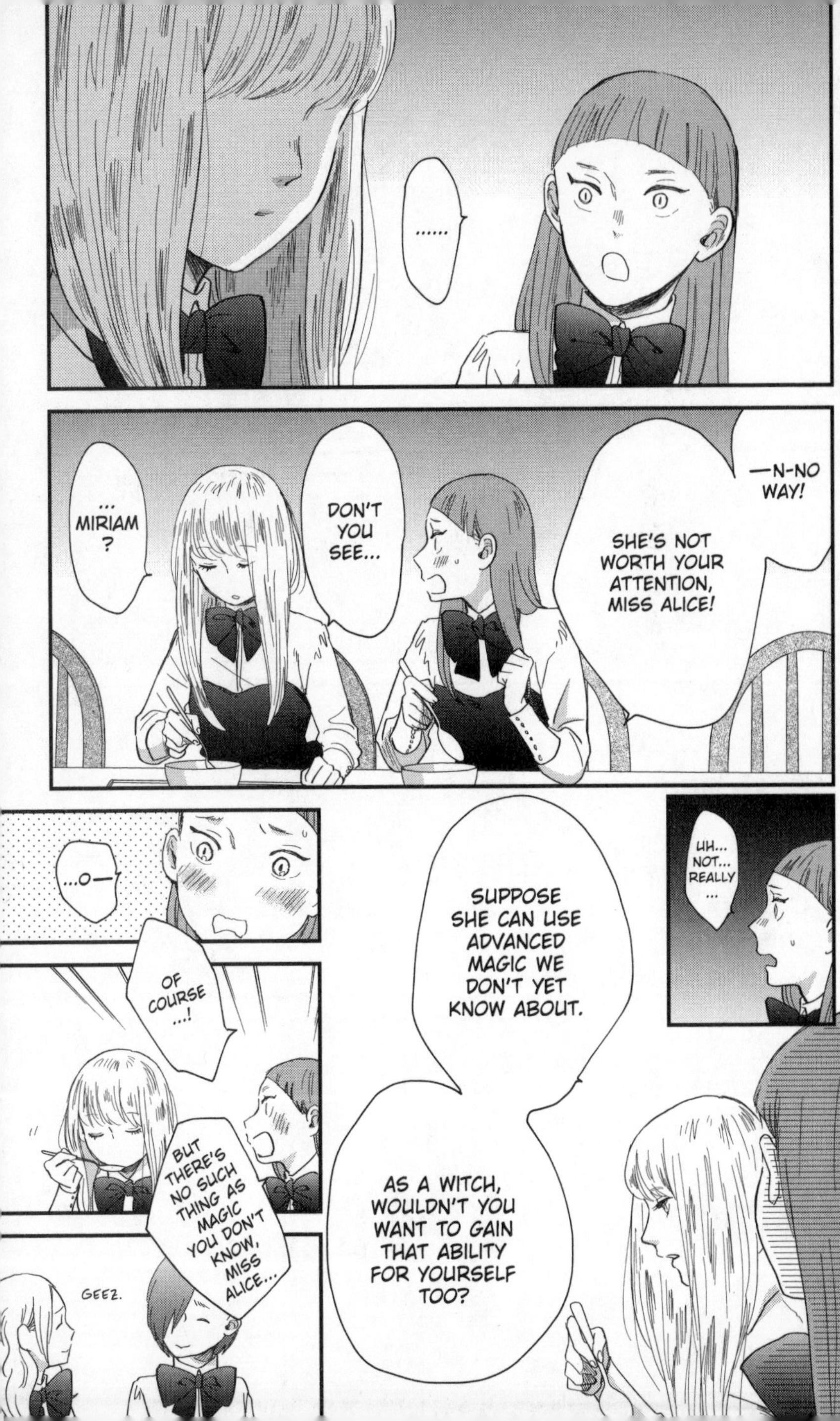
......
—N-NO WAY!
SHE'S NOT WORTH YOUR ATTENTION, MISS ALICE!
DON'T YOU SEE...
...MIRIAM?
UH... NOT... REALLY...
SUPPOSE SHE CAN USE ADVANCED MAGIC WE DON'T YET KNOW ABOUT.
AS A WITCH, WOULDN'T YOU WANT TO GAIN THAT ABILITY FOR YOURSELF TOO?
...O—
OF COURSE...!
BUT THERE'S NO SUCH THING AS MAGIC YOU DON'T KNOW, MISS ALICE...
GEEZ.

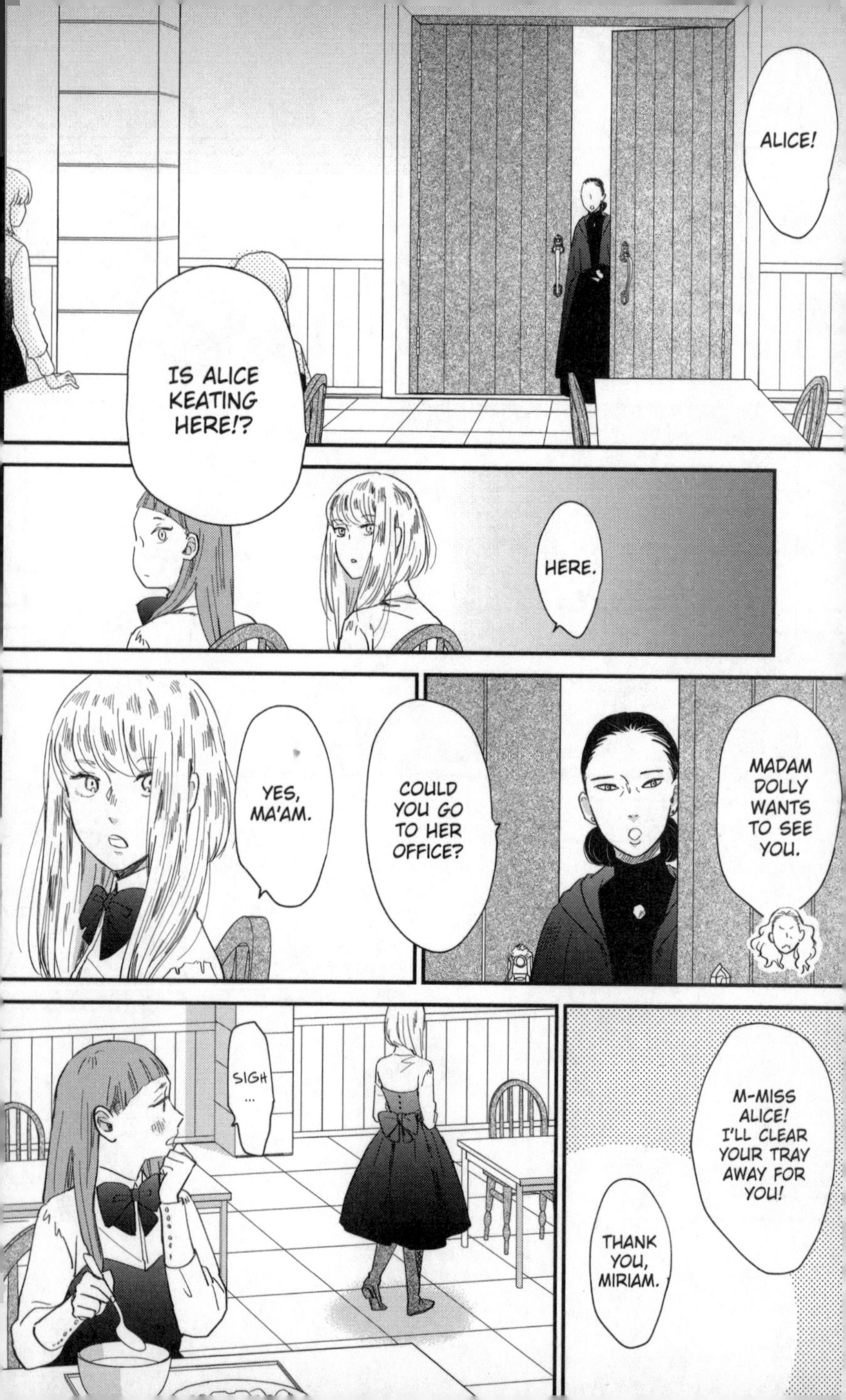
ALICE!
IS ALICE KEATING HERE!?
HERE.
MADAM DOLLY WANTS TO SEE YOU.
COULD YOU GO TO HER OFFICE?
YES, MA'AM.
M-MISS ALICE! I'LL CLEAR YOUR TRAY AWAY FOR YOU!
THANK YOU, MIRIAM.
SIGH ...

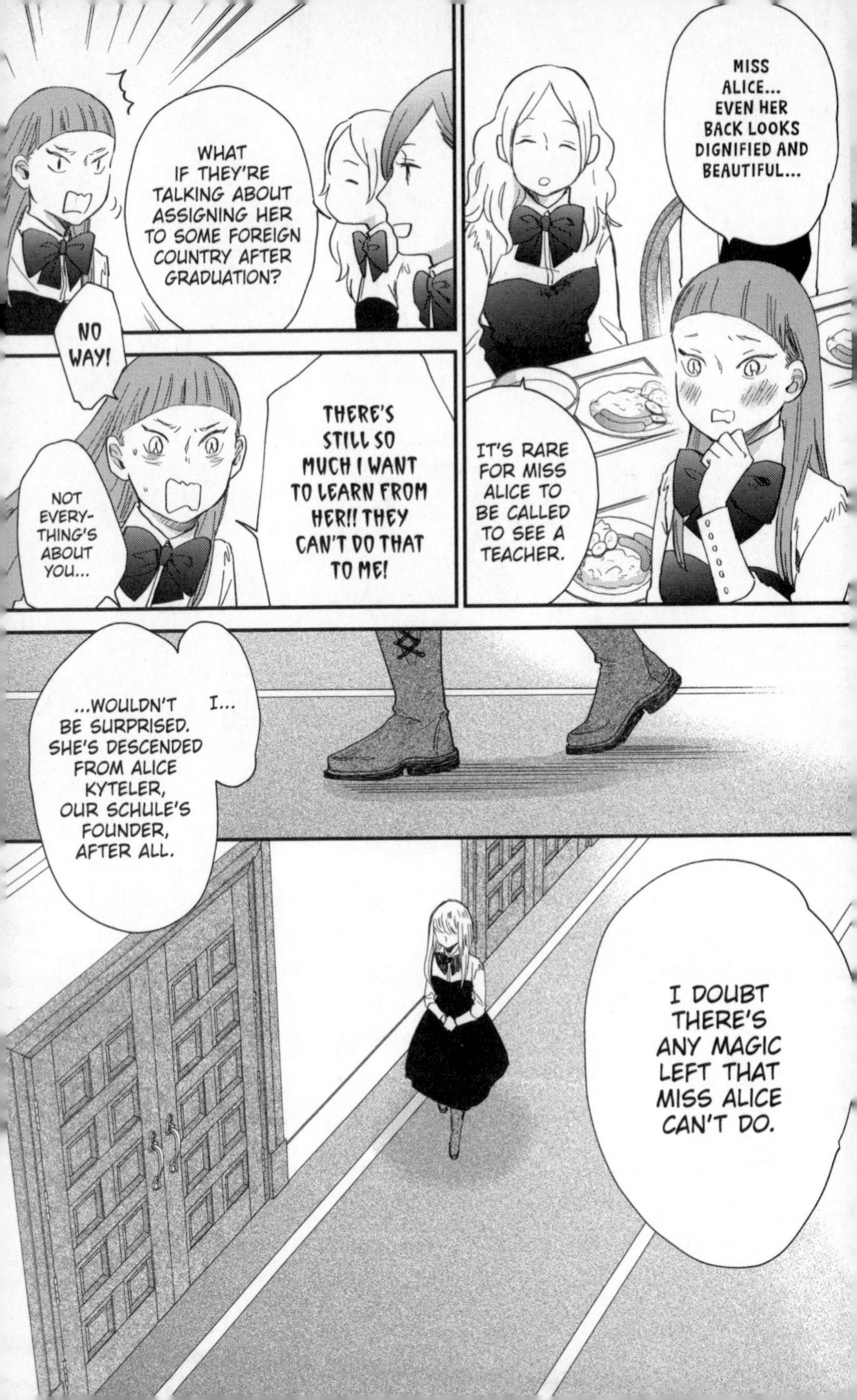
MISS ALICE... EVEN HER BACK LOOKS DIGNIFIED AND BEAUTIFUL...
IT'S RARE FOR MISS ALICE TO BE CALLED TO SEE A TEACHER.
WHAT IF THEY'RE TALKING ABOUT ASSIGNING HER TO SOME FOREIGN COUNTRY AFTER GRADUATION?
NO WAY!
THERE'S STILL SO MUCH I WANT TO LEARN FROM HER!! THEY CAN'T DO THAT TO ME!
NOT EVERY-THING'S ABOUT YOU...
I...
...WOULDN'T BE SURPRISED. SHE'S DESCENDED FROM ALICE KYTELER, OUR SCHULE'S FOUNDER, AFTER ALL.
I DOUBT THERE'S ANY MAGIC LEFT THAT MISS ALICE CAN'T DO.

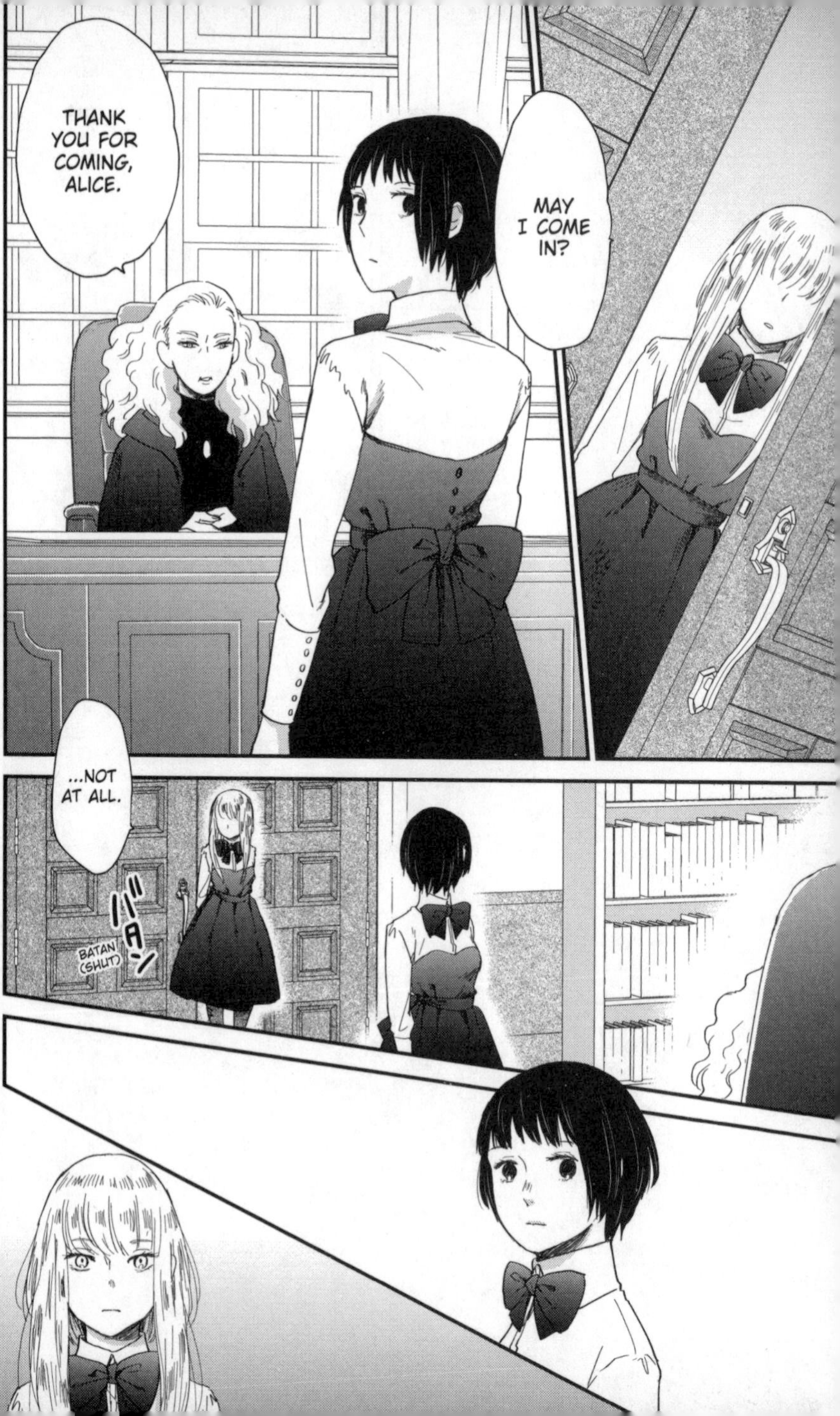
MAY I COME IN?
THANK YOU FOR COMING, ALICE.
...NOT AT ALL.
BATAN (SHUT)

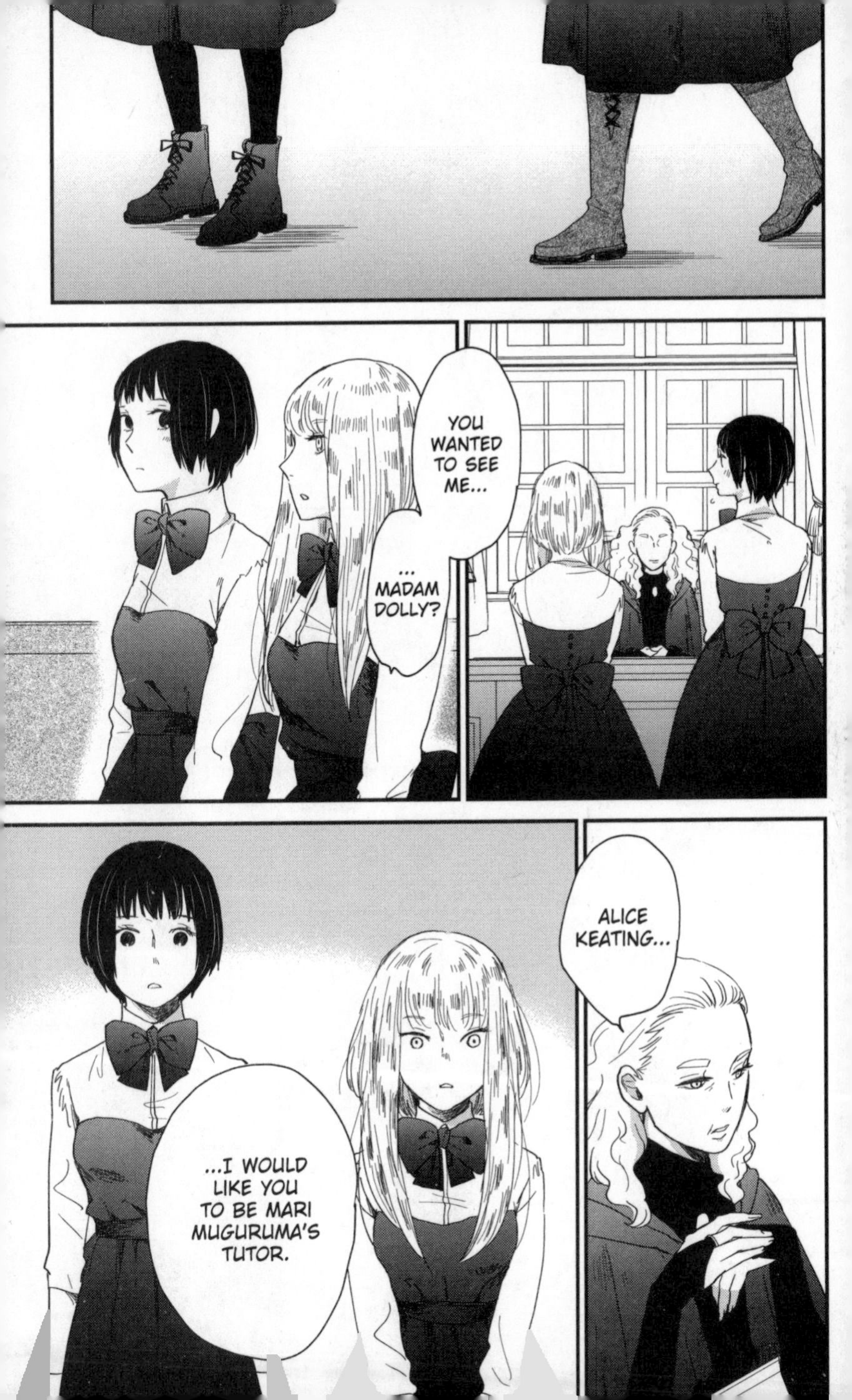
YOU WANTED TO SEE ME...
... MADAM DOLLY?
ALICE KEATING...
...I WOULD LIKE YOU TO BE MARI MUGURUMA'S TUTOR.

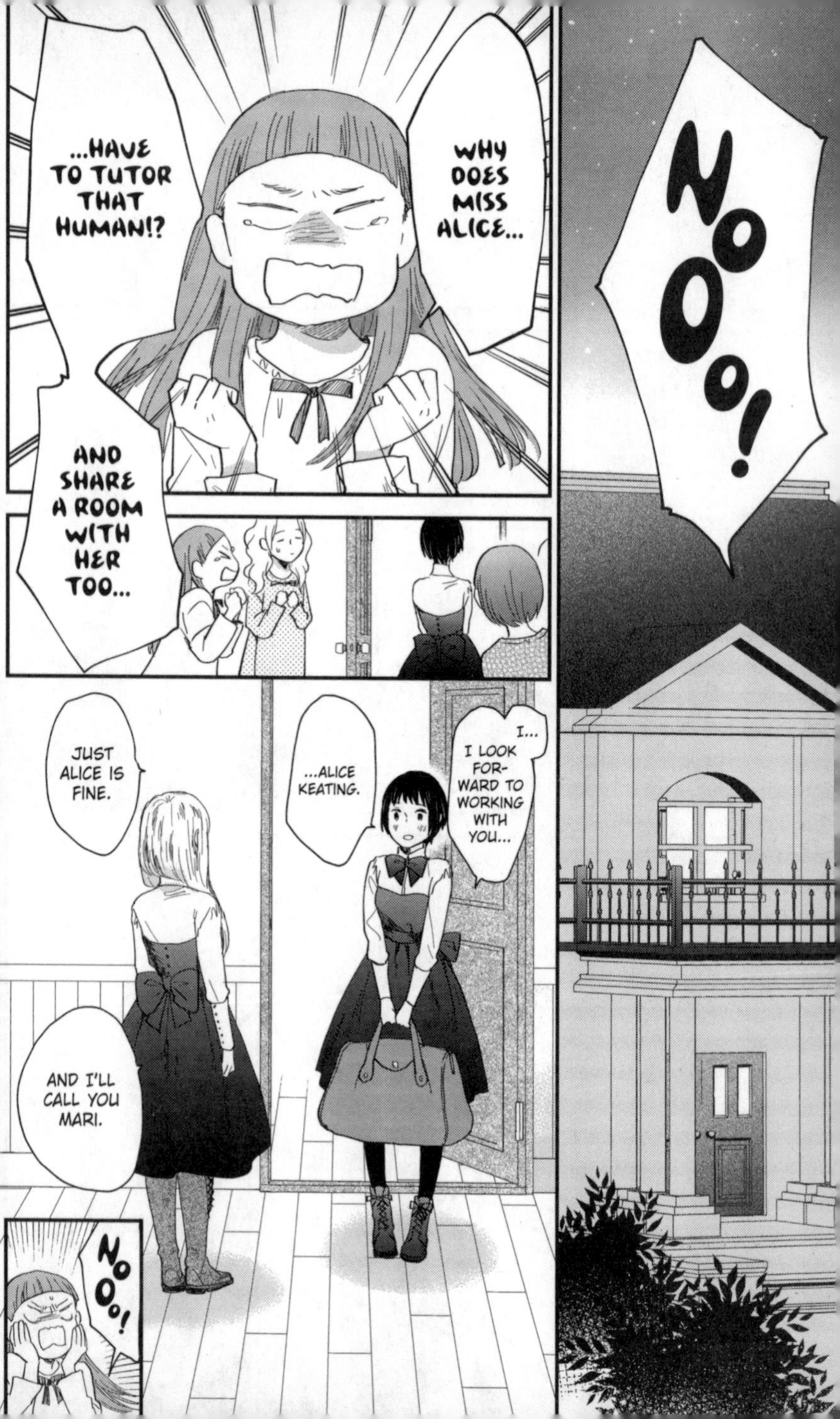
NOOOo!
WHY DOES MISS ALICE...
...HAVE TO TUTOR THAT HUMAN!?
AND SHARE A ROOM WITH HER TOO...
I... I LOOK FOR-WARD TO WORKING WITH YOU...
...ALICE KEATING.
JUST ALICE IS FINE.
AND I'LL CALL YOU MARI.
NOOo!

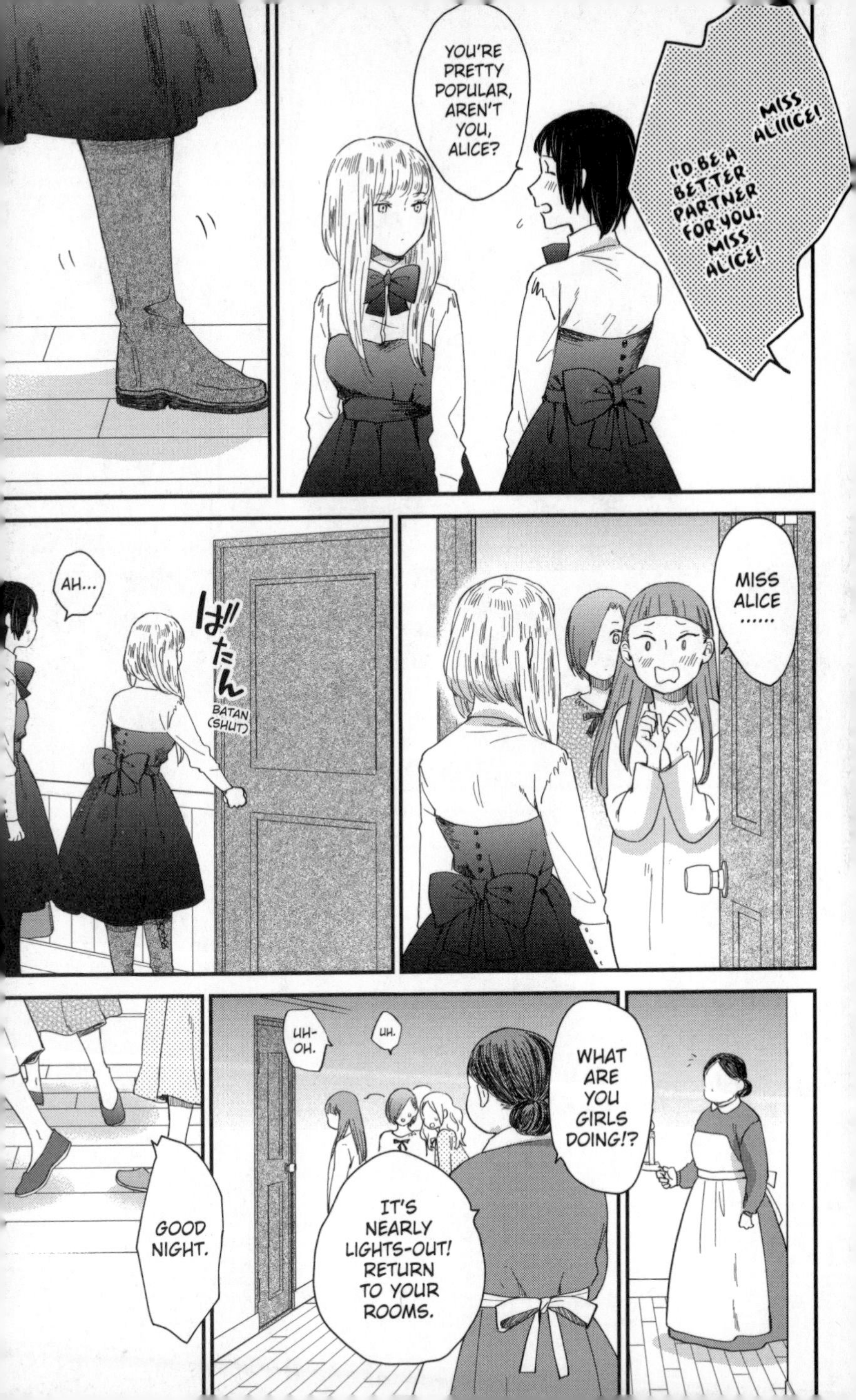
MISS ALIIICE!
I'D BE A BETTER PARTNER FOR YOU, MISS ALICE!
YOU'RE PRETTY POPULAR, AREN'T YOU, ALICE?
MISS ALICE ......
AH...
ばたん
BATAN (SHUT)
WHAT ARE YOU GIRLS DOING!?
UH.
UH-OH.
IT'S NEARLY LIGHTS-OUT! RETURN TO YOUR ROOMS.
GOOD NIGHT.

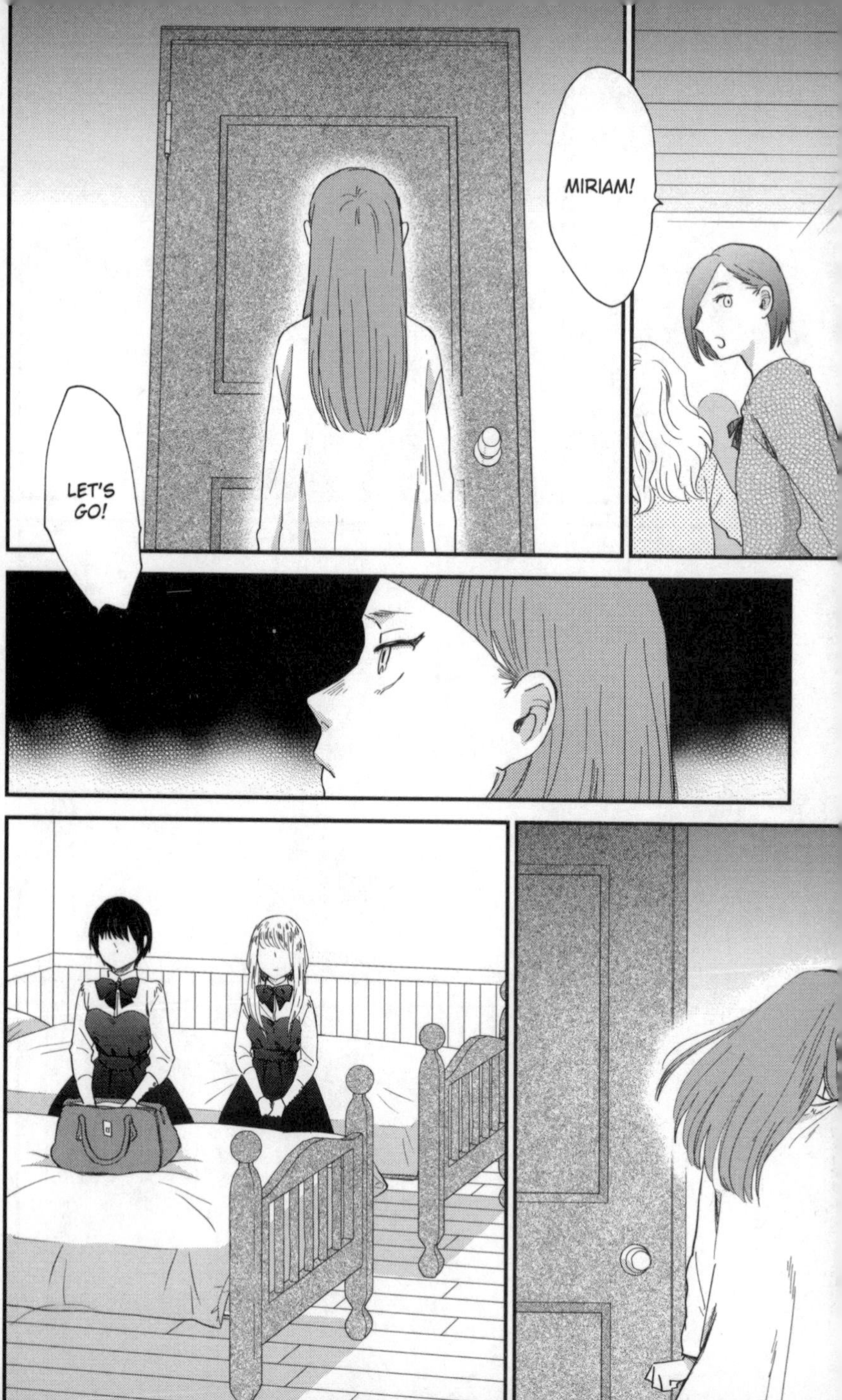
MIRIAM!
LET'S GO!

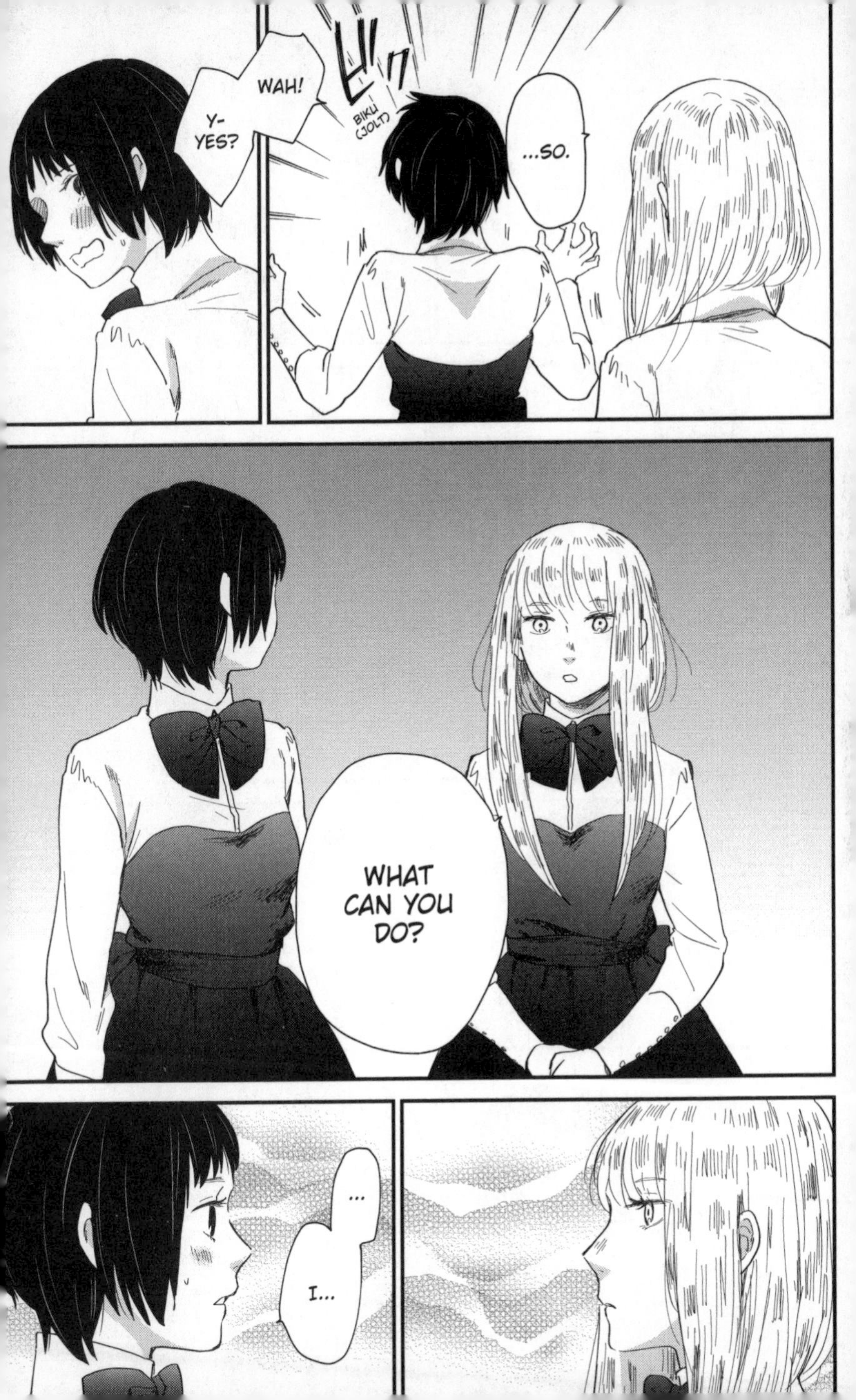
...SO.
BIKU (JOLT)
WAH!
Y- YES?
WHAT CAN YOU DO?
...
I...

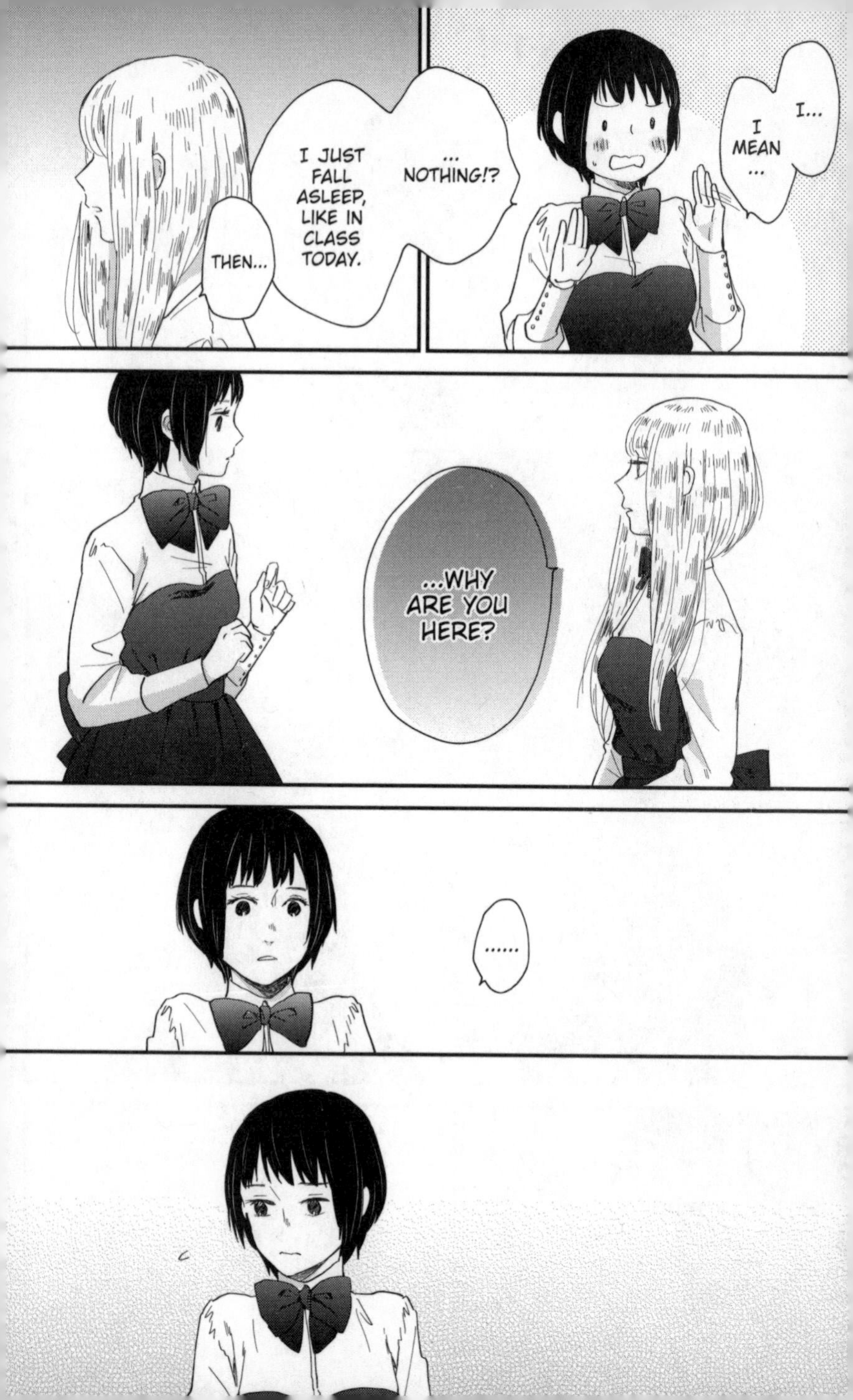

I... I MEAN ...
... NOTHING!? I JUST FALL ASLEEP, LIKE IN CLASS TODAY.
THEN...
...WHY ARE YOU HERE?
......

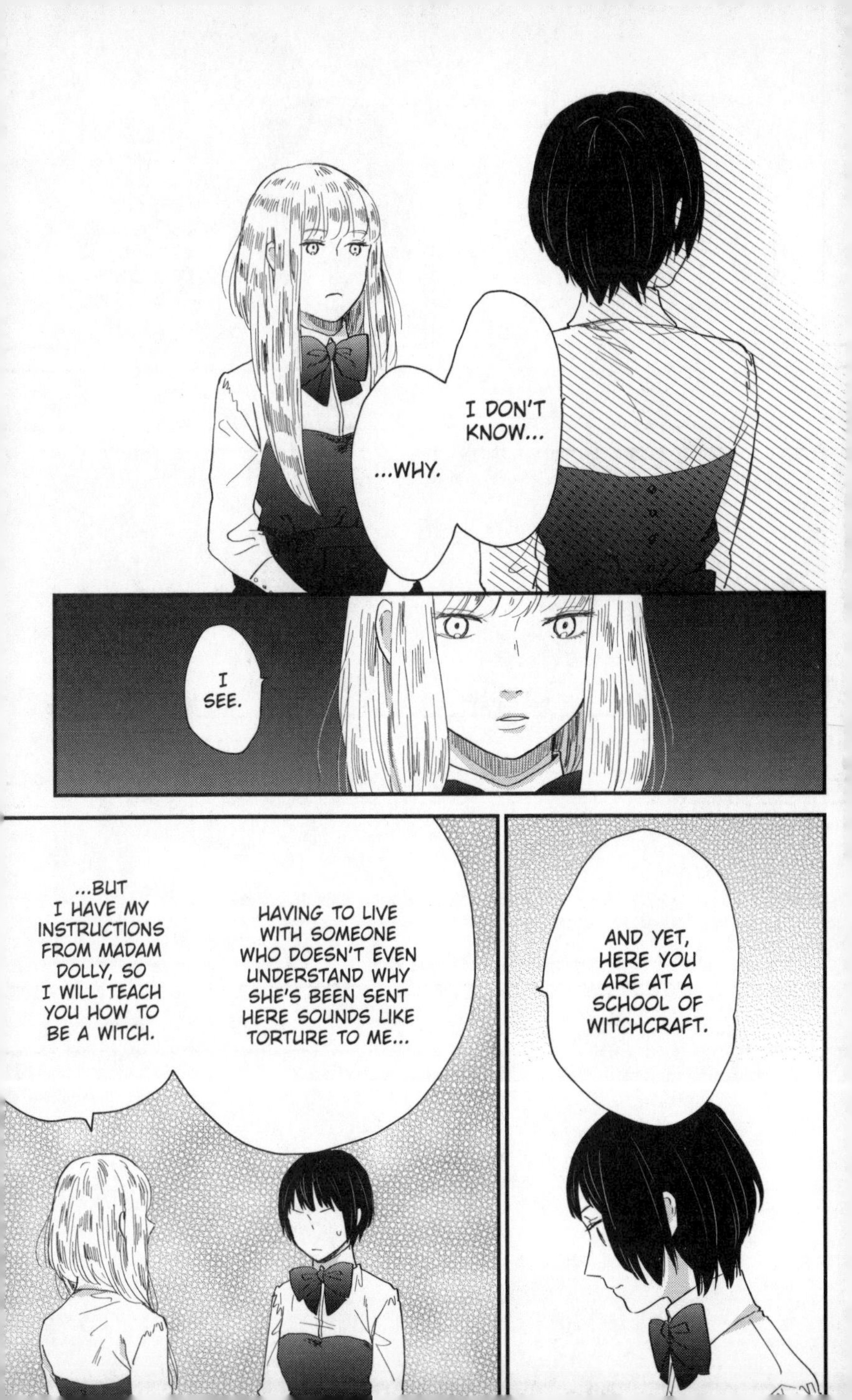
I DON'T KNOW...
...WHY.
I SEE.
AND YET, HERE YOU ARE AT A SCHOOL OF WITCHCRAFT.
HAVING TO LIVE WITH SOMEONE WHO DOESN'T EVEN UNDERSTAND WHY SHE'S BEEN SENT HERE SOUNDS LIKE TORTURE TO ME...
...BUT I HAVE MY INSTRUCTIONS FROM MADAM DOLLY, SO I WILL TEACH YOU HOW TO BE A WITCH.

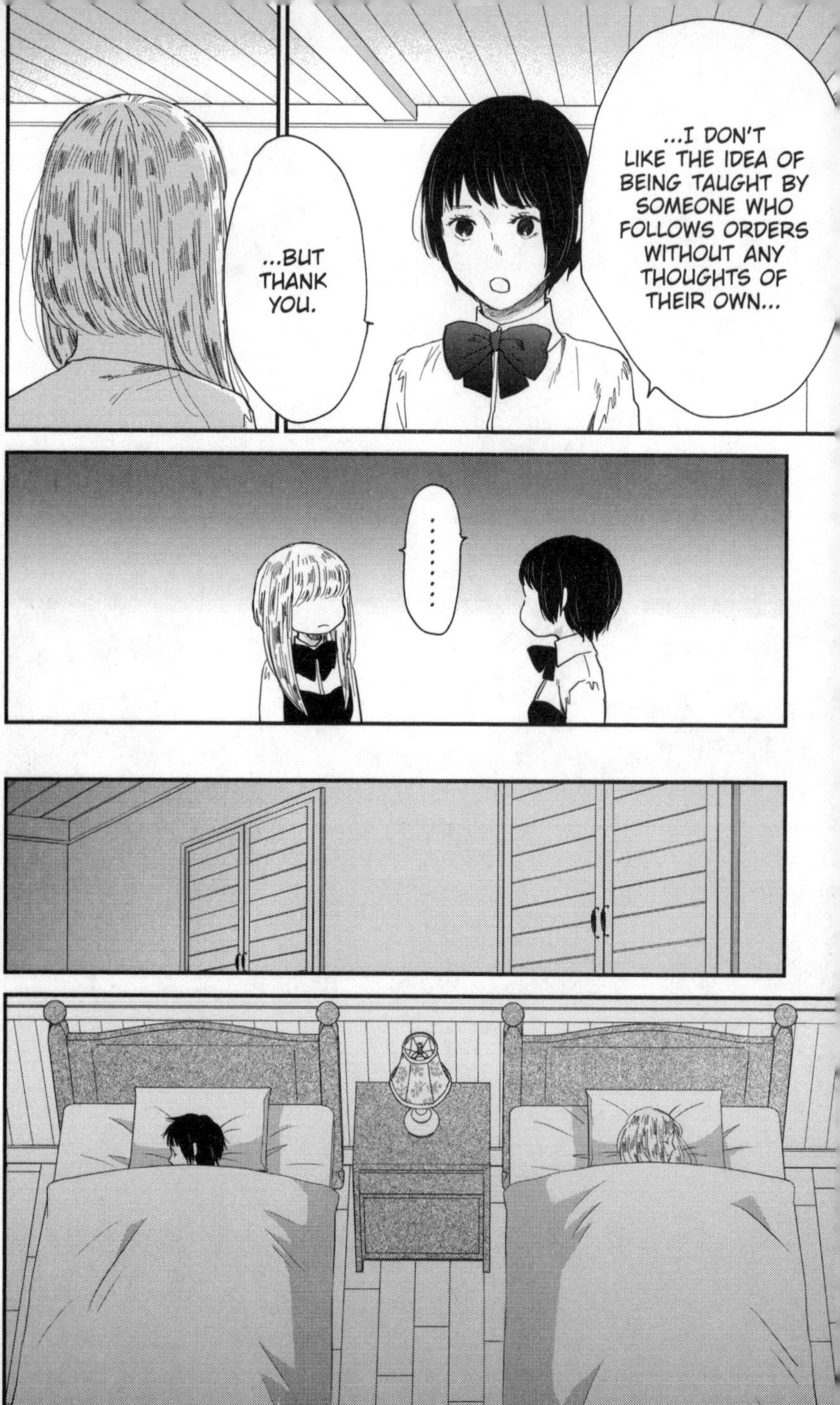
...I DON'T LIKE THE IDEA OF BEING TAUGHT BY SOMEONE WHO FOLLOWS ORDERS WITHOUT ANY THOUGHTS OF THEIR OWN...
...BUT THANK YOU.
....

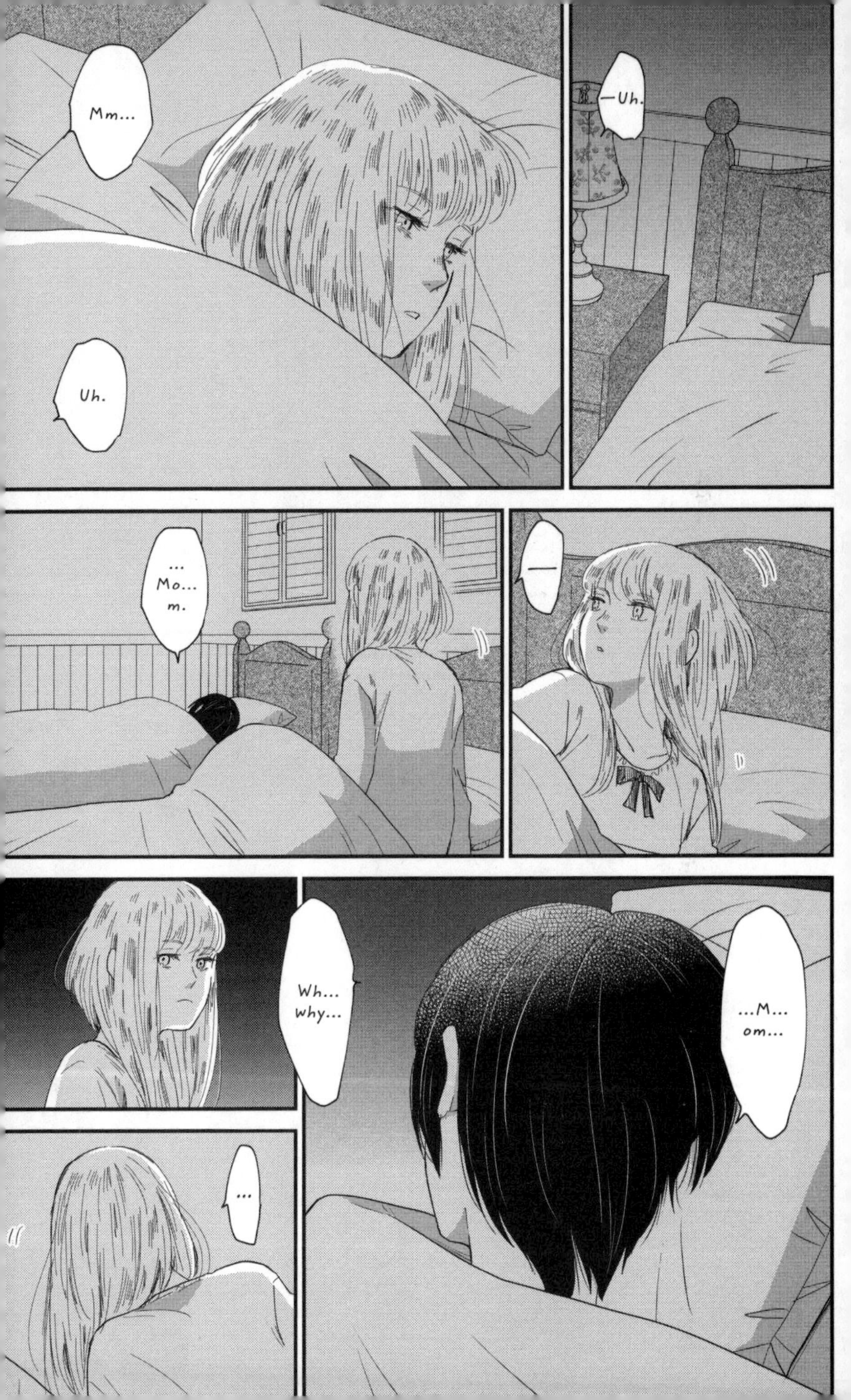
—Uh.
Mm...
Uh.
—
... Mo... m.
...M... om...
Wh... why...
...

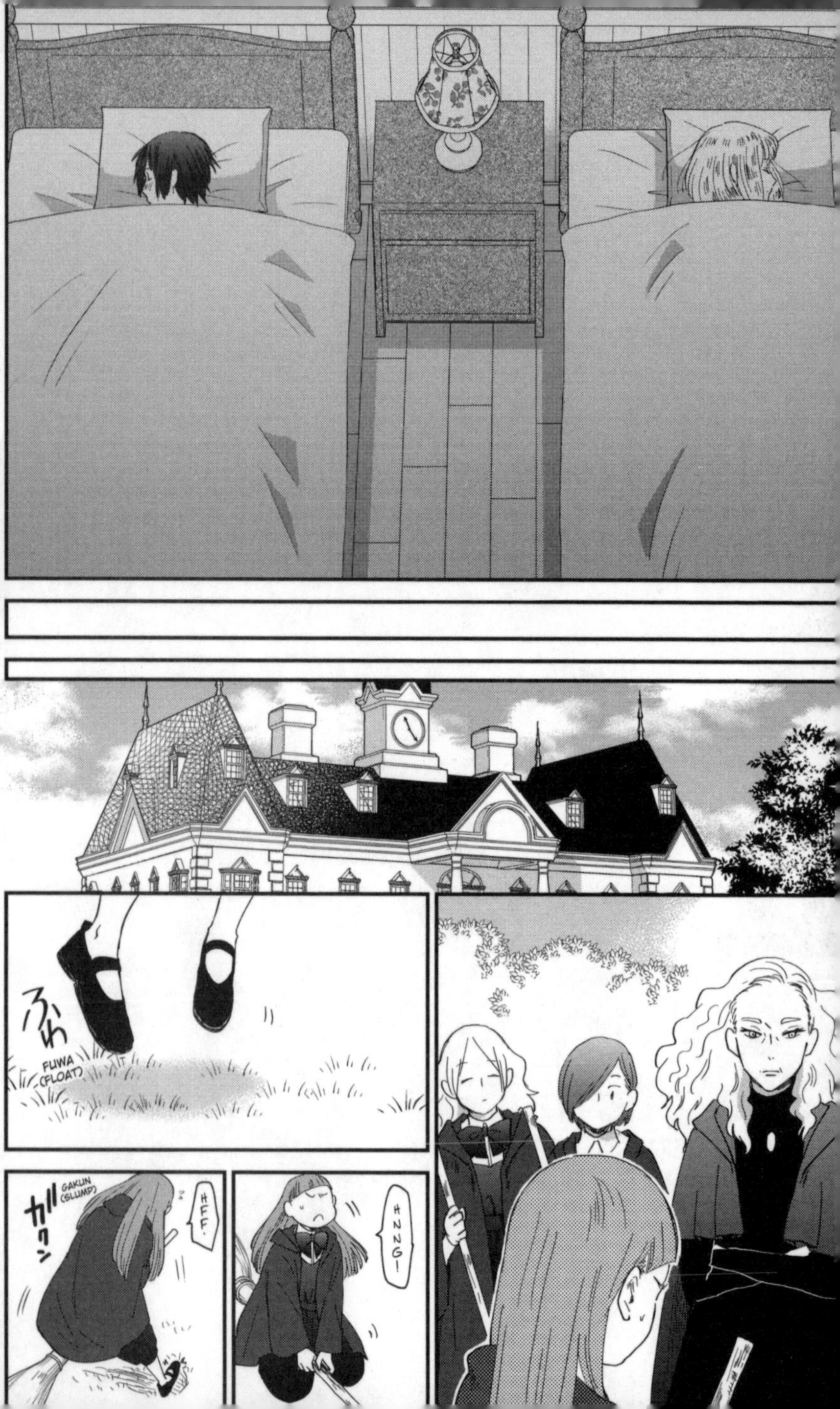
ふわ
FUWA (FLOAT)
HNNG!
HFF.
ガクン
GAKUN (SLUMP)

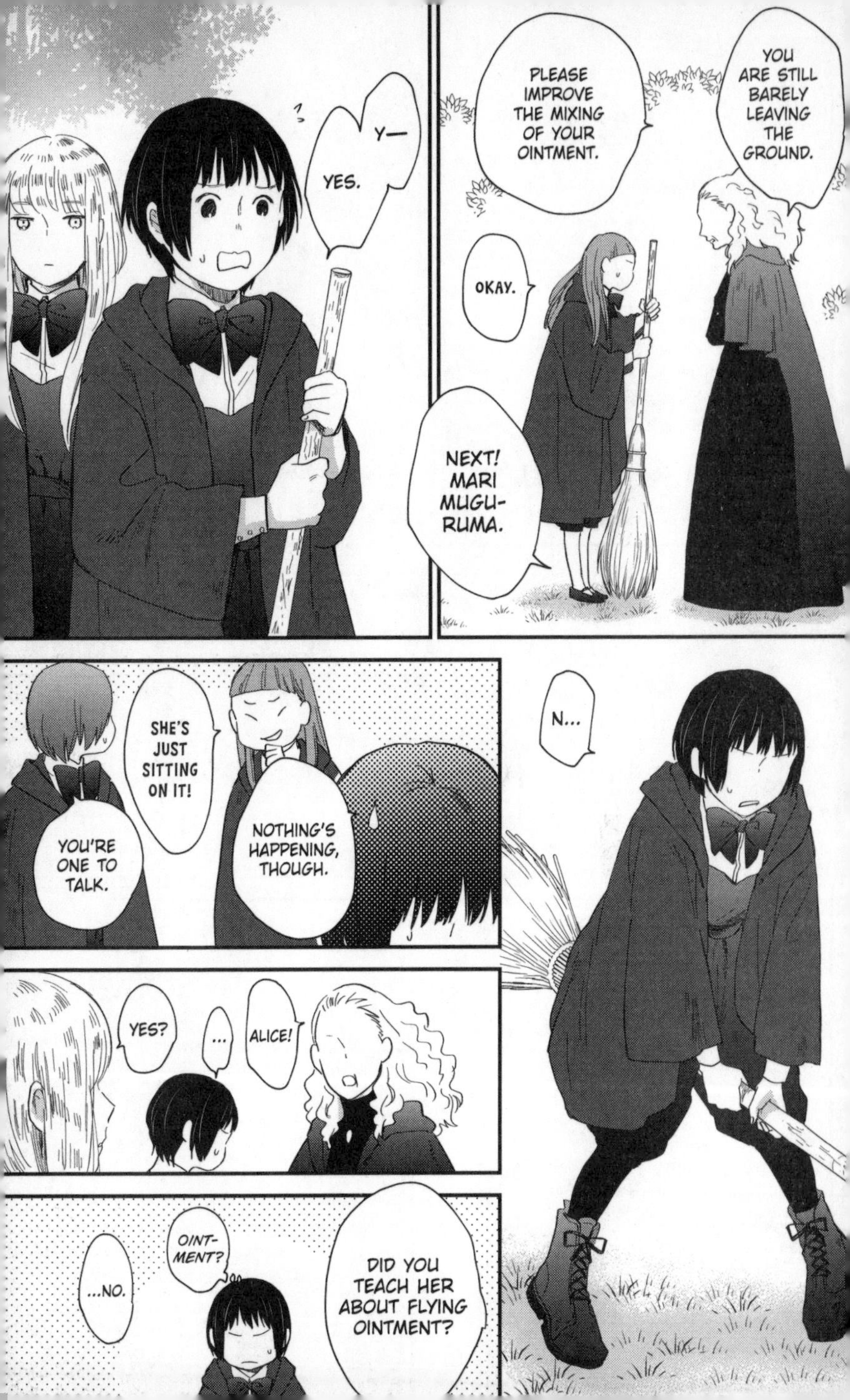
YOU ARE STILL BARELY LEAVING THE GROUND.
PLEASE IMPROVE THE MIXING OF YOUR OINTMENT.
OKAY.
NEXT! MARI MUGU-RUMA.
Y—
YES.
N...
SHE'S JUST SITTING ON IT!
NOTHING'S HAPPENING, THOUGH.
YOU'RE ONE TO TALK.
ALICE!
...
YES?
DID YOU TEACH HER ABOUT FLYING OINTMENT?
OINT-MENT?
...NO.

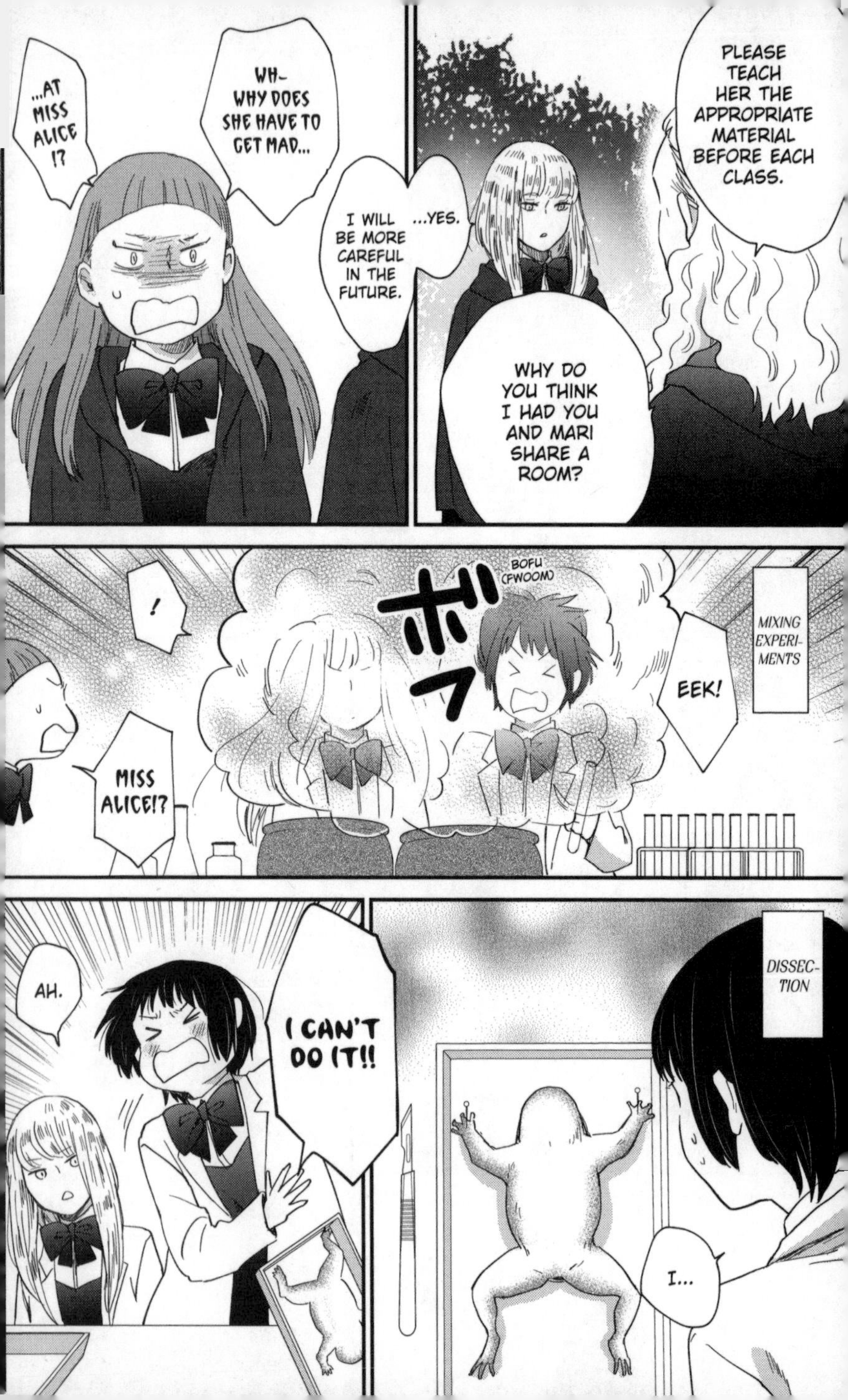
PLEASE TEACH HER THE APPROPRIATE MATERIAL BEFORE EACH CLASS.
...YES.
WHY DO YOU THINK I HAD YOU AND MARI SHARE A ROOM?
I WILL BE MORE CAREFUL IN THE FUTURE.
WH- WHY DOES SHE HAVE TO GET MAD...
...AT MISS ALICE!?
MIXING EXPERI-MENTS
EEK!
BOFU (FWOOM)
ボフ
!
MISS ALICE!?
DISSEC-TION
I...
I CAN'T DO IT!!
AH.

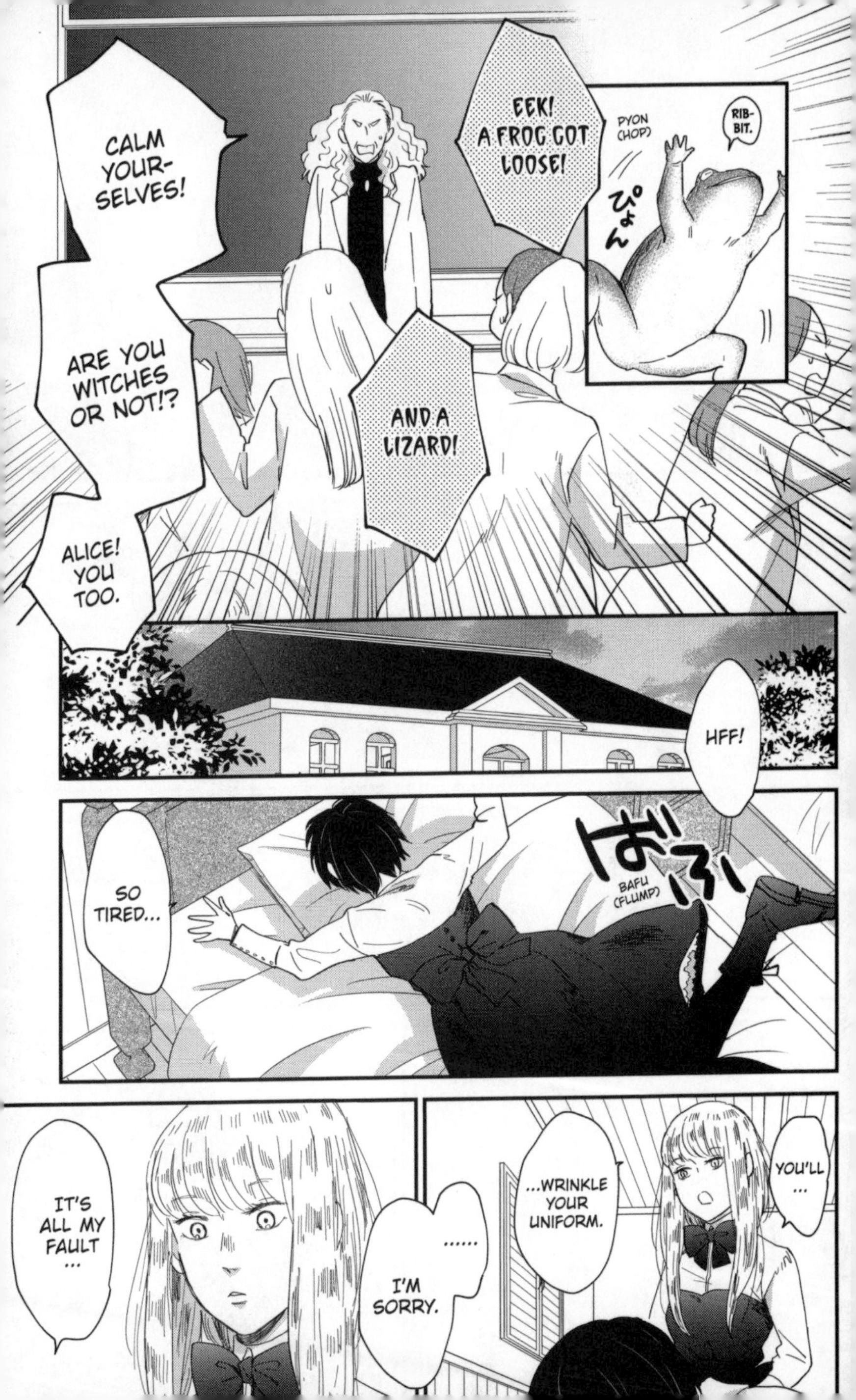
RIB-BIT.
PYON (HOP)
ぴょん
EEK! A FROG GOT LOOSE!
AND A LIZARD!
CALM YOURSELVES!
ARE YOU WITCHES OR NOT!?
ALICE! YOU TOO.
HFF!
ぼふ
BAFU (FLUMP)
SO TIRED...
YOU'LL ...
...WRINKLE YOUR UNIFORM.
IT'S ALL MY FAULT ...
......
I'M SORRY.

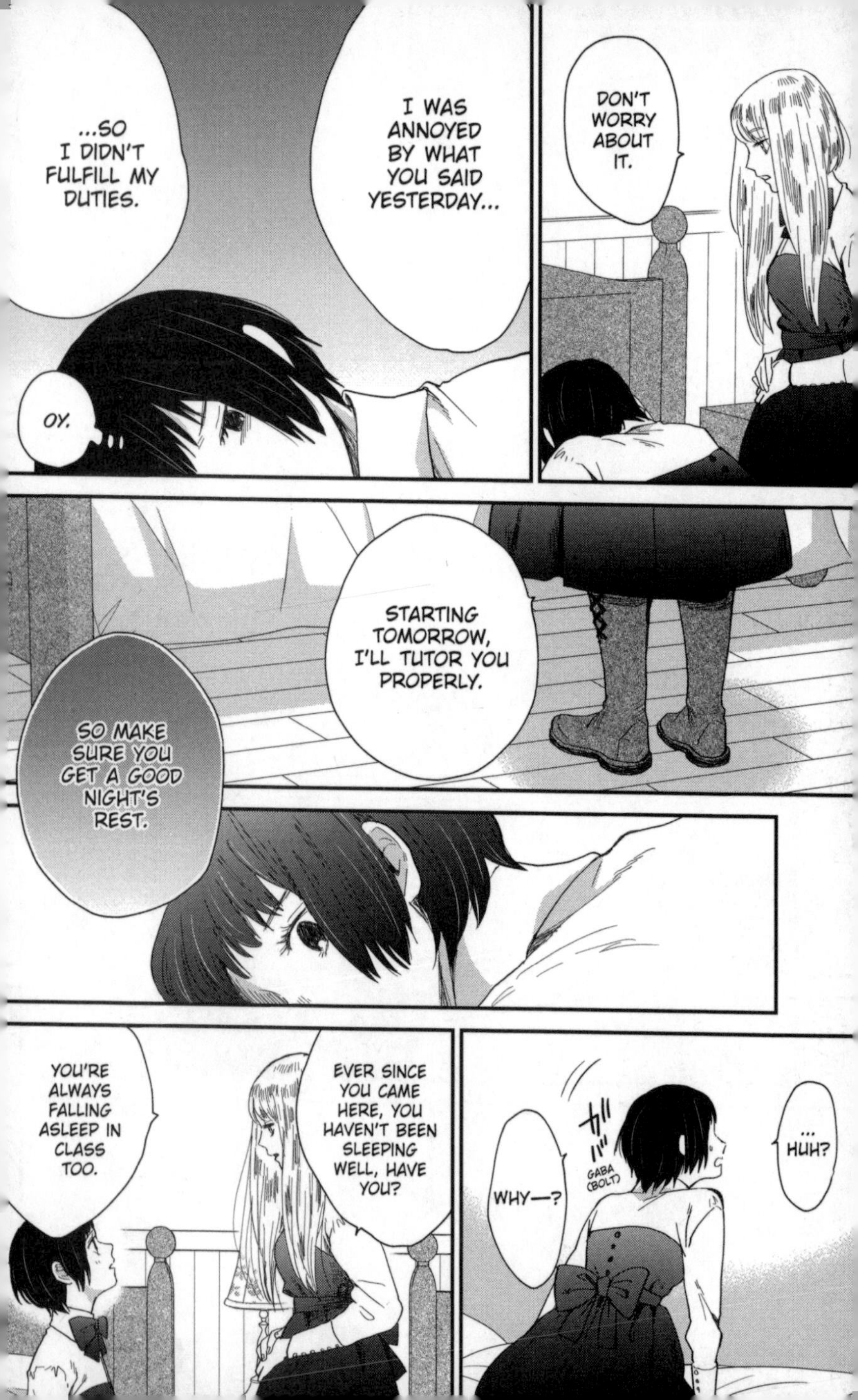
DON'T WORRY ABOUT IT.
I WAS ANNOYED BY WHAT YOU SAID YESTERDAY...
...SO I DIDN'T FULFILL MY DUTIES.
OY.
STARTING TOMORROW, I'LL TUTOR YOU PROPERLY.
SO MAKE SURE YOU GET A GOOD NIGHT'S REST.
...HUH?
ガバ
GABA (BOLT)
WHY—?
EVER SINCE YOU CAME HERE, YOU HAVEN'T BEEN SLEEPING WELL, HAVE YOU?
YOU'RE ALWAYS FALLING ASLEEP IN CLASS TOO.

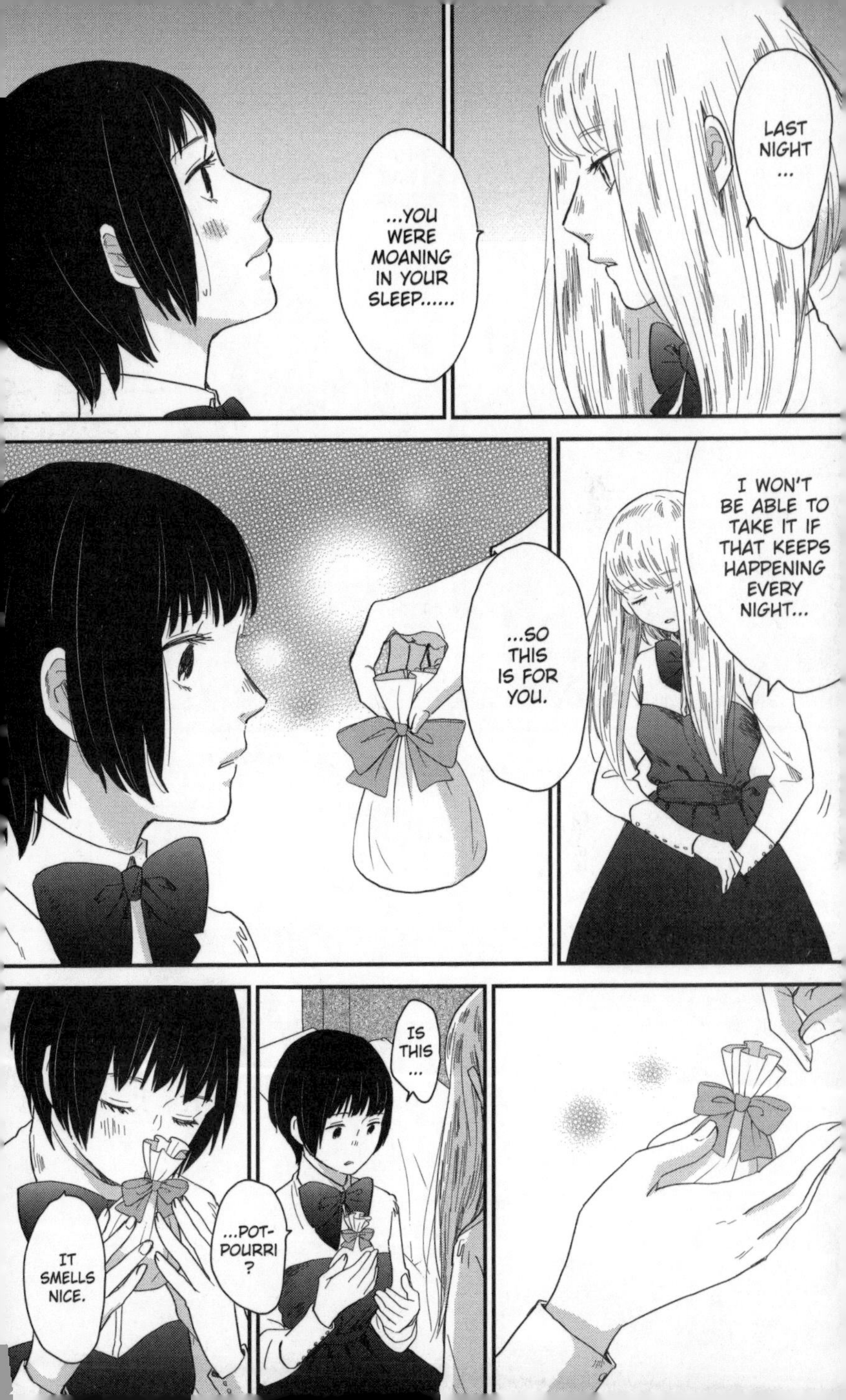
LAST NIGHT ...
...YOU WERE MOANING IN YOUR SLEEP......
I WON'T BE ABLE TO TAKE IT IF THAT KEEPS HAPPENING EVERY NIGHT...
...SO THIS IS FOR YOU.
IS THIS ...
...POT-POURRI ?
IT SMELLS NICE.

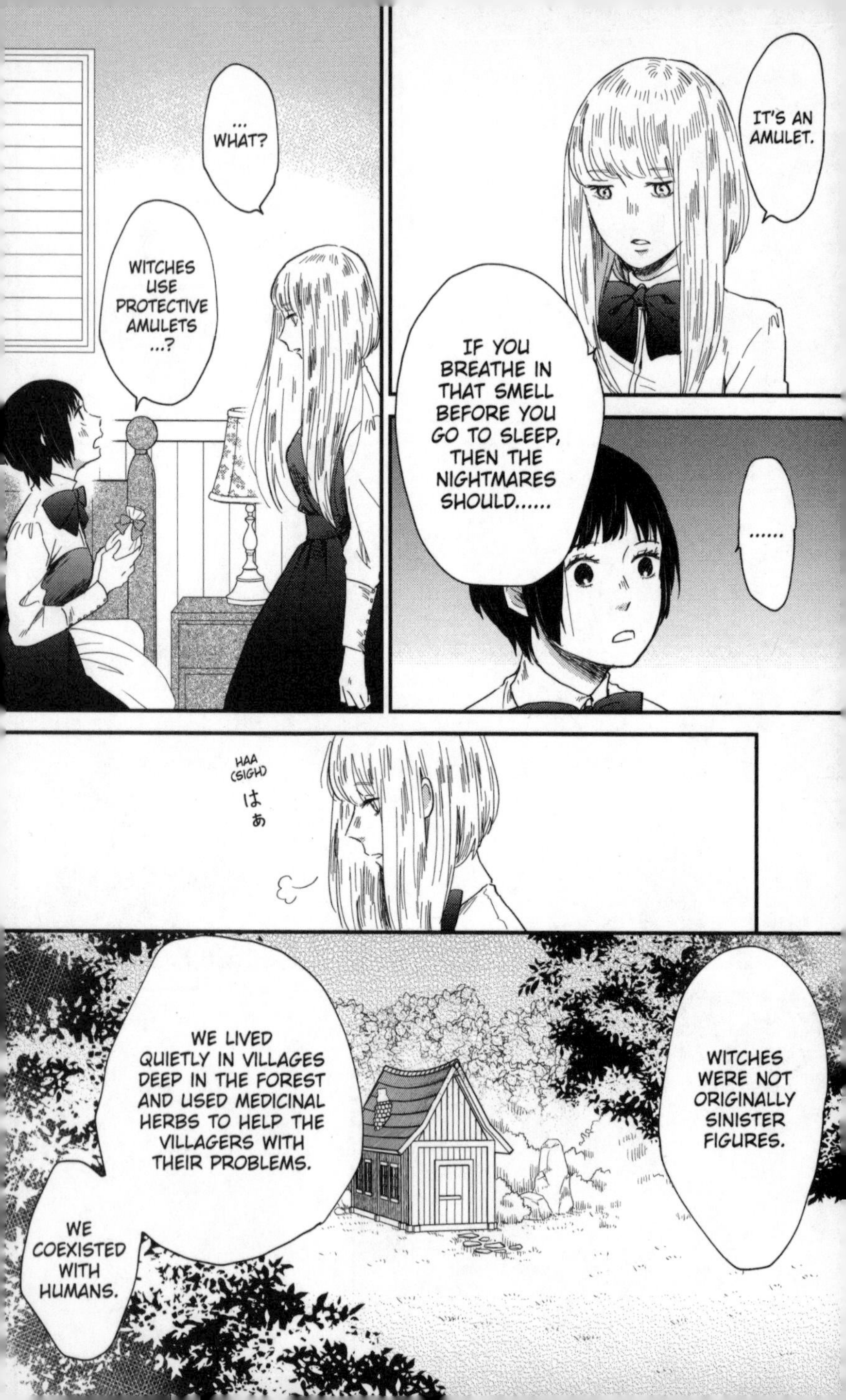
IT'S AN AMULET.
IF YOU BREATHE IN THAT SMELL BEFORE YOU GO TO SLEEP, THEN THE NIGHTMARES SHOULD......
......
... WHAT?
WITCHES USE PROTECTIVE AMULETS ...?
HAA (SIGH) はぁ
WITCHES WERE NOT ORIGINALLY SINISTER FIGURES.
WE LIVED QUIETLY IN VILLAGES DEEP IN THE FOREST AND USED MEDICINAL HERBS TO HELP THE VILLAGERS WITH THEIR PROBLEMS.
WE COEXISTED WITH HUMANS.

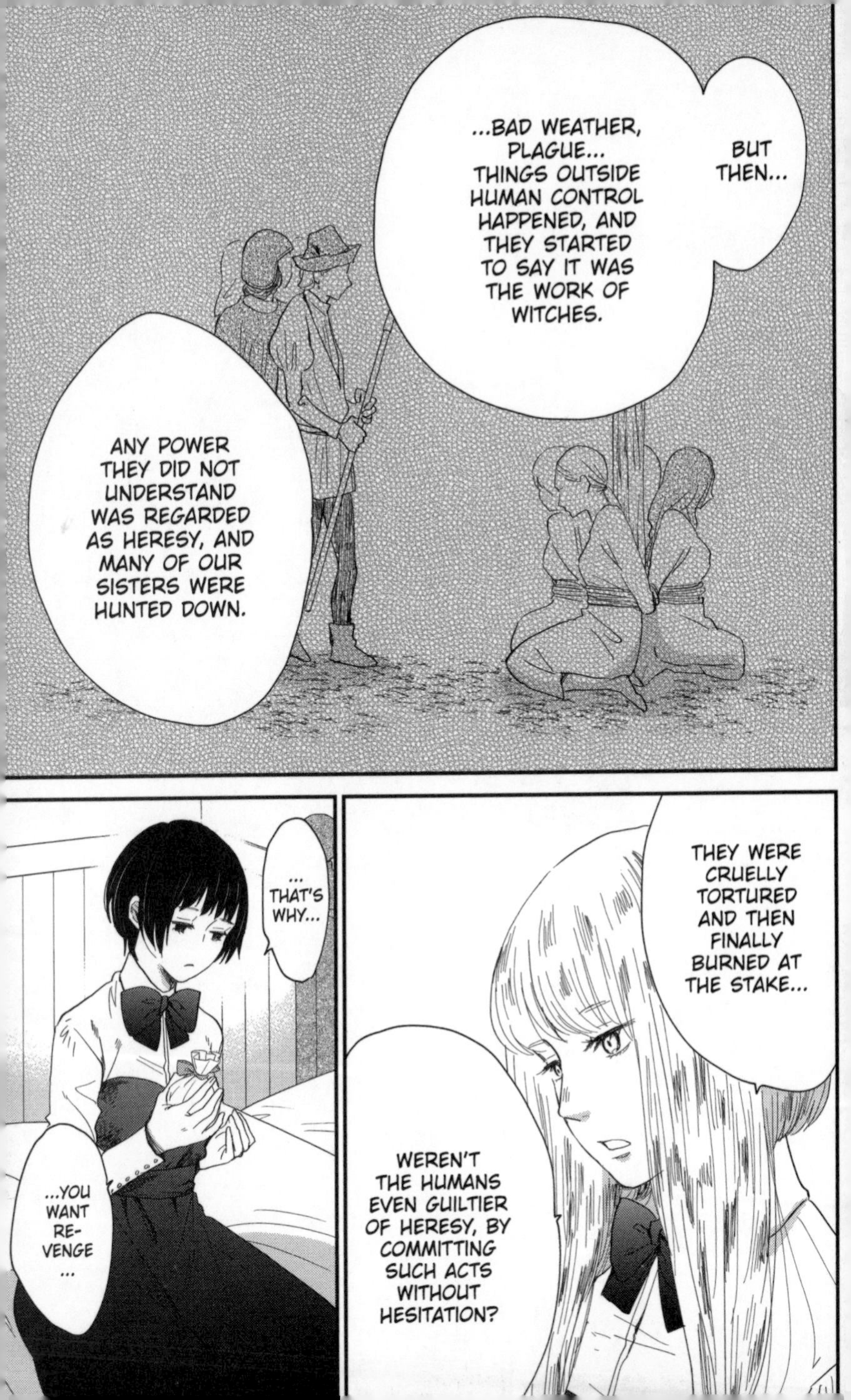
BUT THEN...
...BAD WEATHER, PLAGUE... THINGS OUTSIDE HUMAN CONTROL HAPPENED, AND THEY STARTED TO SAY IT WAS THE WORK OF WITCHES.
ANY POWER THEY DID NOT UNDERSTAND WAS REGARDED AS HERESY, AND MANY OF OUR SISTERS WERE HUNTED DOWN.
THEY WERE CRUELLY TORTURED AND THEN FINALLY BURNED AT THE STAKE...
WEREN'T THE HUMANS EVEN GUILTIER OF HERESY, BY COMMITTING SUCH ACTS WITHOUT HESITATION?
... THAT'S WHY...
...YOU WANT RE-VENGE...

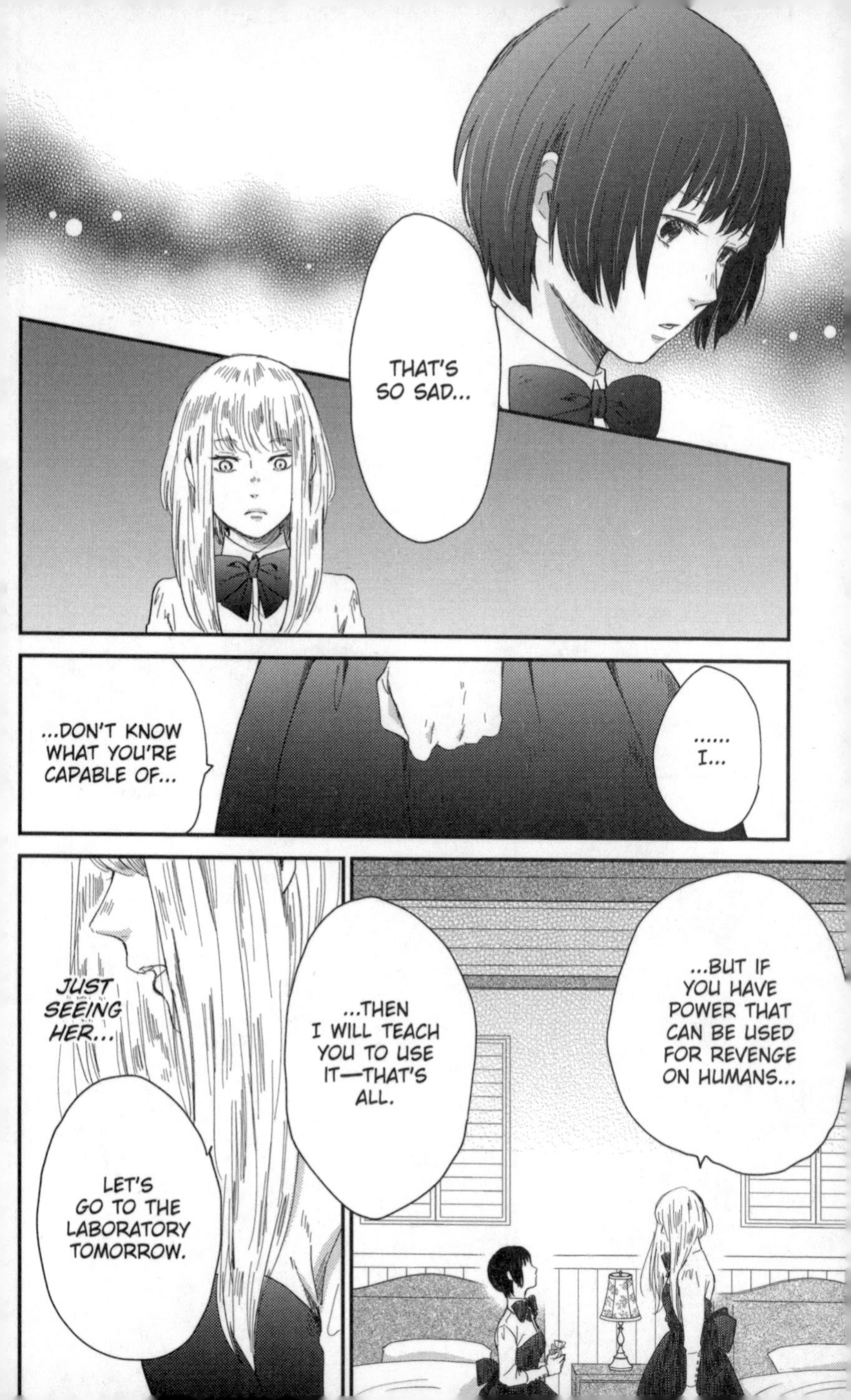
THAT'S SO SAD...
...... I...
...DON'T KNOW WHAT YOU'RE CAPABLE OF...
...BUT IF YOU HAVE POWER THAT CAN BE USED FOR REVENGE ON HUMANS...
...THEN I WILL TEACH YOU TO USE IT—THAT'S ALL.
JUST SEEING HER...
LET'S GO TO THE LABORATORY TOMORROW.

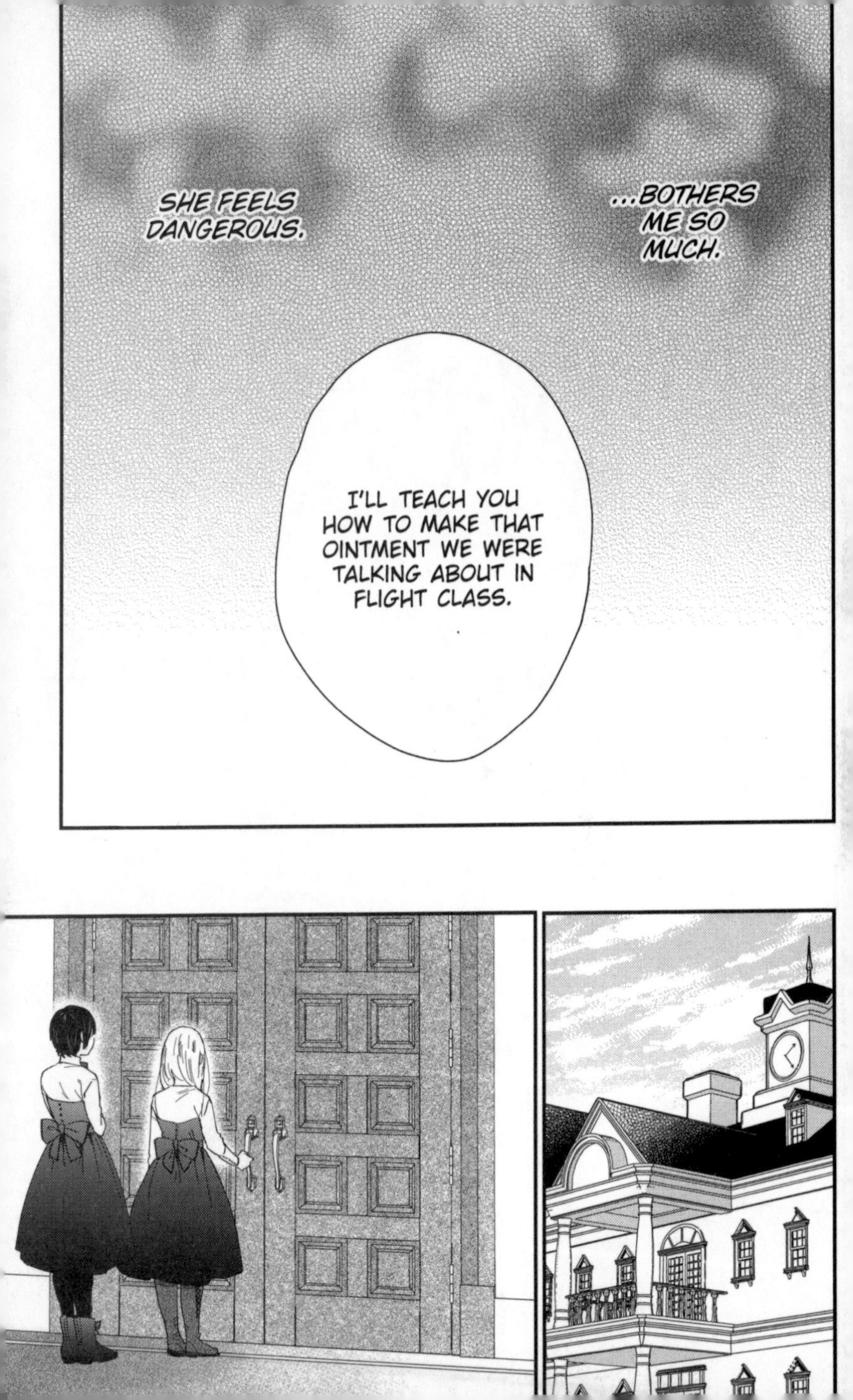
...BOTHERS ME SO MUCH.
SHE FEELS DANGEROUS.
I'LL TEACH YOU HOW TO MAKE THAT OINTMENT WE WERE TALKING ABOUT IN FLIGHT CLASS.

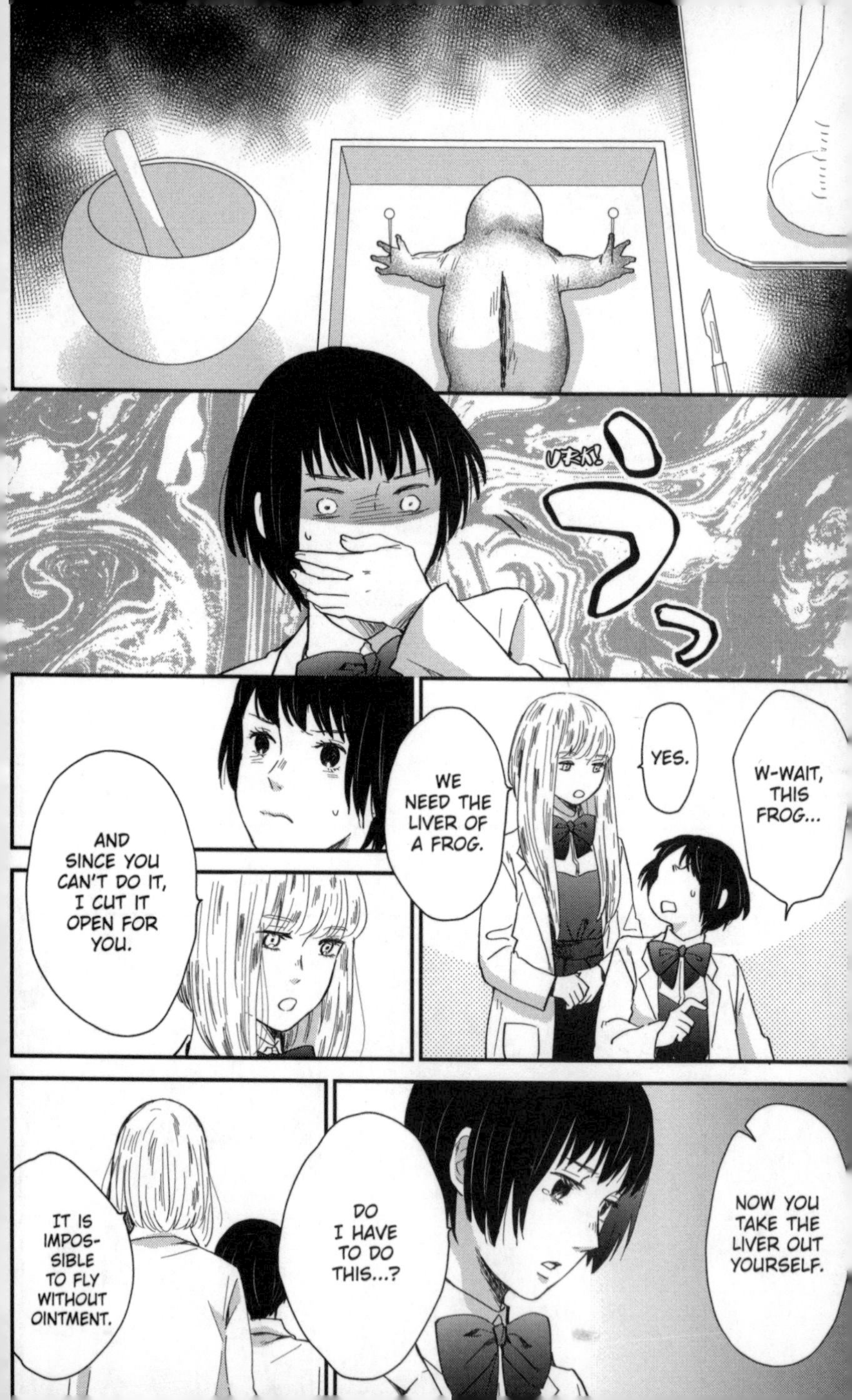
URK!
うっっ
W-WAIT, THIS FROG...
YES.
WE NEED THE LIVER OF A FROG.
AND SINCE YOU CAN'T DO IT, I CUT IT OPEN FOR YOU.
NOW YOU TAKE THE LIVER OUT YOURSELF.
DO I HAVE TO DO THIS...?
IT IS IMPOSSIBLE TO FLY WITHOUT OINTMENT.

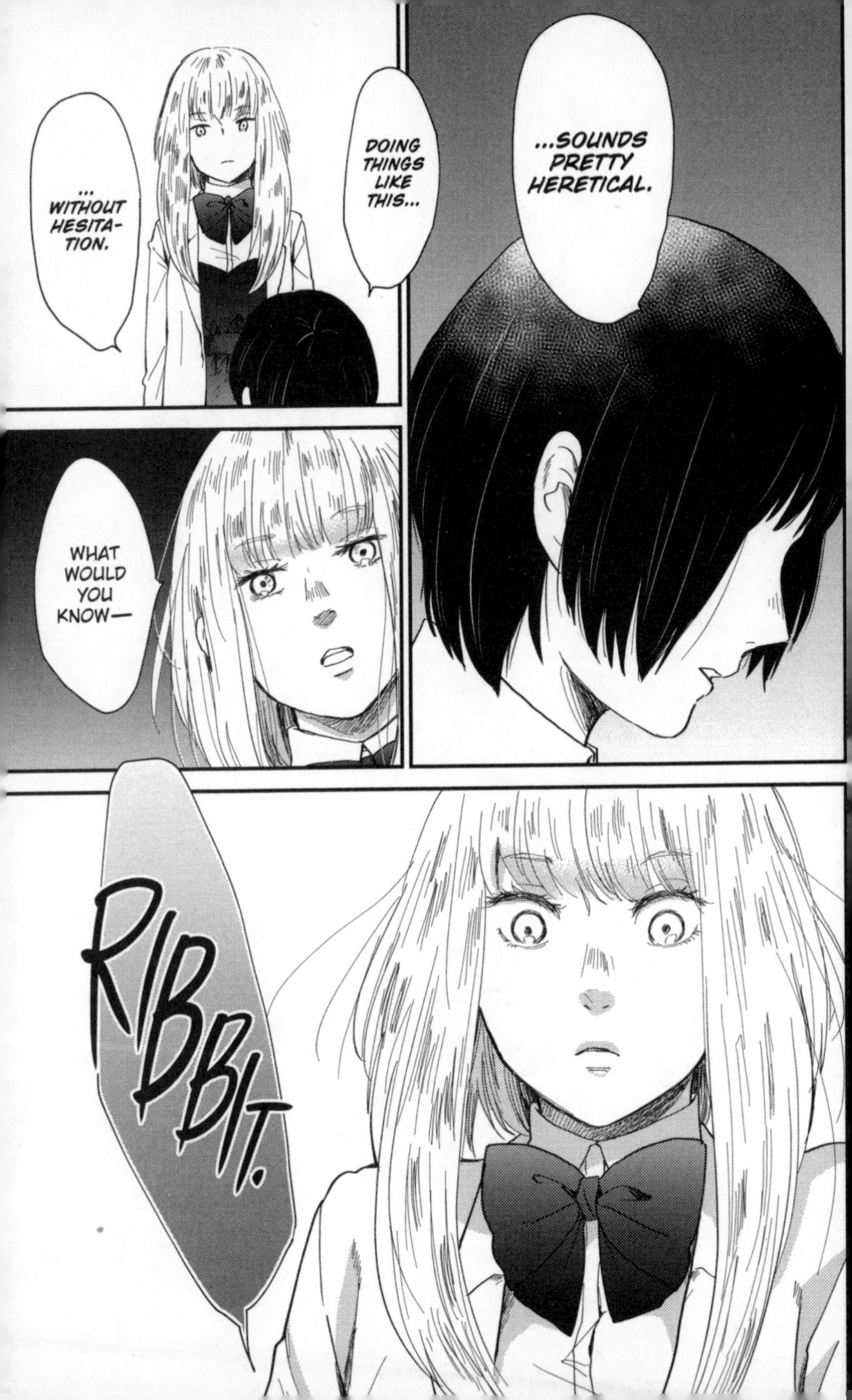
DOING THINGS LIKE THIS...
...WITHOUT HESITA-TION.
...SOUNDS PRETTY HERETICAL.
WHAT WOULD YOU KNOW—
RIBBIT.

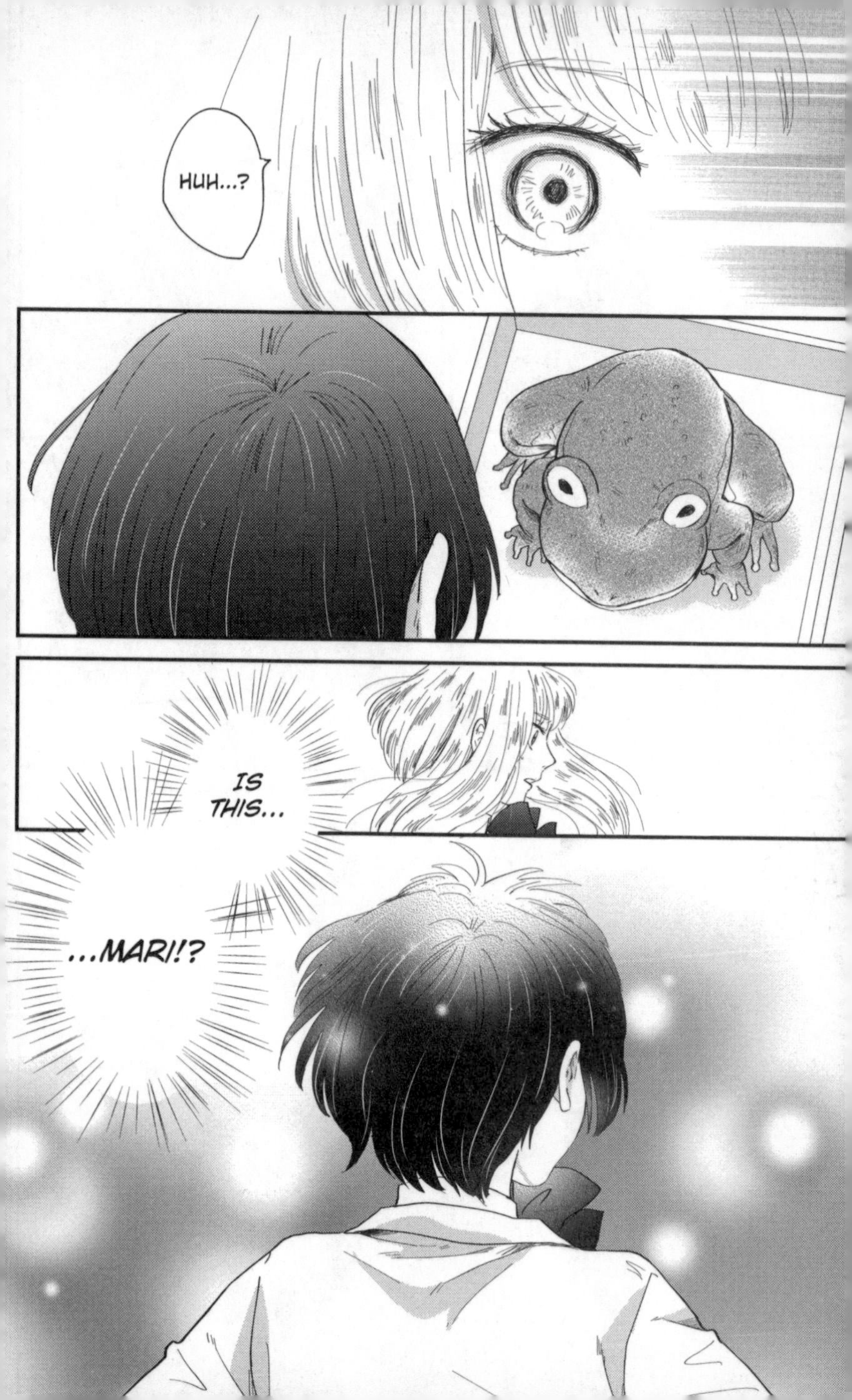
HUH...?
IS THIS...
...MARI!?

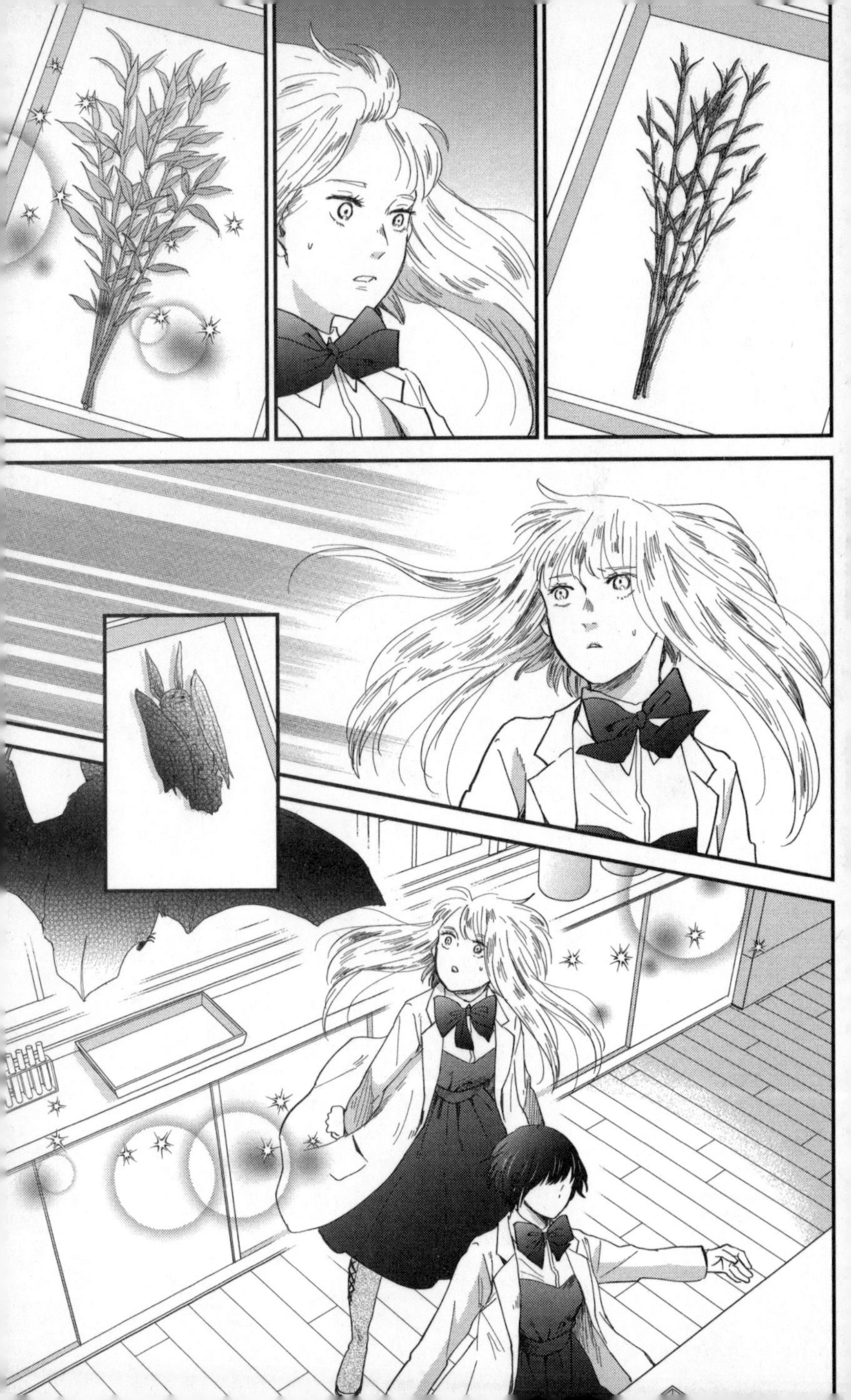

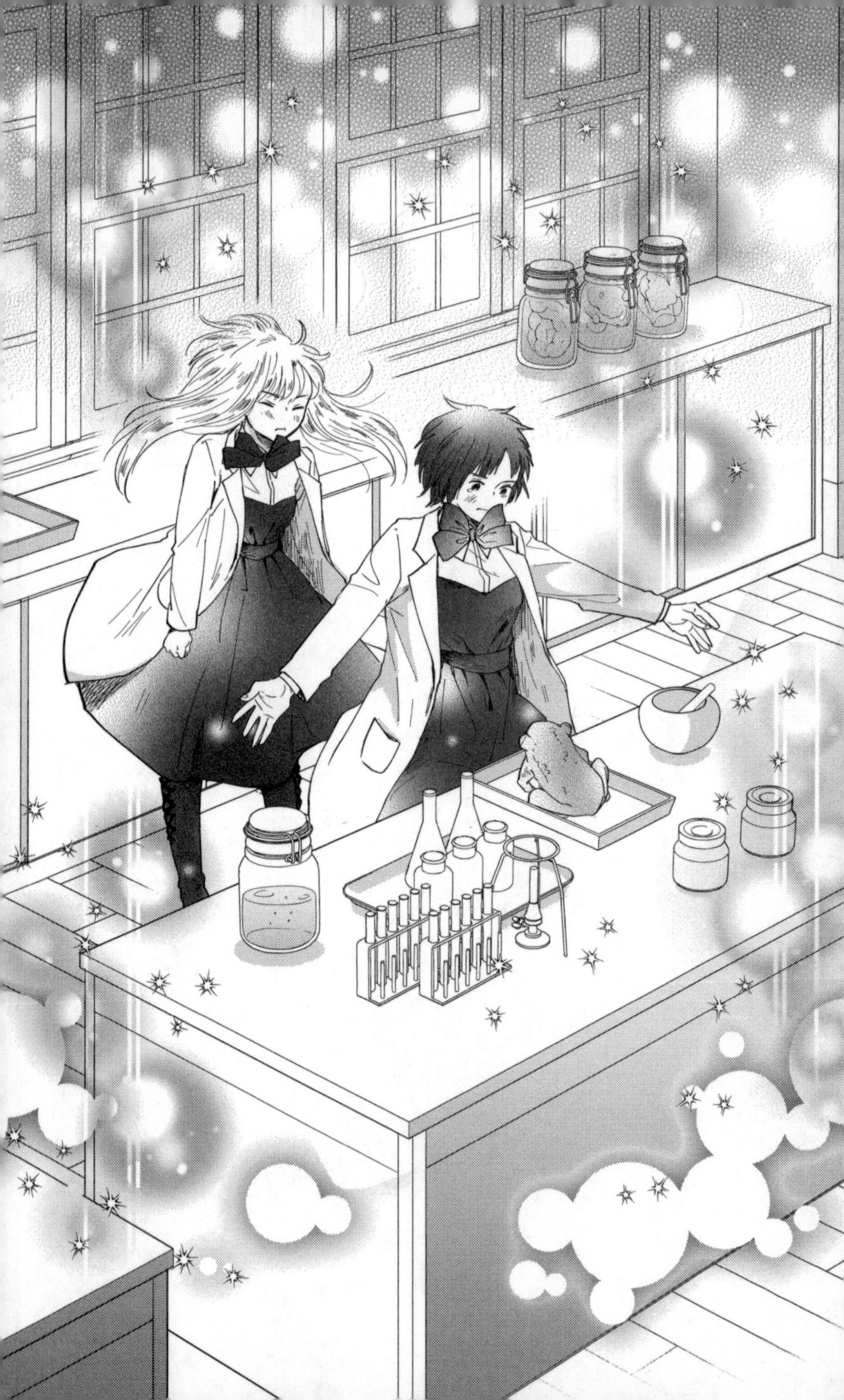

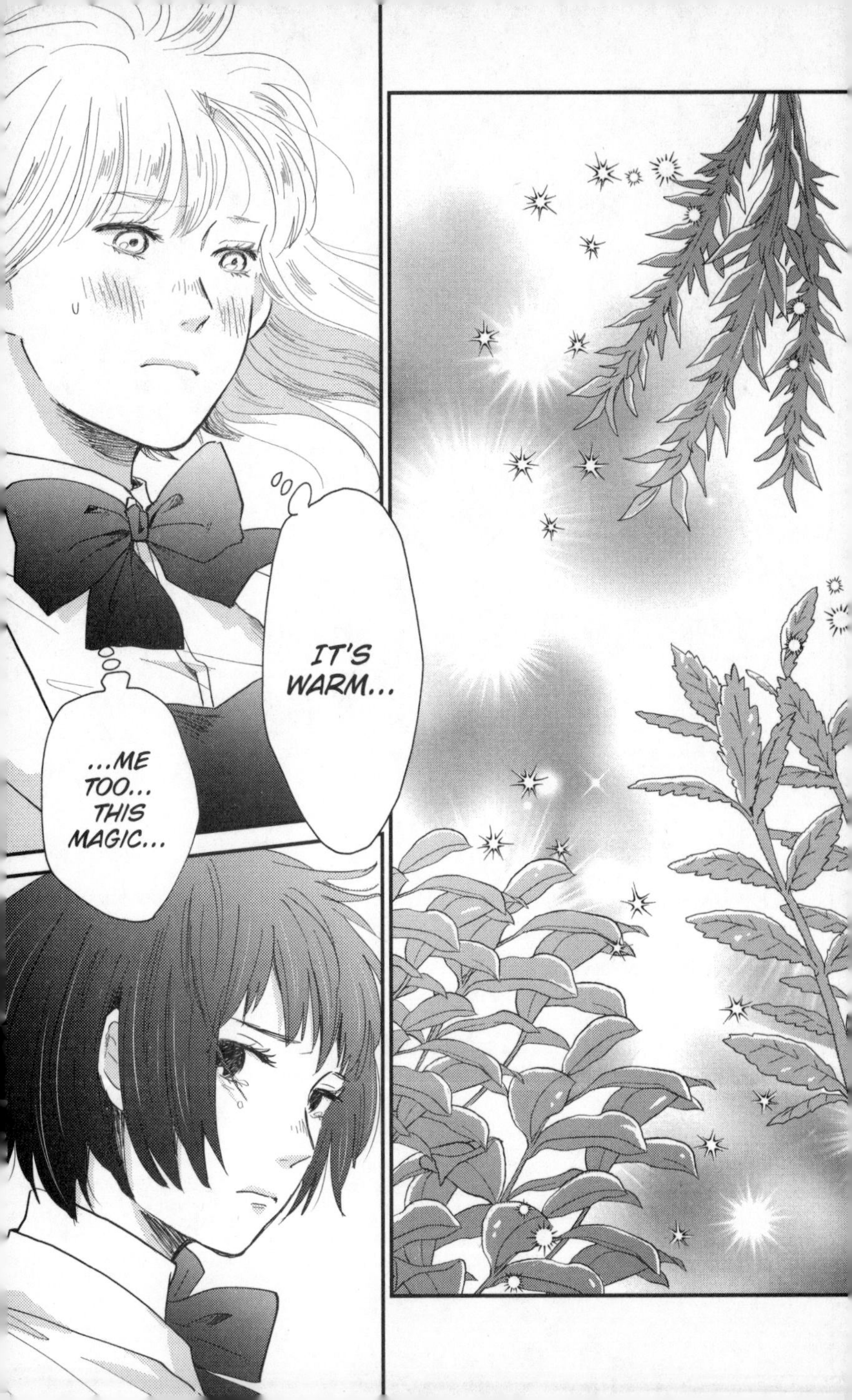
IT'S WARM...
...ME TOO... THIS MAGIC...

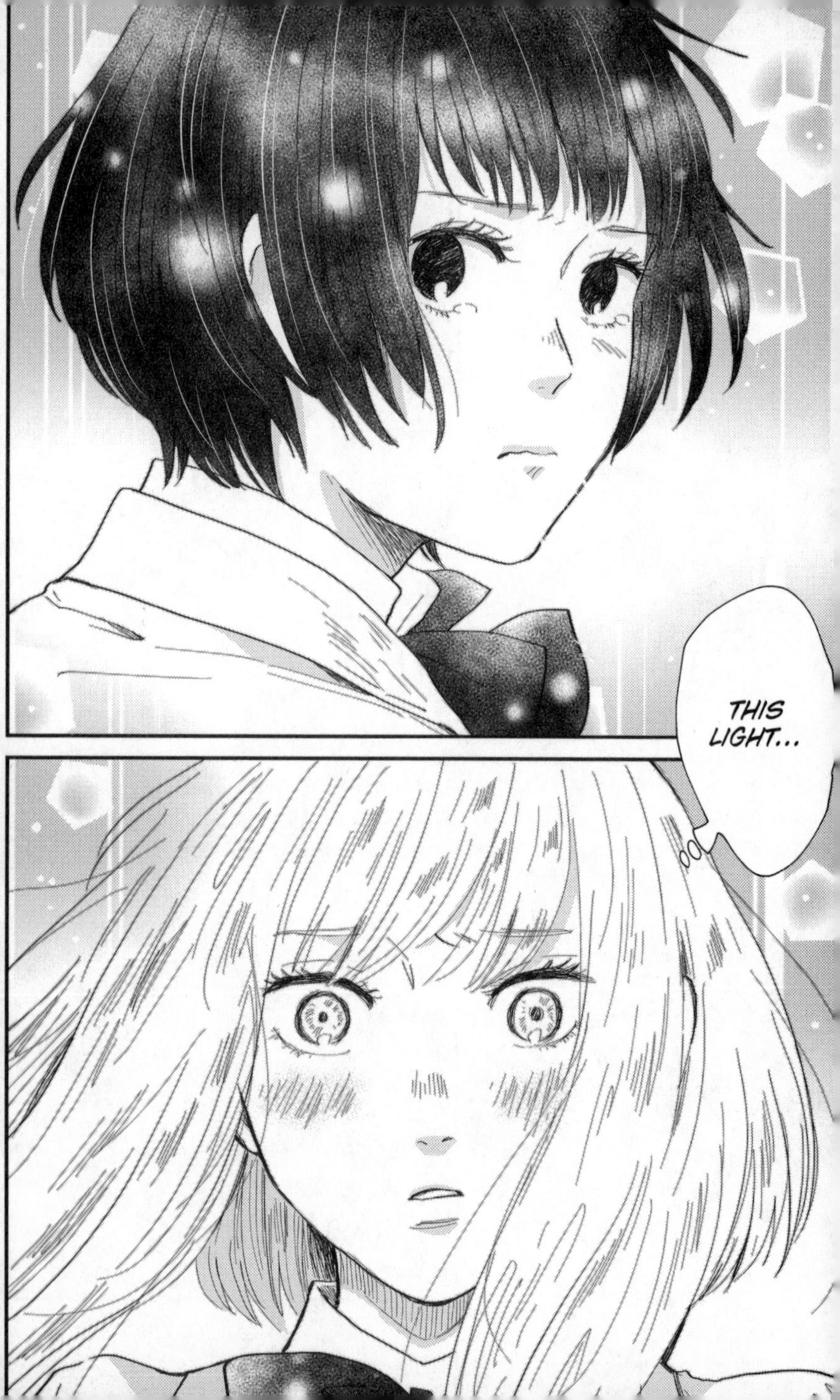
THIS LIGHT...

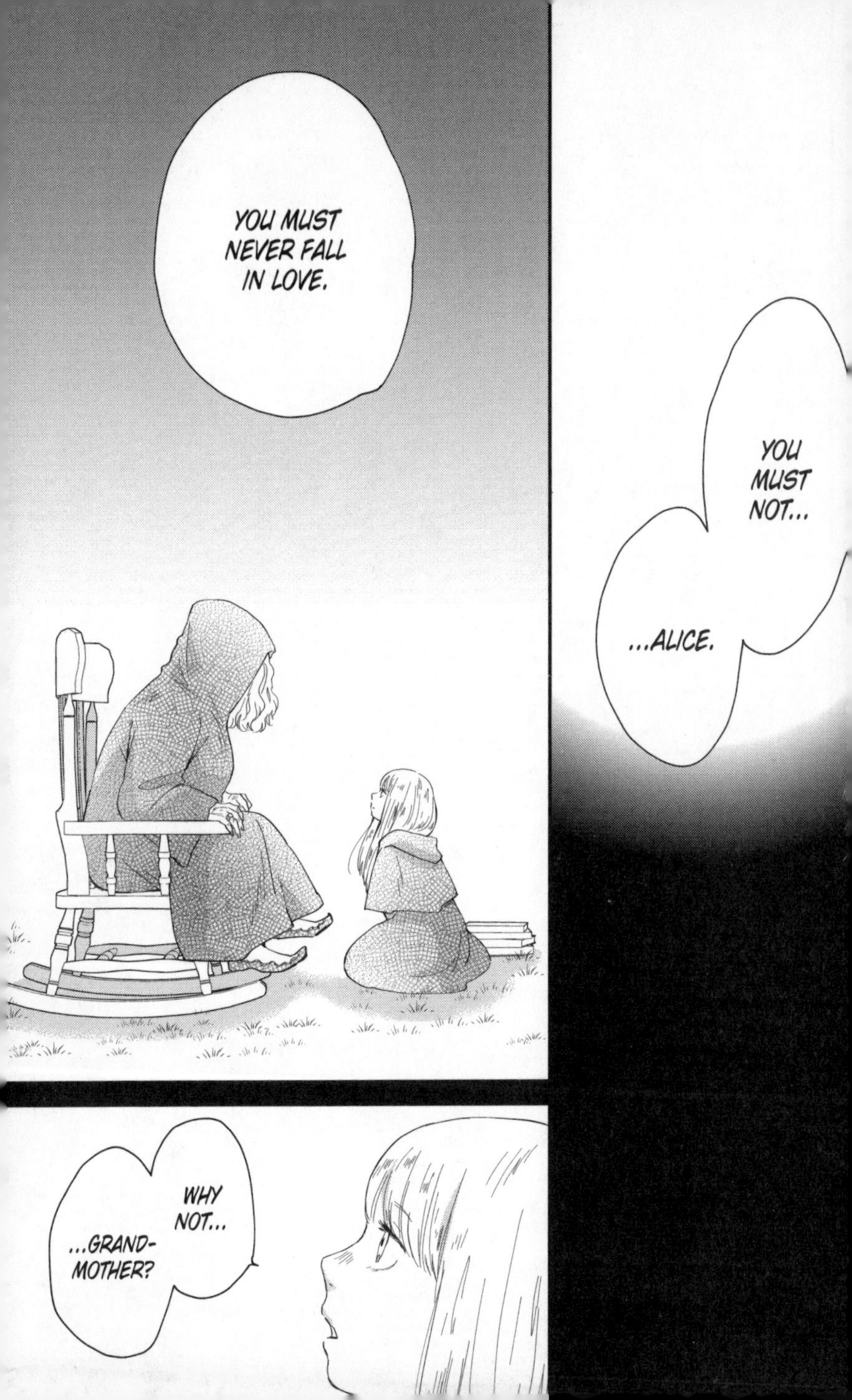
YOU MUST NOT...
...ALICE.
YOU MUST NEVER FALL IN LOVE.
WHY NOT... ...GRAND-MOTHER?

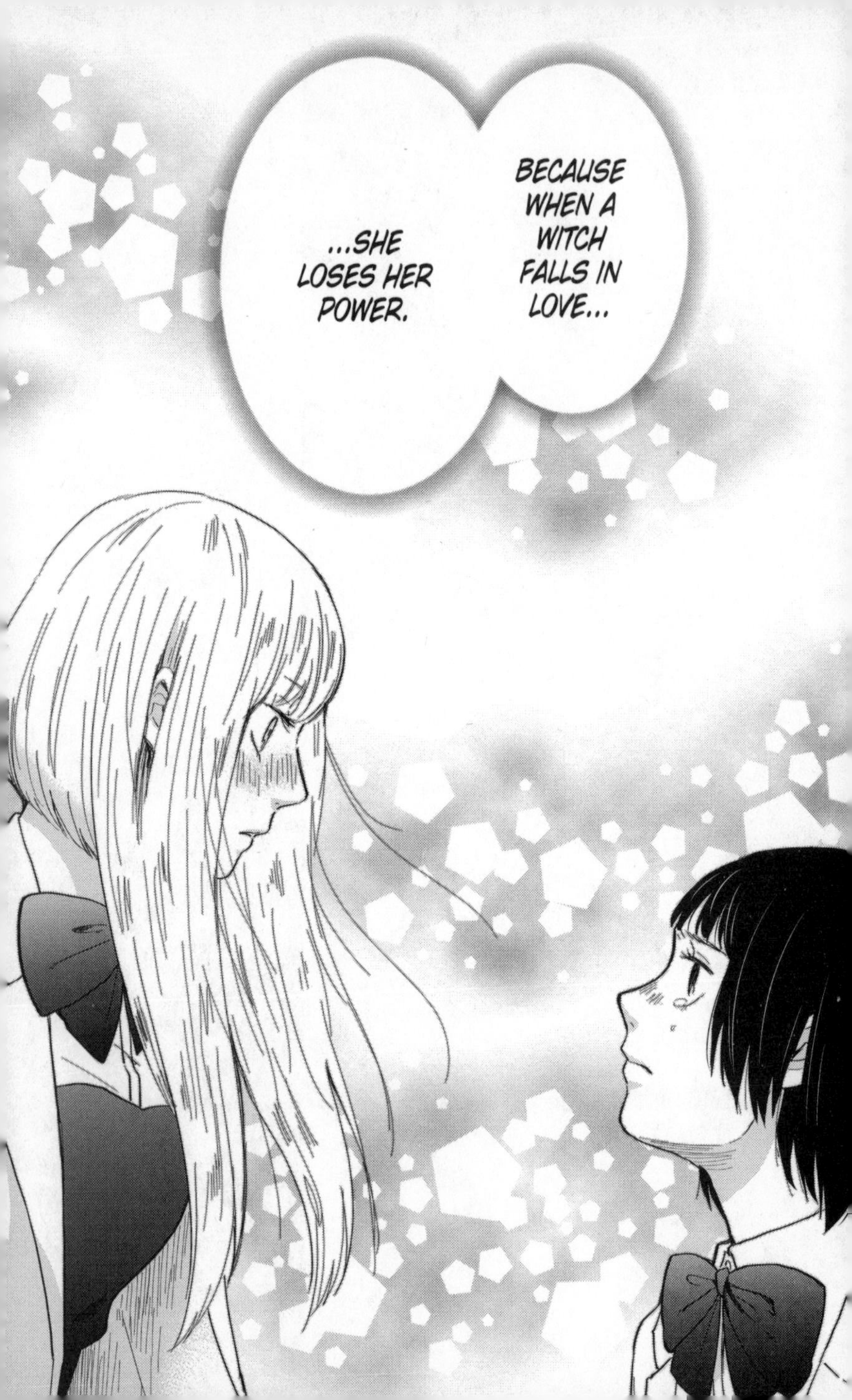
BECAUSE WHEN A WITCH FALLS IN LOVE...
...SHE LOSES HER POWER.

A Witch's Love at the End of the World

A Witch's Love at the End of the World

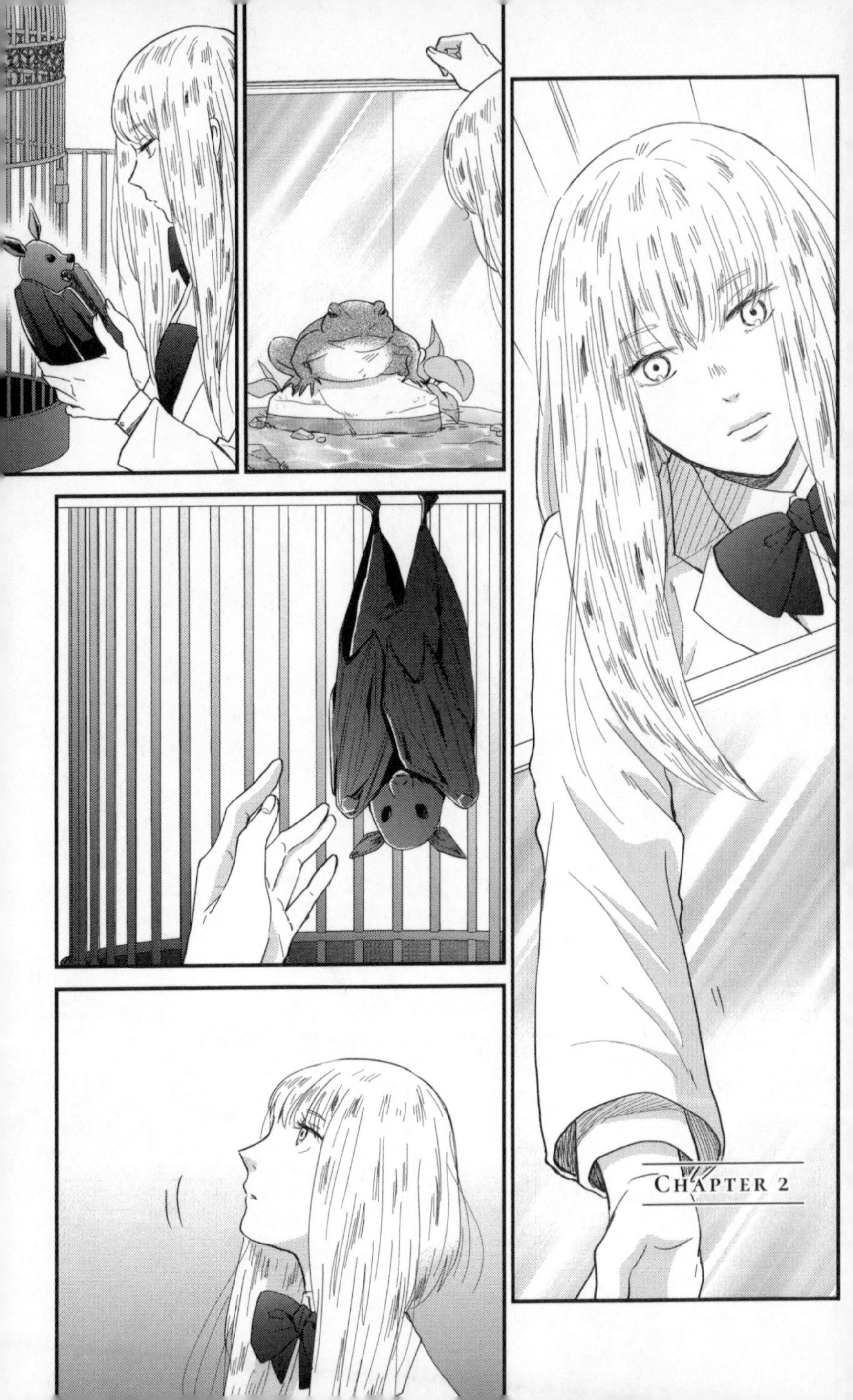
CHAPTER 2

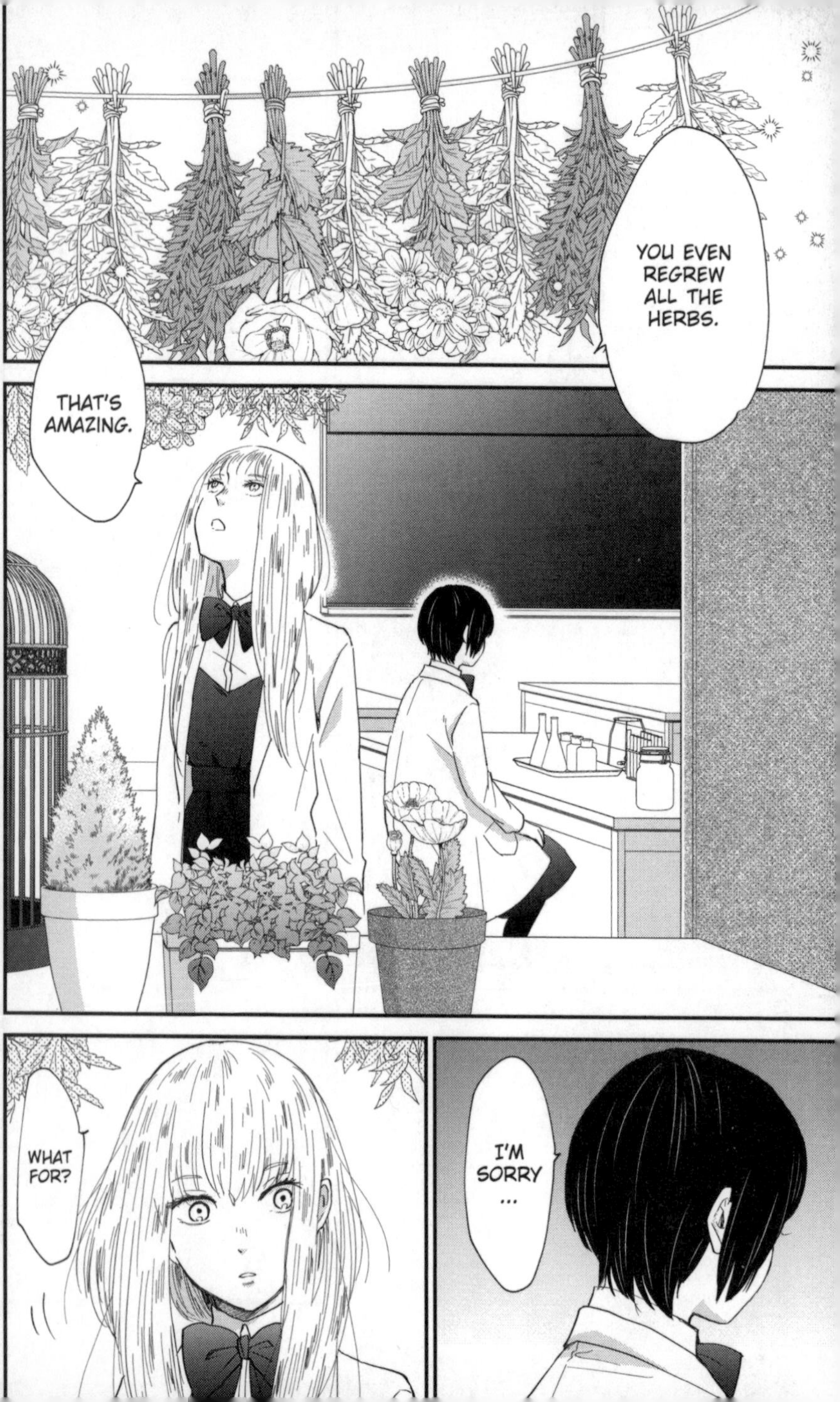
YOU EVEN REGREW ALL THE HERBS.
THAT'S AMAZING.
I'M SORRY ...
WHAT FOR?

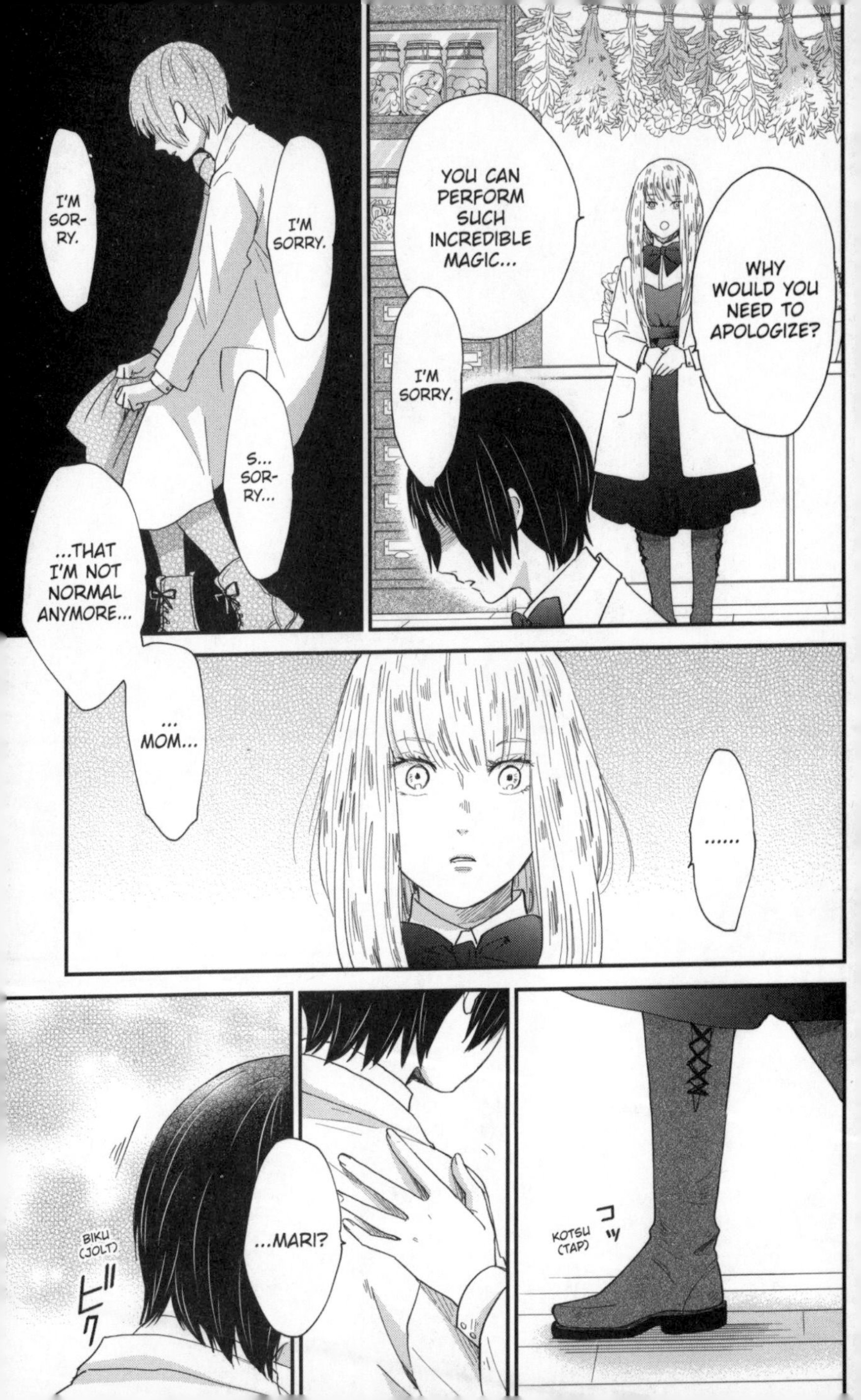
YOU CAN PERFORM SUCH INCREDIBLE MAGIC...
WHY WOULD YOU NEED TO APOLOGIZE?
I'M SORRY.
I'M SORRY.
I'M SOR-RY.
S... SOR-RY...
...THAT I'M NOT NORMAL ANYMORE...
... MOM...
......
KOTSU (TAP)
コッ
...MARI?
BIKU (JOLT)
ビク

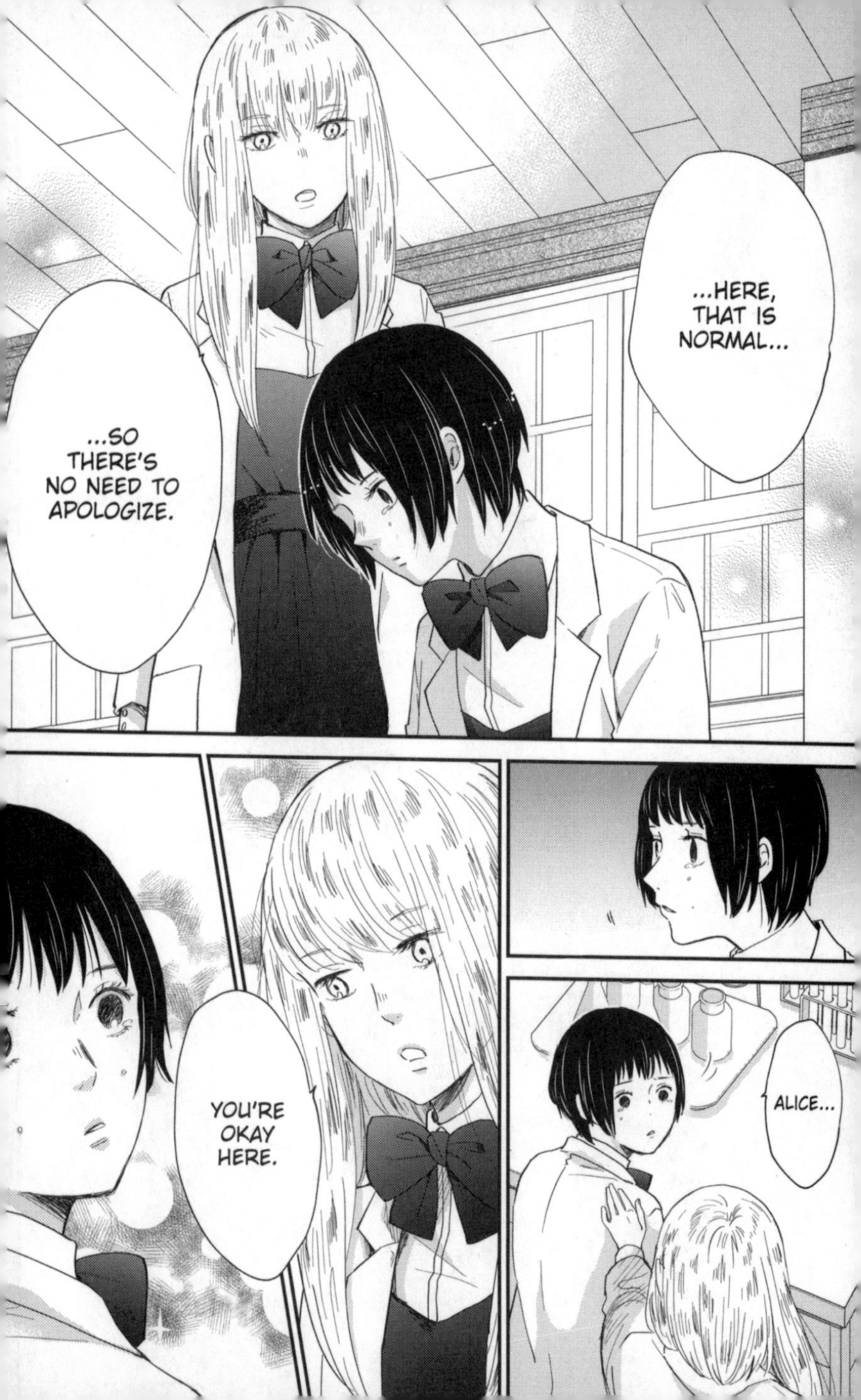
...HERE, THAT IS NORMAL...
...SO THERE'S NO NEED TO APOLOGIZE.
ALICE...
YOU'RE OKAY HERE.

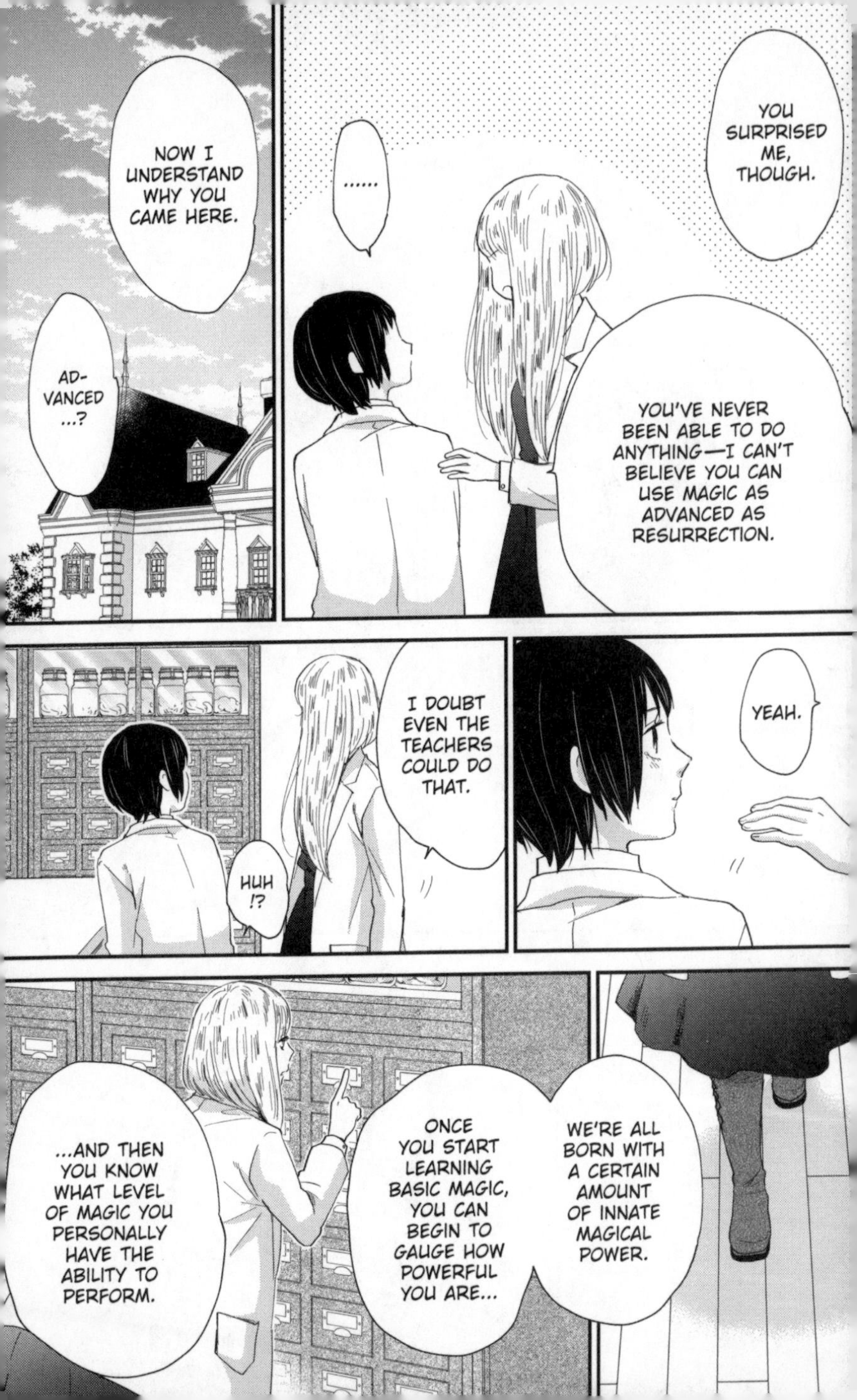
YOU SURPRISED ME, THOUGH.
......
YOU'VE NEVER BEEN ABLE TO DO ANYTHING—I CAN'T BELIEVE YOU CAN USE MAGIC AS ADVANCED AS RESURRECTION.
NOW I UNDERSTAND WHY YOU CAME HERE.
AD-VANCED ...?
YEAH.
I DOUBT EVEN THE TEACHERS COULD DO THAT.
HUH !?
WE'RE ALL BORN WITH A CERTAIN AMOUNT OF INNATE MAGICAL POWER.
ONCE YOU START LEARNING BASIC MAGIC, YOU CAN BEGIN TO GAUGE HOW POWERFUL YOU ARE...
...AND THEN YOU KNOW WHAT LEVEL OF MAGIC YOU PERSONALLY HAVE THE ABILITY TO PERFORM.

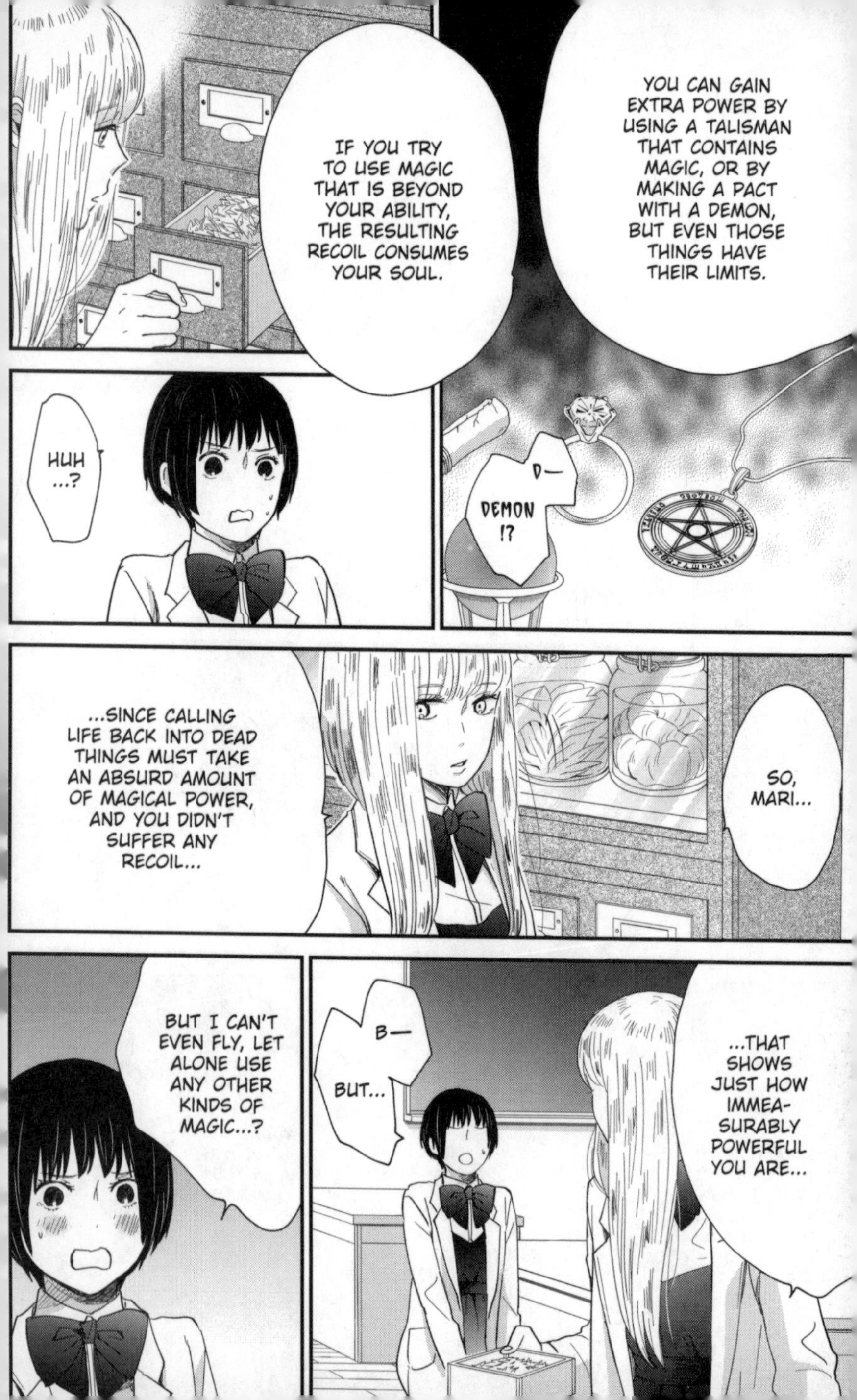
IF YOU TRY TO USE MAGIC THAT IS BEYOND YOUR ABILITY, THE RESULTING RECOIL CONSUMES YOUR SOUL.
HUH ...?
YOU CAN GAIN EXTRA POWER BY USING A TALISMAN THAT CONTAINS MAGIC, OR BY MAKING A PACT WITH A DEMON, BUT EVEN THOSE THINGS HAVE THEIR LIMITS.
D— DEMON !?
SO, MARI...
...SINCE CALLING LIFE BACK INTO DEAD THINGS MUST TAKE AN ABSURD AMOUNT OF MAGICAL POWER, AND YOU DIDN'T SUFFER ANY RECOIL...
...THAT SHOWS JUST HOW IMMEA-SURABLY POWERFUL YOU ARE...
B— BUT...
BUT I CAN'T EVEN FLY, LET ALONE USE ANY OTHER KINDS OF MAGIC...?

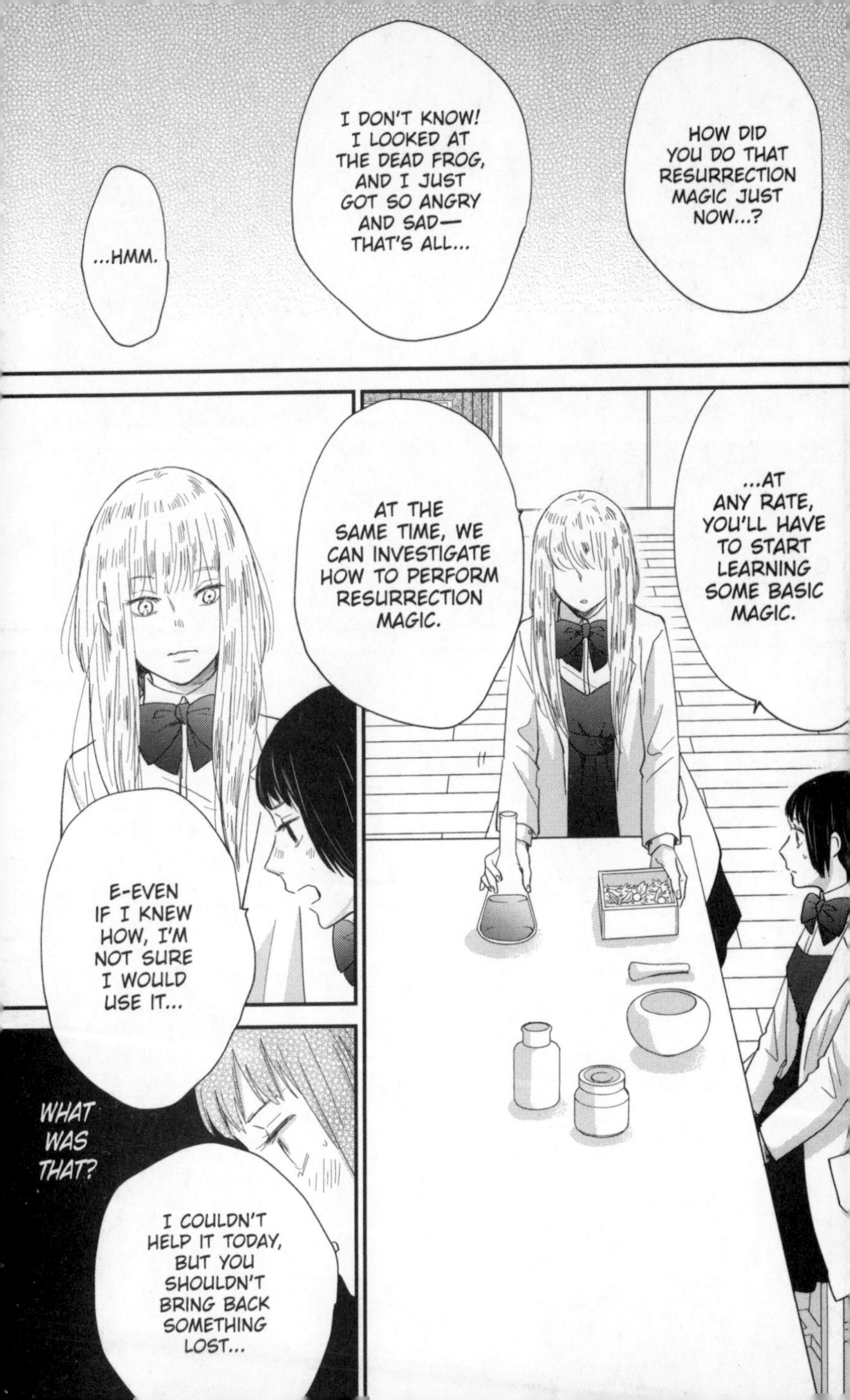
HOW DID YOU DO THAT RESURRECTION MAGIC JUST NOW...?
I DON'T KNOW! I LOOKED AT THE DEAD FROG, AND I JUST GOT SO ANGRY AND SAD— THAT'S ALL...
...HMM.
...AT ANY RATE, YOU'LL HAVE TO START LEARNING SOME BASIC MAGIC.
AT THE SAME TIME, WE CAN INVESTIGATE HOW TO PERFORM RESURRECTION MAGIC.
E-EVEN IF I KNEW HOW, I'M NOT SURE I WOULD USE IT...
WHAT WAS THAT?
I COULDN'T HELP IT TODAY, BUT YOU SHOULDN'T BRING BACK SOMETHING LOST...

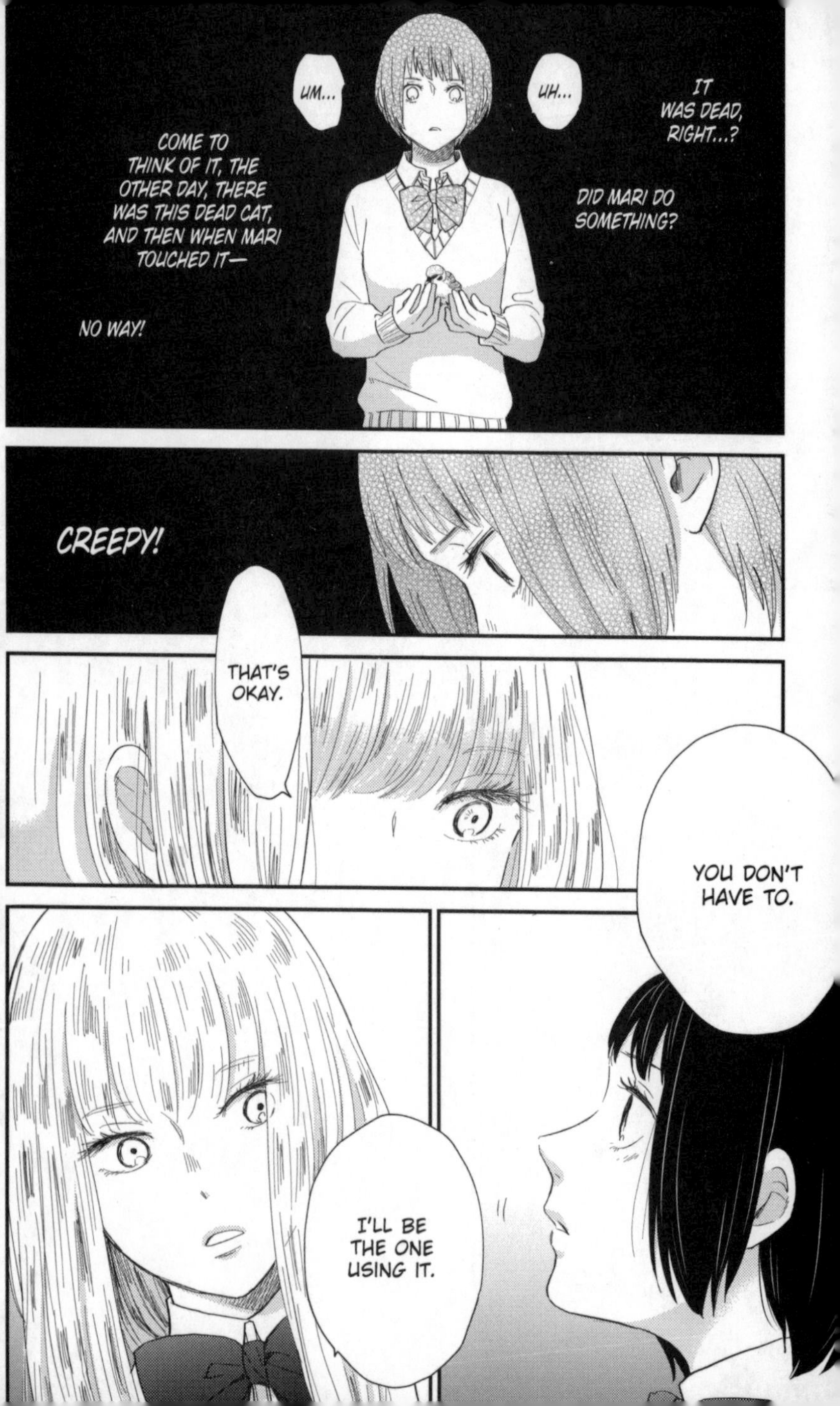
IT WAS DEAD, RIGHT...?
UH...
UM...
DID MARI DO SOMETHING?
COME TO THINK OF IT, THE OTHER DAY, THERE WAS THIS DEAD CAT, AND THEN WHEN MARI TOUCHED IT—
NO WAY!
CREEPY!
THAT'S OKAY.
YOU DON'T HAVE TO.
I'LL BE THE ONE USING IT.

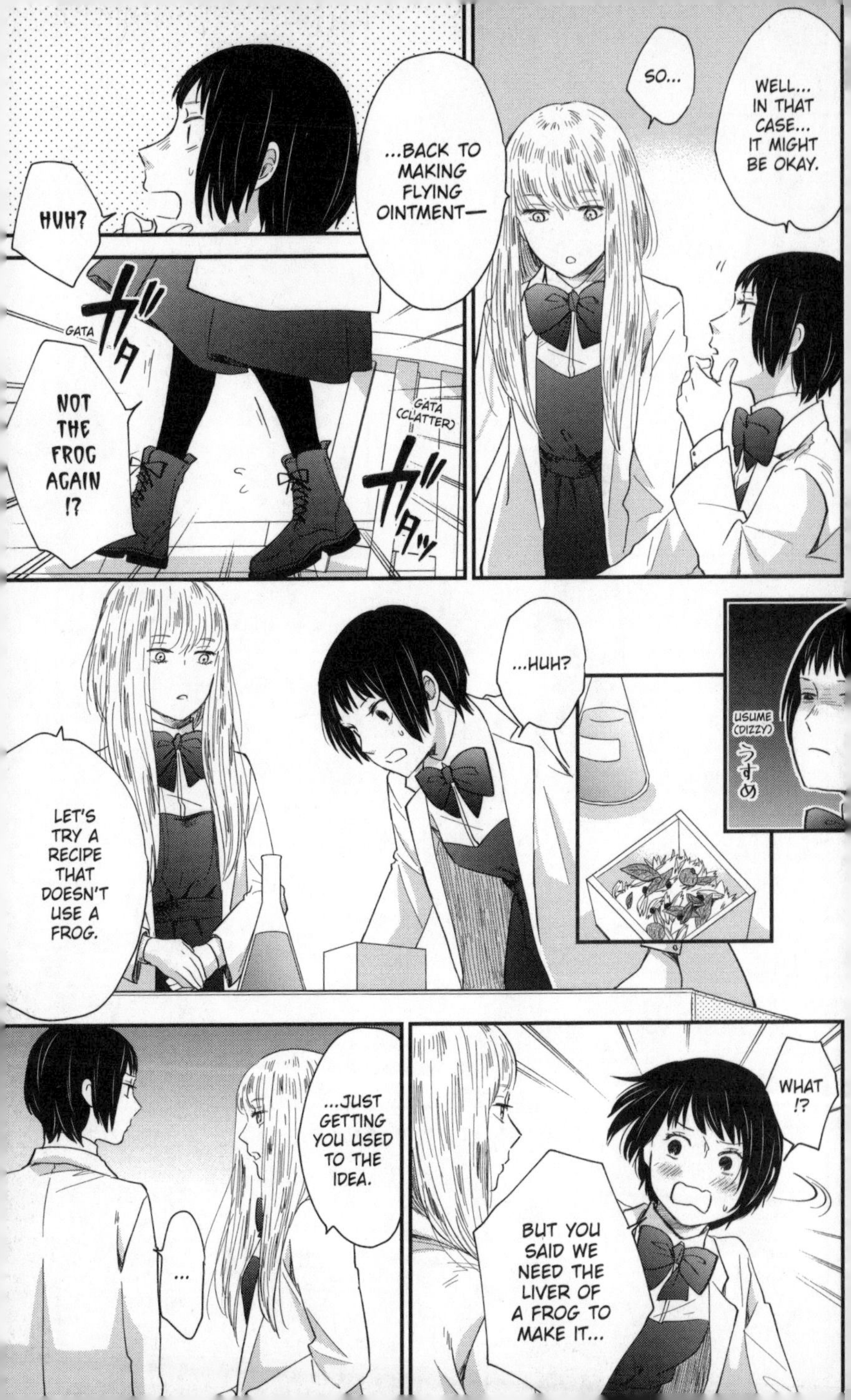

WELL... IN THAT CASE... IT MIGHT BE OKAY.
SO...
...BACK TO MAKING FLYING OINTMENT—
HUH?
GATA
ガタ
NOT THE FROG AGAIN !?
GATA (CLATTER)
ガタッ
USUME (DIZZY)
うすめ
...HUH?
LET'S TRY A RECIPE THAT DOESN'T USE A FROG.
WHAT !?
BUT YOU SAID WE NEED THE LIVER OF A FROG TO MAKE IT...
...JUST GETTING YOU USED TO THE IDEA.
...

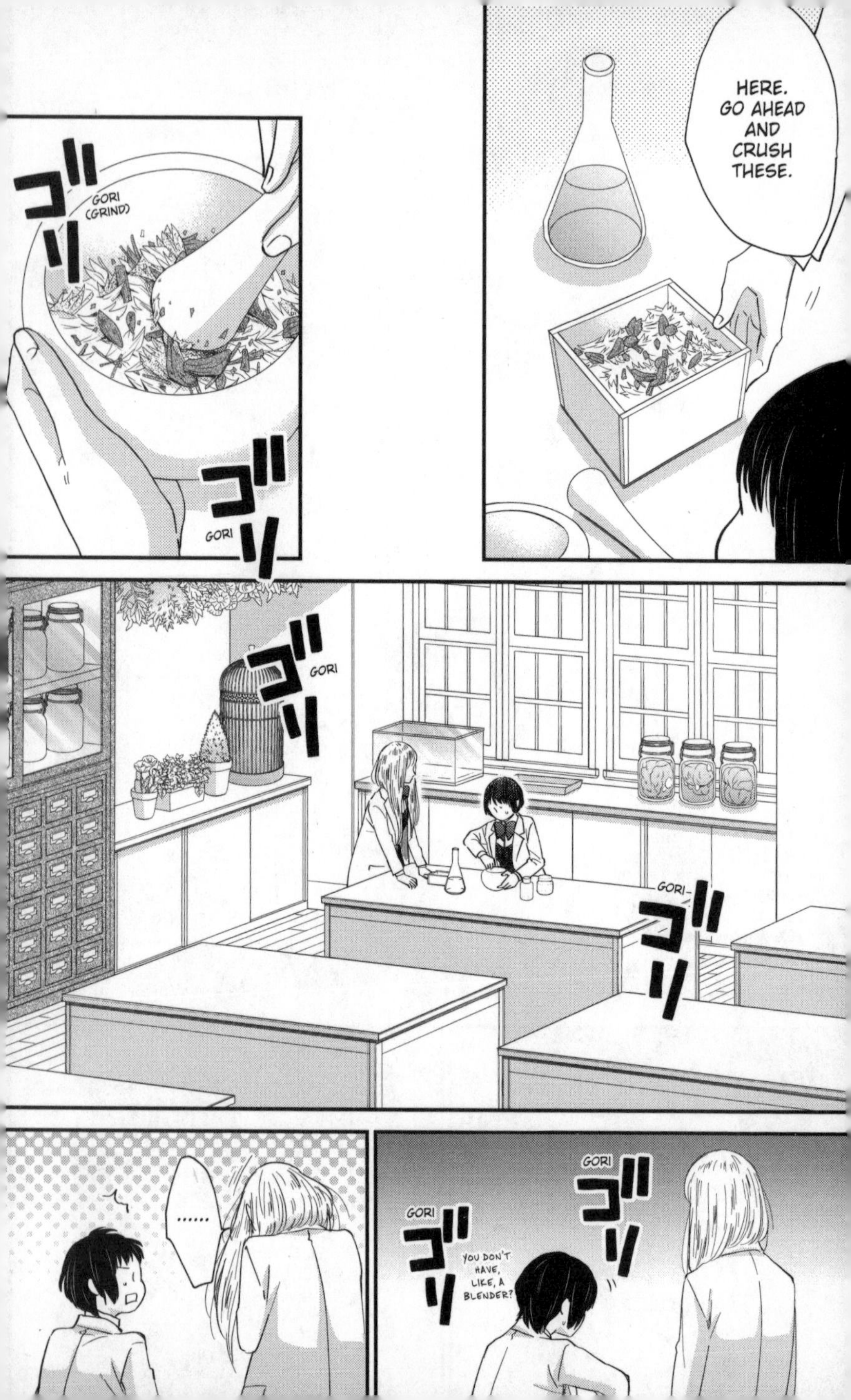
HERE. GO AHEAD AND CRUSH THESE.
GORI (GRIND)
GORI
GORI
GORI
GORI
GORI
YOU DON'T HAVE, LIKE, A BLENDER?
......

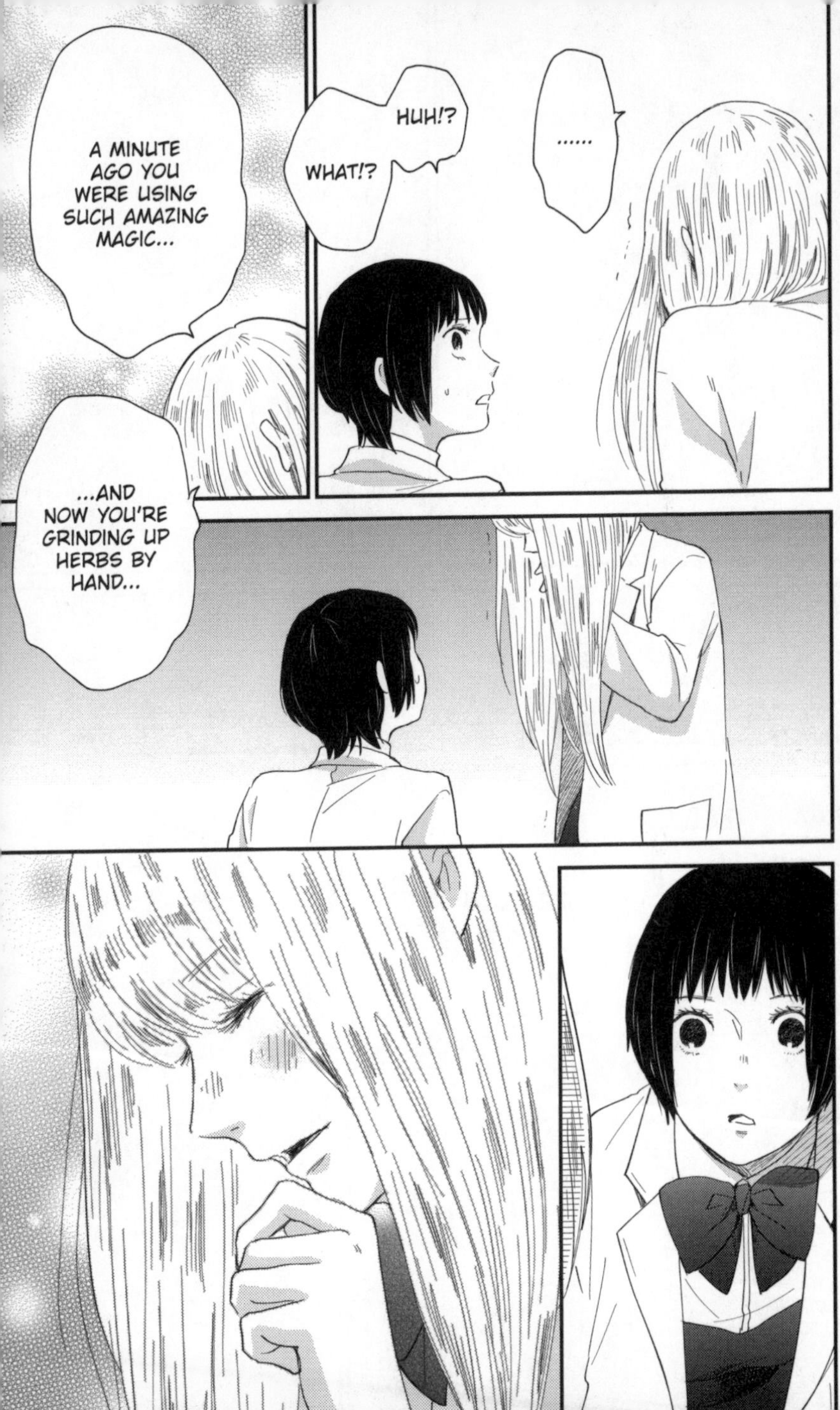
......
HUH!? WHAT!?
A MINUTE AGO YOU WERE USING SUCH AMAZING MAGIC...
...AND NOW YOU'RE GRINDING UP HERBS BY HAND...

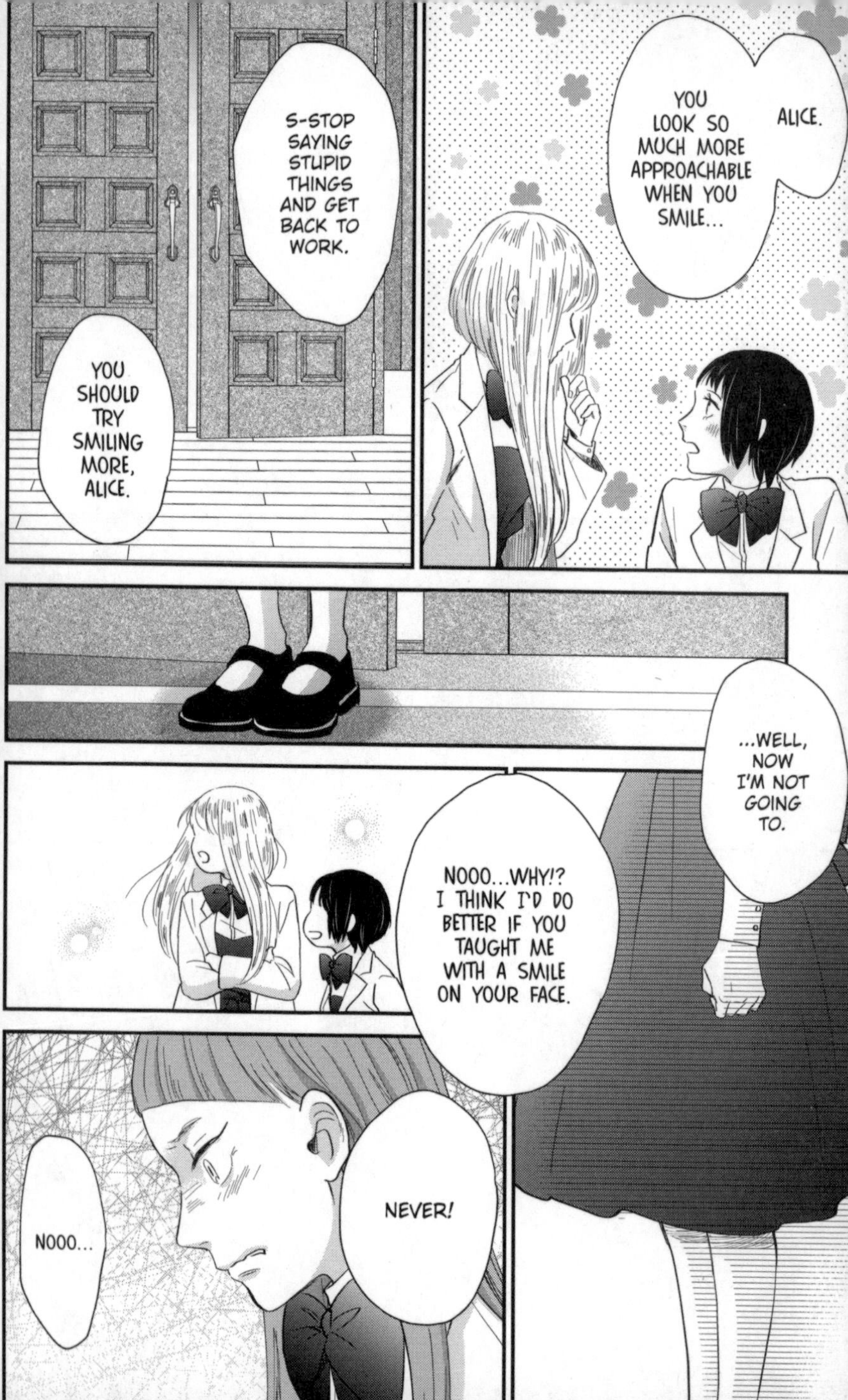
YOU LOOK SO MUCH MORE APPROACHABLE WHEN YOU SMILE... ALICE.
S-STOP SAYING STUPID THINGS AND GET BACK TO WORK.
YOU SHOULD TRY SMILING MORE, ALICE.
...WELL, NOW I'M NOT GOING TO.
NOOO...WHY!? I THINK I'D DO BETTER IF YOU TAUGHT ME WITH A SMILE ON YOUR FACE.
NEVER!
NOOO...

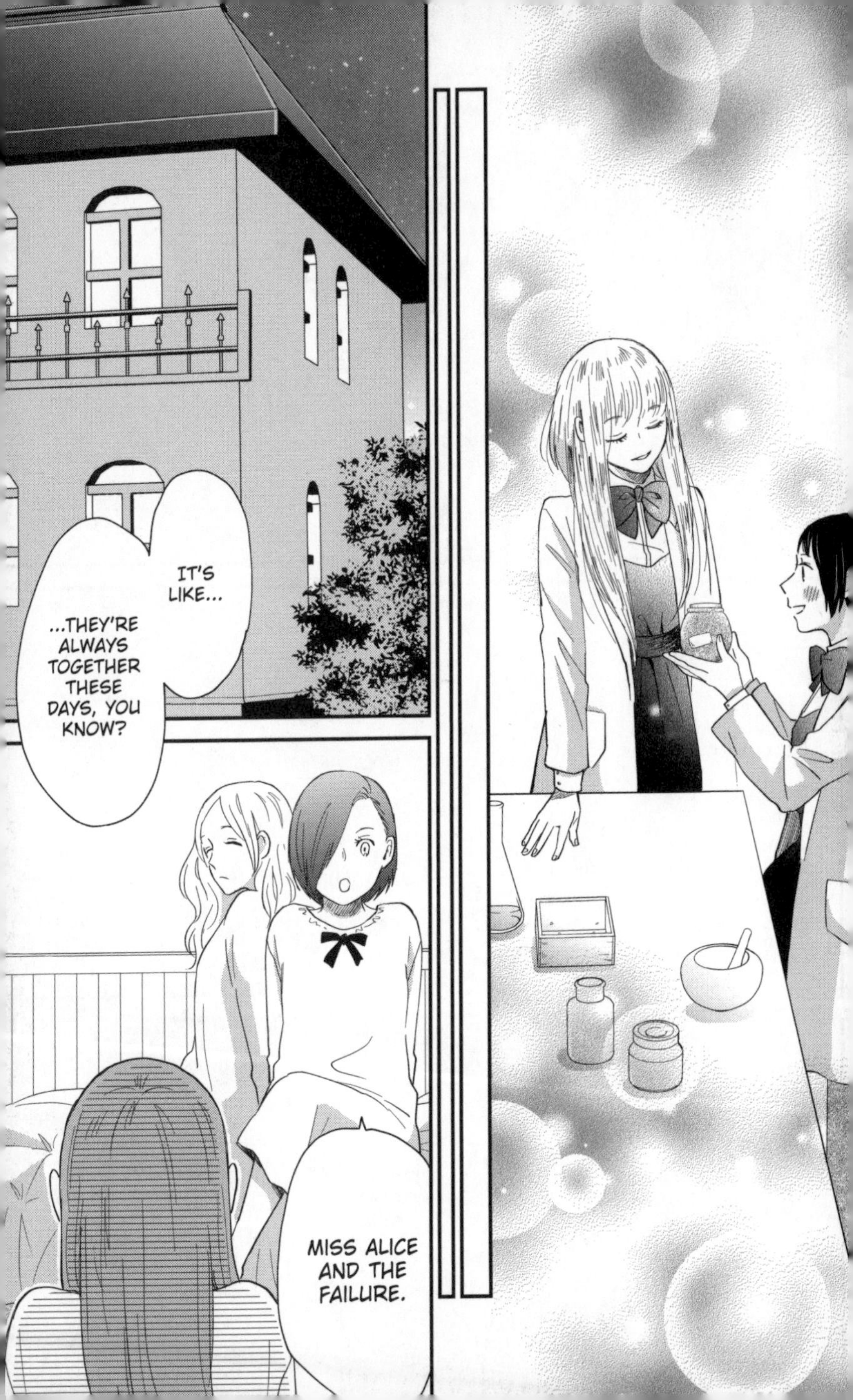
IT'S LIKE... ...THEY'RE ALWAYS TOGETHER THESE DAYS, YOU KNOW?
MISS ALICE AND THE FAILURE.

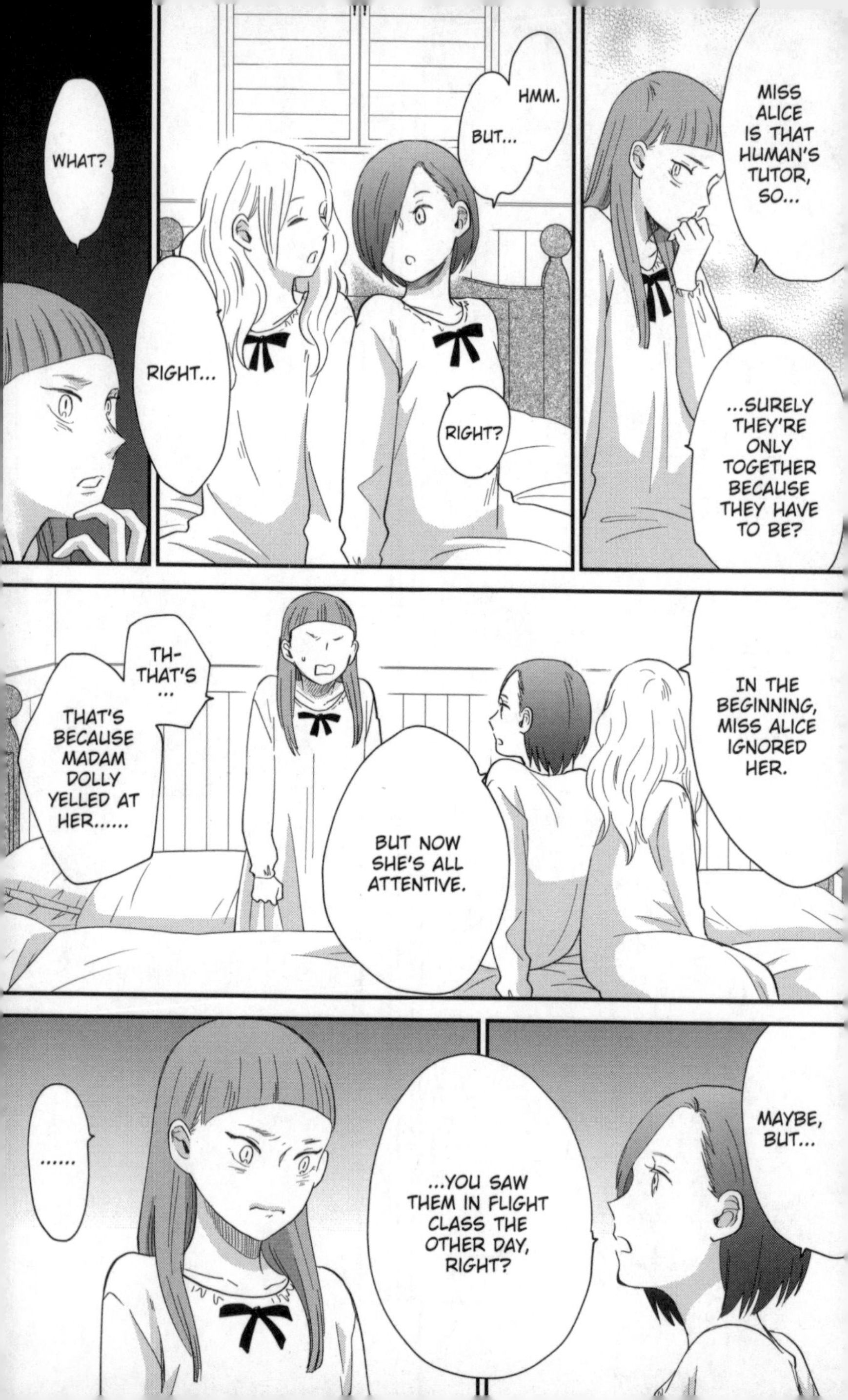
MISS ALICE IS THAT HUMAN'S TUTOR, SO...
...SURELY THEY'RE ONLY TOGETHER BECAUSE THEY HAVE TO BE?
HMM.
BUT...
RIGHT?
RIGHT...
WHAT?
IN THE BEGINNING, MISS ALICE IGNORED HER.
BUT NOW SHE'S ALL ATTENTIVE.
TH-THAT'S...
THAT'S BECAUSE MADAM DOLLY YELLED AT HER......
MAYBE, BUT...
...YOU SAW THEM IN FLIGHT CLASS THE OTHER DAY, RIGHT?
......

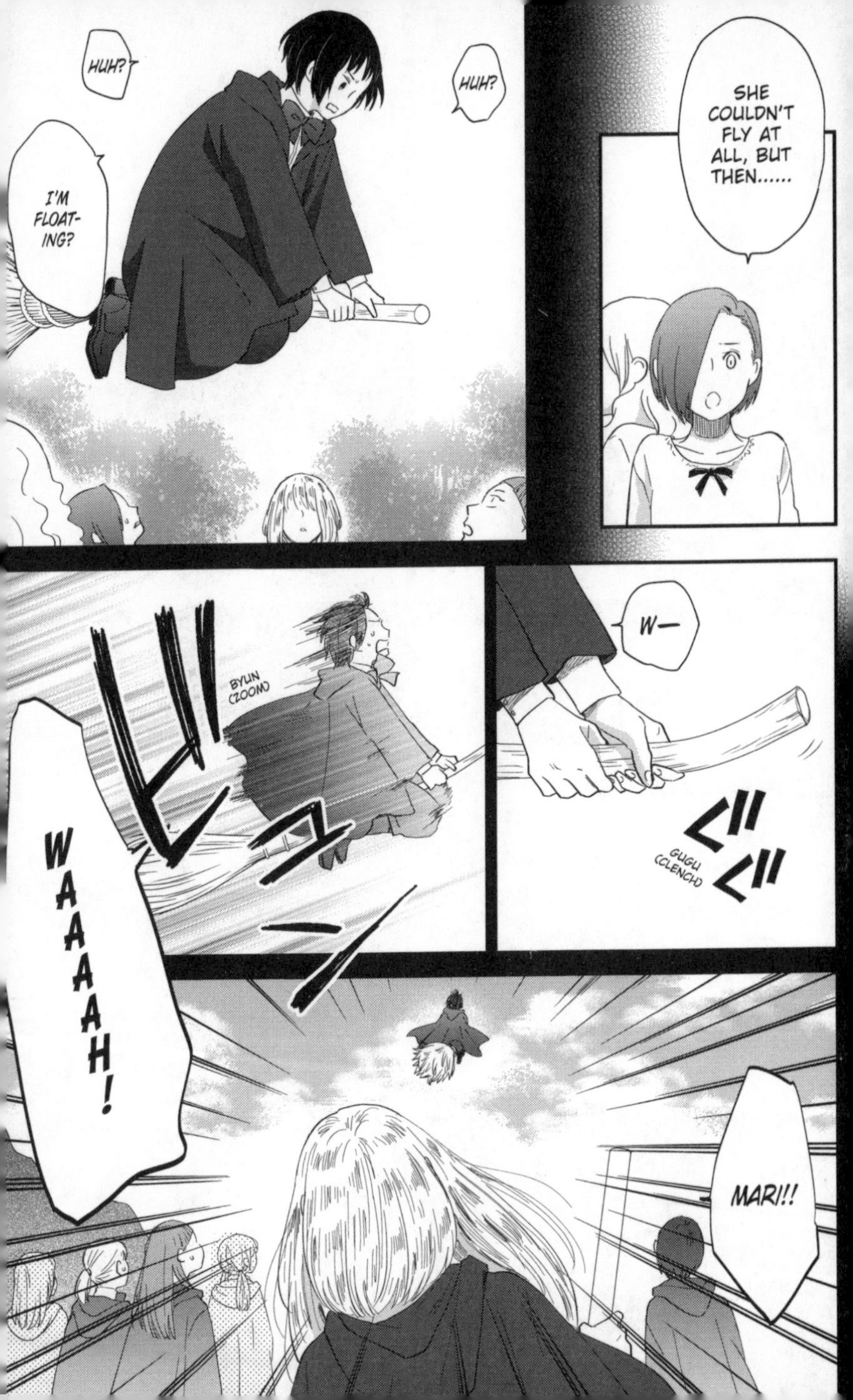
SHE COULDN'T FLY AT ALL, BUT THEN......
HUH?
HUH?
I'M FLOAT-ING?
W—
ぐぐ
GUGU (CLENCH)
BYUN (ZOOM)
WAAAAAH!
MARI!!

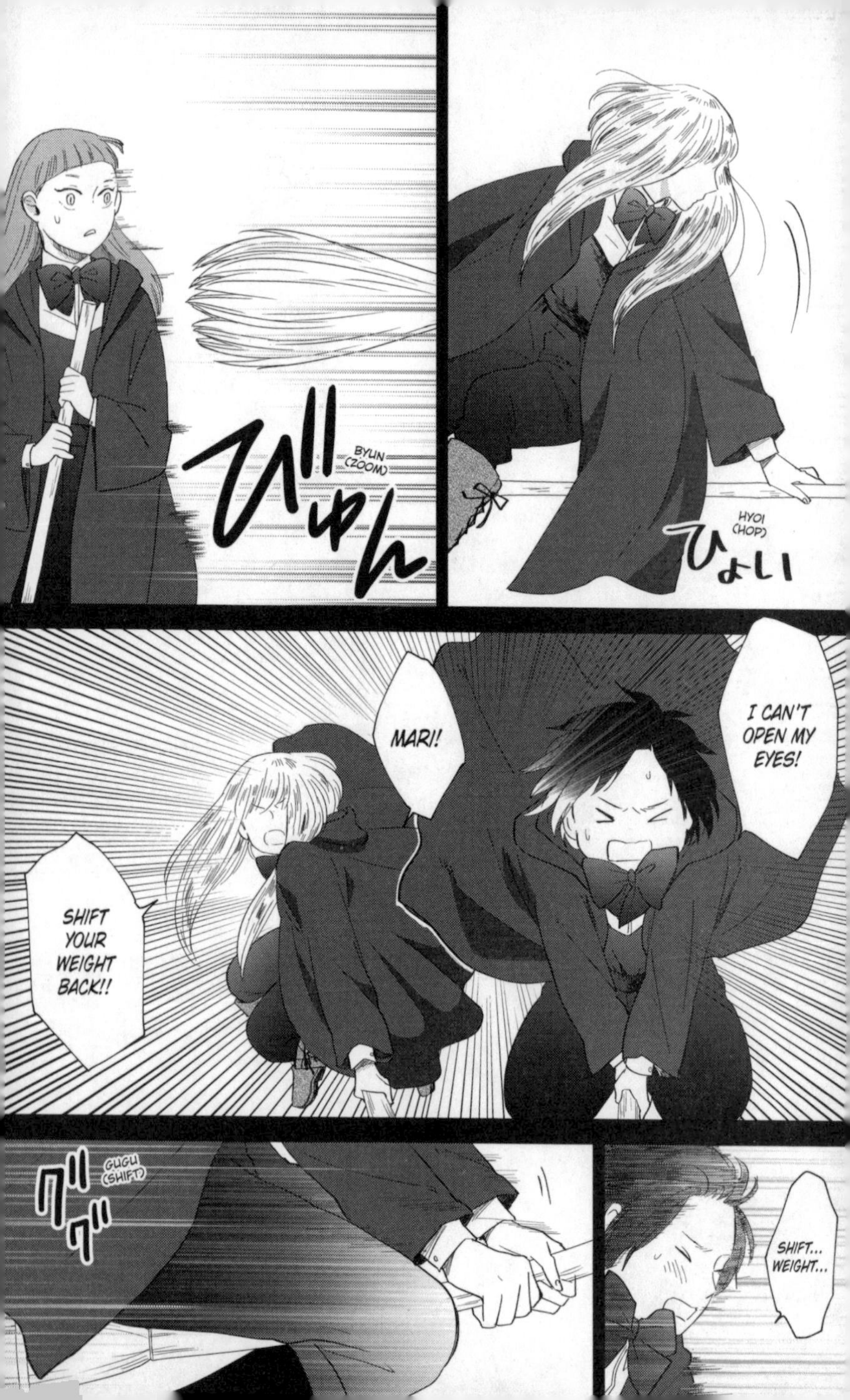
HYOI (HOP)
ひょい
BYUN (ZOOM)
びゅん
I CAN'T OPEN MY EYES!
MARI!
SHIFT YOUR WEIGHT BACK!!
SHIFT... WEIGHT...
GUGU (SHIFT)
ググ

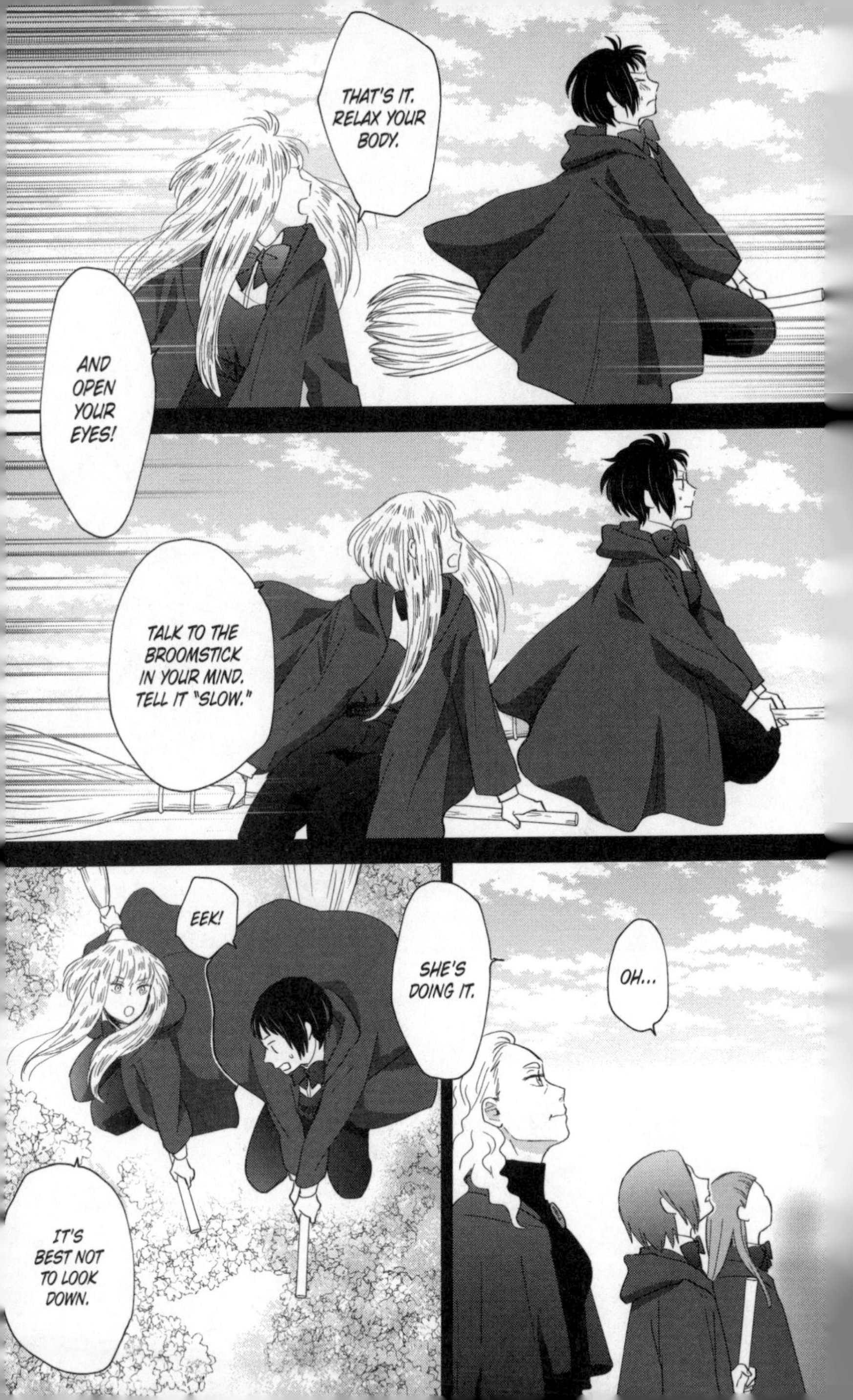
THAT'S IT. RELAX YOUR BODY.
AND OPEN YOUR EYES!
TALK TO THE BROOMSTICK IN YOUR MIND. TELL IT "SLOW."
OH...
SHE'S DOING IT.
EEK!
IT'S BEST NOT TO LOOK DOWN.

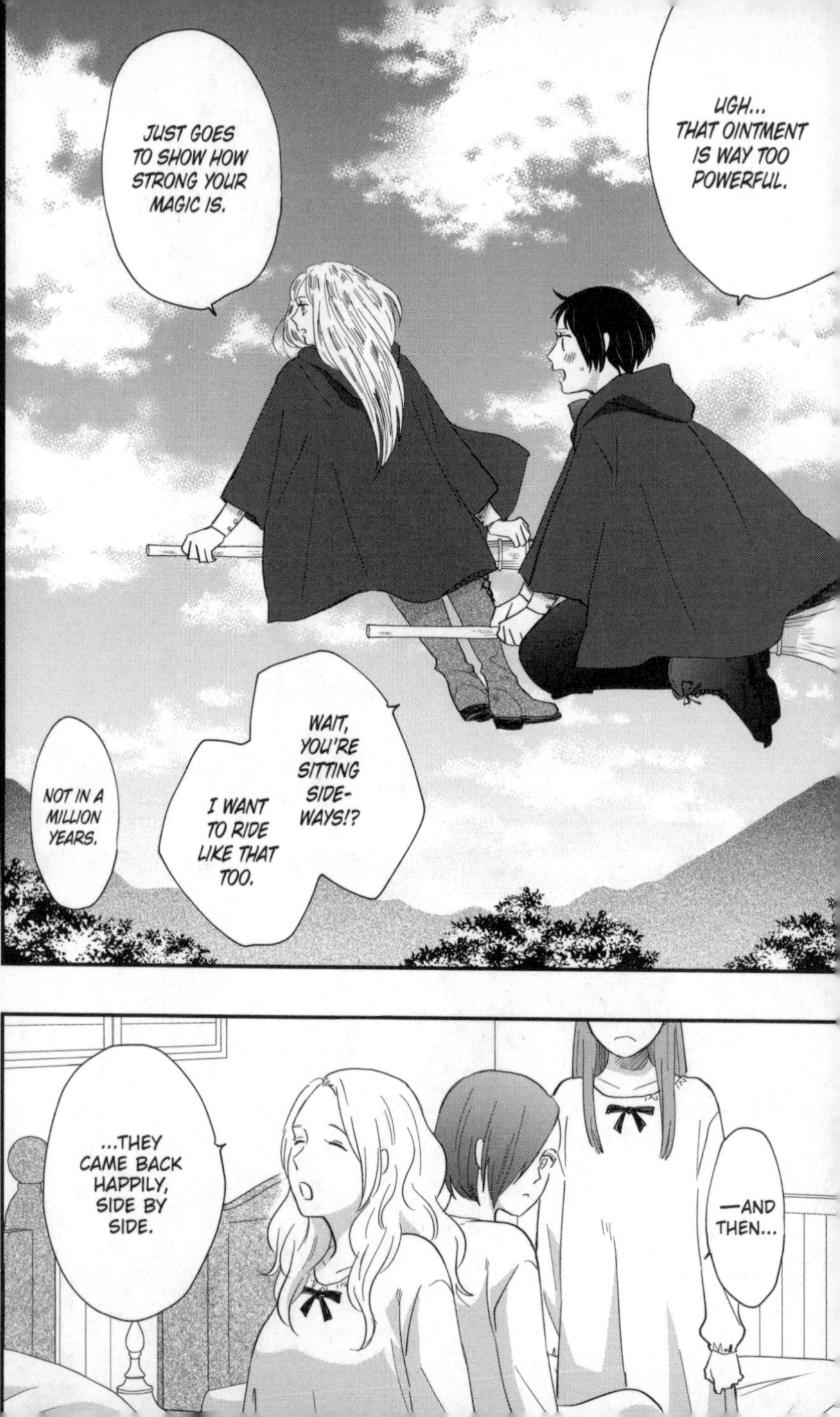
UGH... THAT OINTMENT IS WAY TOO POWERFUL.
JUST GOES TO SHOW HOW STRONG YOUR MAGIC IS.
WAIT, YOU'RE SITTING SIDE-WAYS!?
I WANT TO RIDE LIKE THAT TOO.
NOT IN A MILLION YEARS.
—AND THEN...
...THEY CAME BACK HAPPILY, SIDE BY SIDE.

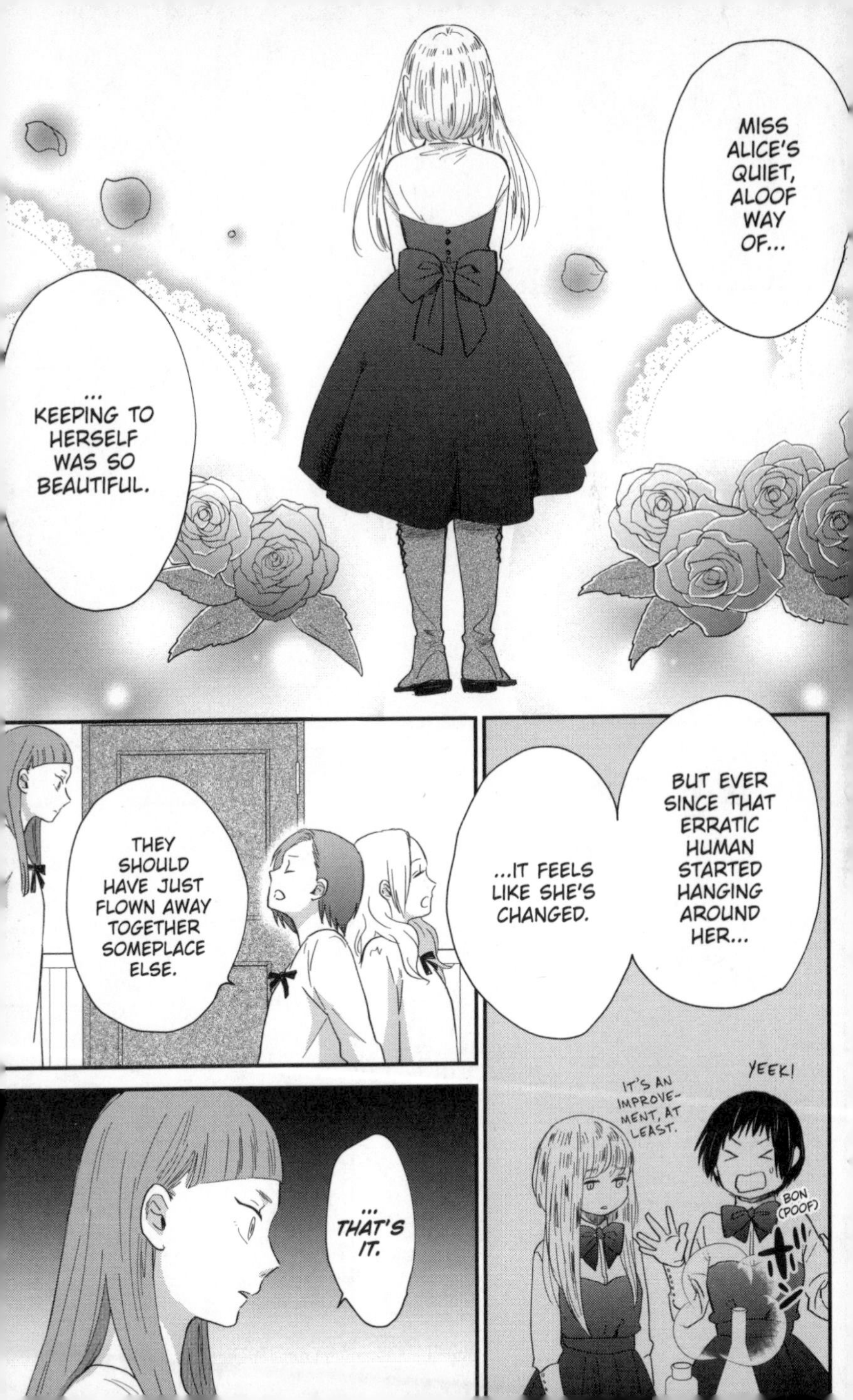
MISS ALICE'S QUIET, ALOOF WAY OF...
...KEEPING TO HERSELF WAS SO BEAUTIFUL.
BUT EVER SINCE THAT ERRATIC HUMAN STARTED HANGING AROUND HER...
...IT FEELS LIKE SHE'S CHANGED.
YEEK!
IT'S AN IMPROVEMENT, AT LEAST.
BON (POOF)
THEY SHOULD HAVE JUST FLOWN AWAY TOGETHER SOMEPLACE ELSE.
... THAT'S IT.

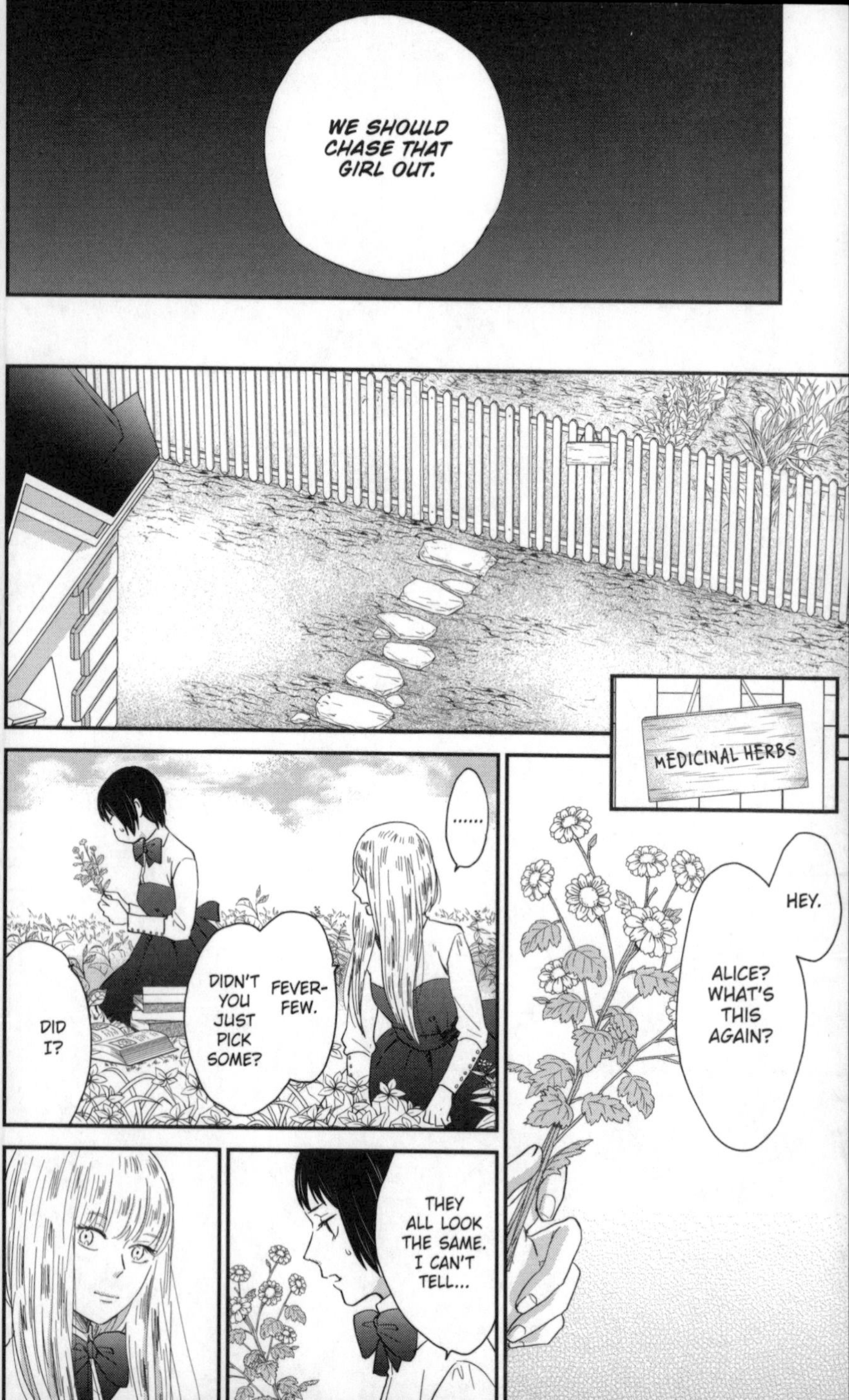
WE SHOULD CHASE THAT GIRL OUT.
MEDICINAL HERBS
HEY.
ALICE? WHAT'S THIS AGAIN?
......
FEVER-FEW.
DIDN'T YOU JUST PICK SOME?
DID I?
THEY ALL LOOK THE SAME. I CAN'T TELL...

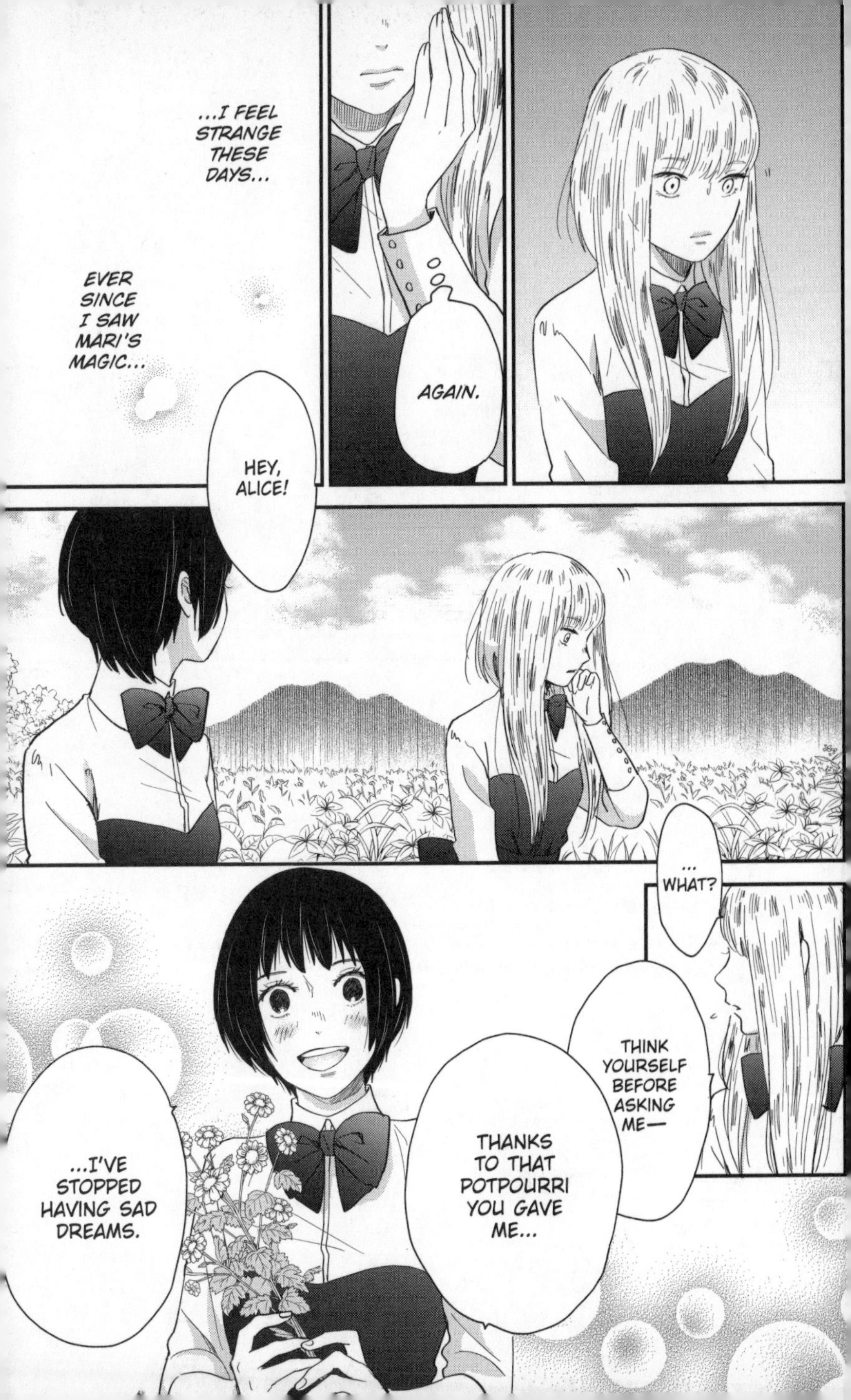
AGAIN.
...I FEEL STRANGE THESE DAYS...
EVER SINCE I SAW MARI'S MAGIC...
HEY, ALICE!
...WHAT?
THINK YOURSELF BEFORE ASKING ME—
THANKS TO THAT POTPOURRI YOU GAVE ME...
...I'VE STOPPED HAVING SAD DREAMS.

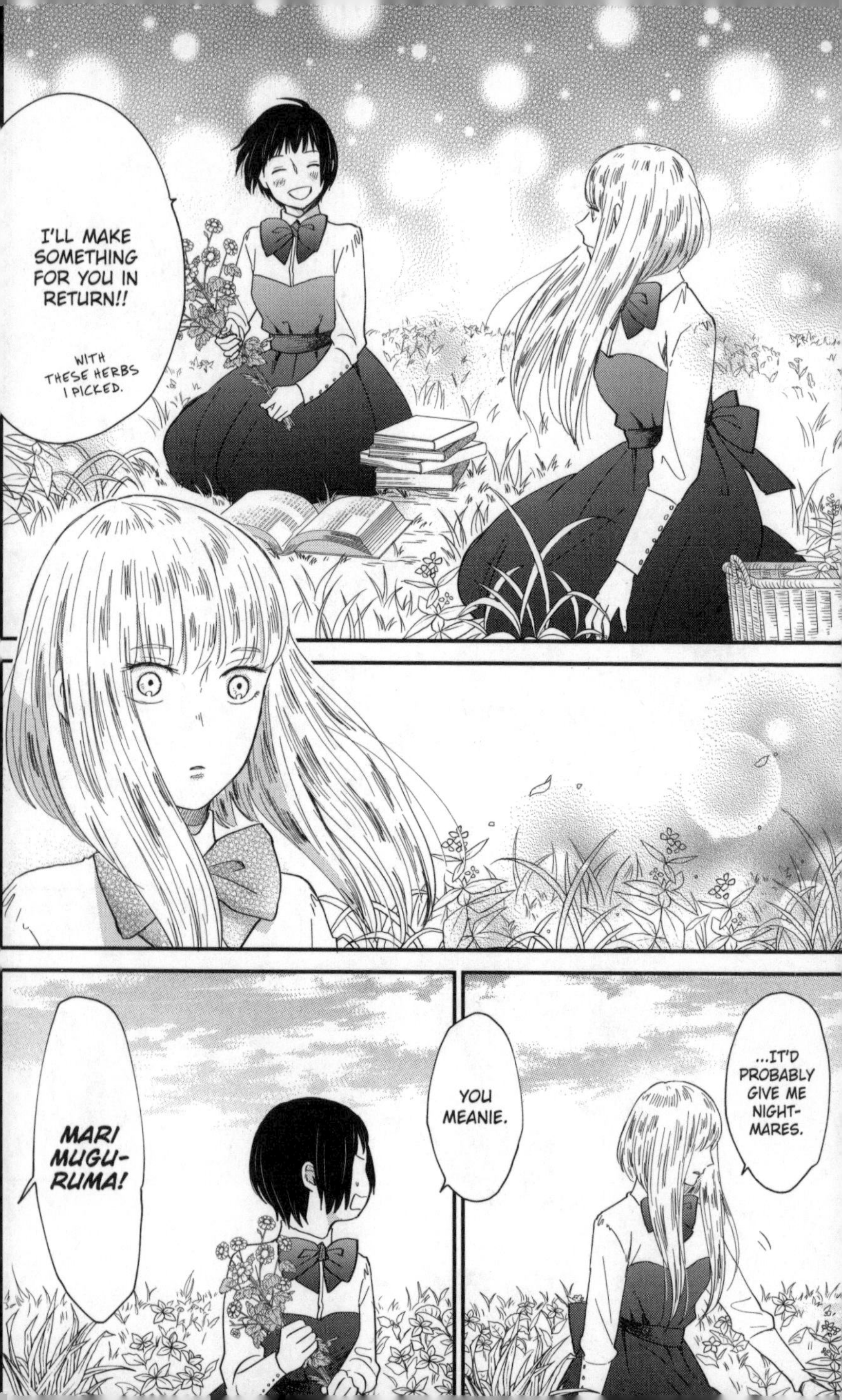
I'LL MAKE SOMETHING FOR YOU IN RETURN!!
WITH THESE HERBS I PICKED.
...IT'D PROBABLY GIVE ME NIGHT-MARES.
YOU MEANIE.
MARI MUGU-RUMA!

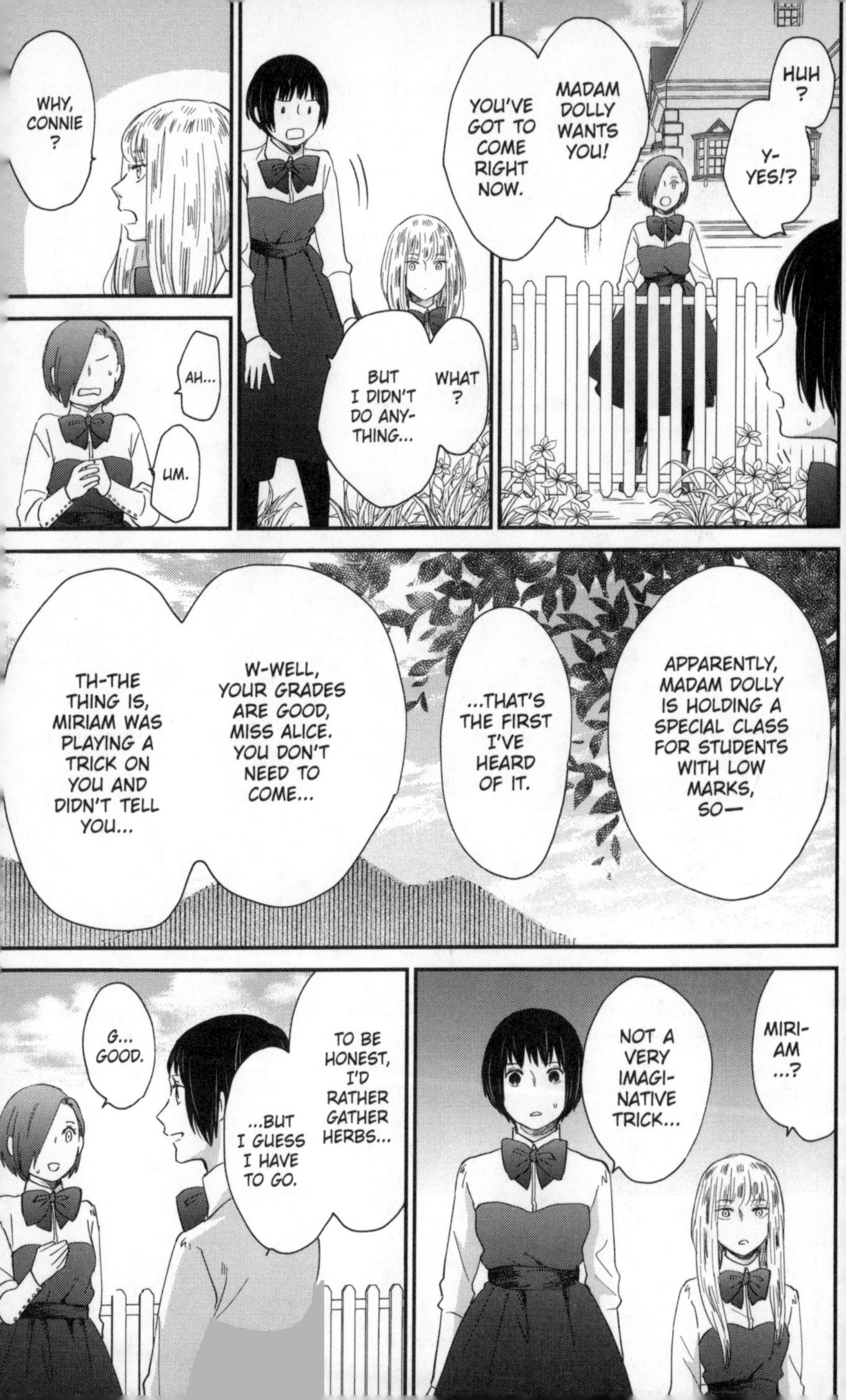
HUH?
Y-YES!?
MADAM DOLLY WANTS YOU!
YOU'VE GOT TO COME RIGHT NOW.
WHAT?
BUT I DIDN'T DO ANYTHING...
WHY, CONNIE?
AH...
UM.
APPARENTLY, MADAM DOLLY IS HOLDING A SPECIAL CLASS FOR STUDENTS WITH LOW MARKS, SO—
...THAT'S THE FIRST I'VE HEARD OF IT.
W-WELL, YOUR GRADES ARE GOOD, MISS ALICE. YOU DON'T NEED TO COME...
TH-THE THING IS, MIRIAM WAS PLAYING A TRICK ON YOU AND DIDN'T TELL YOU...
MIRIAM...?
NOT A VERY IMAGINATIVE TRICK...
TO BE HONEST, I'D RATHER GATHER HERBS...
...BUT I GUESS I HAVE TO GO.
G... GOOD.

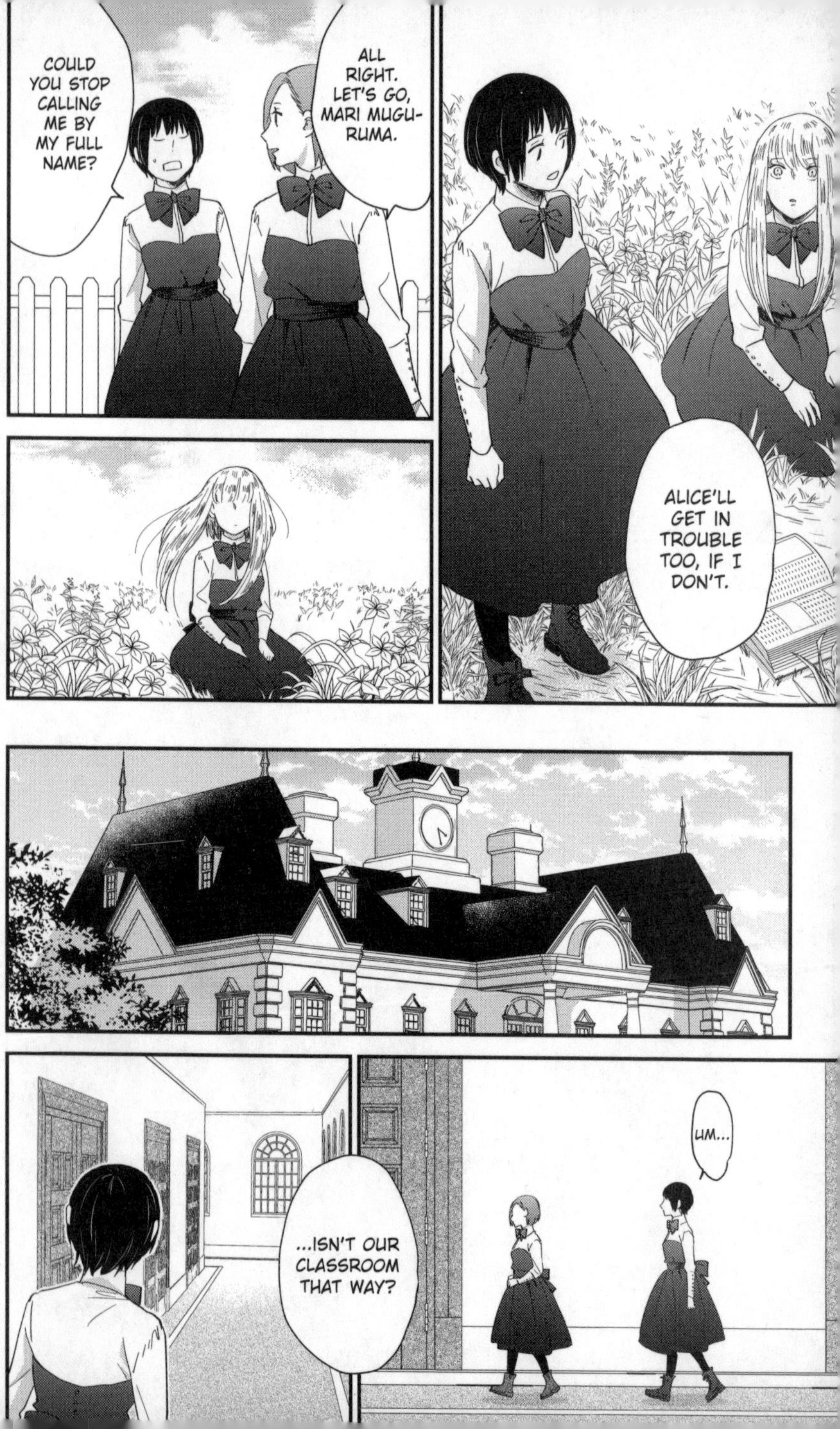
ALICE'LL GET IN TROUBLE TOO, IF I DON'T.
ALL RIGHT. LET'S GO, MARI MUGU-RUMA.
COULD YOU STOP CALLING ME BY MY FULL NAME?
UM...
...ISN'T OUR CLASSROOM THAT WAY?

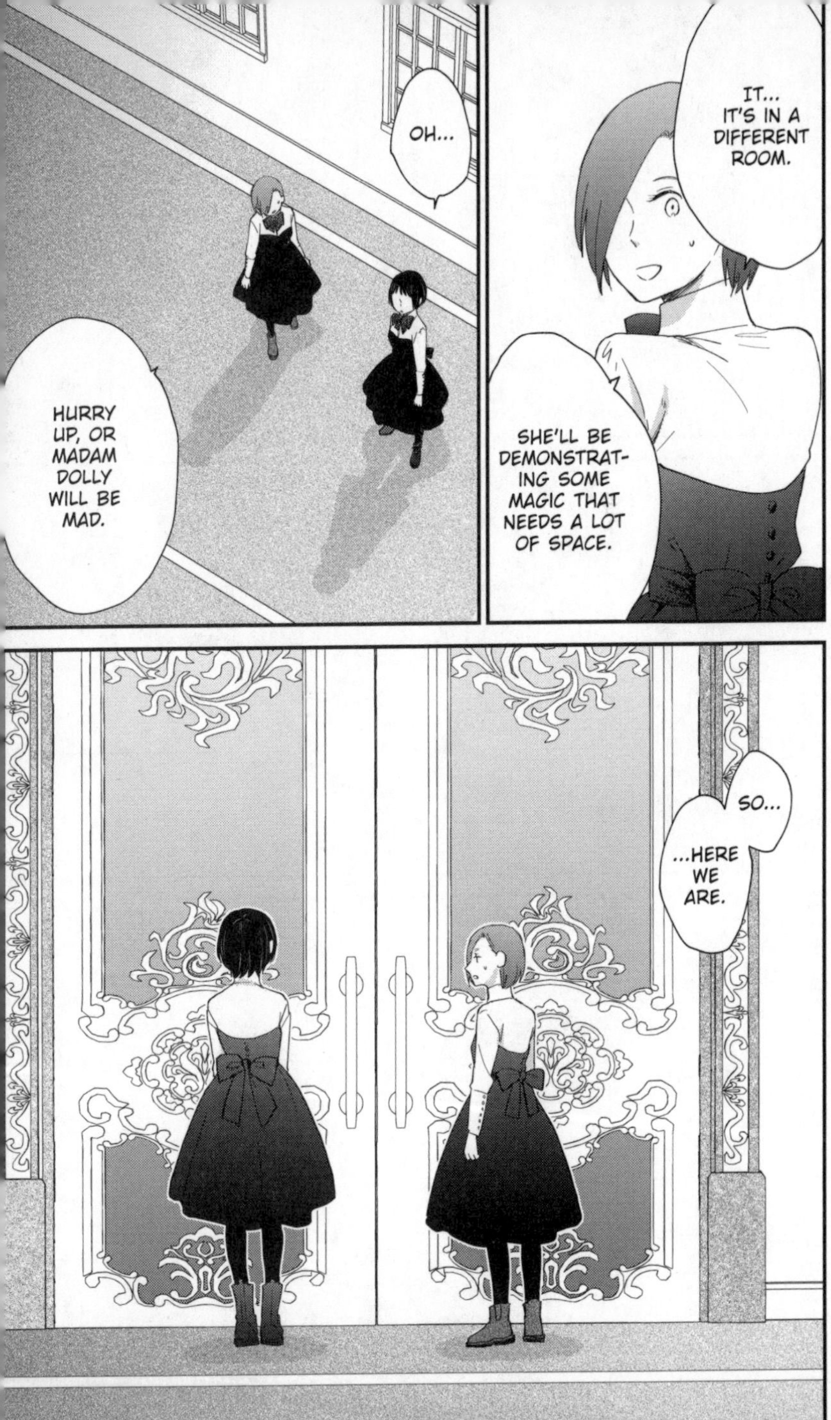
IT... IT'S IN A DIFFERENT ROOM.
SHE'LL BE DEMONSTRATING SOME MAGIC THAT NEEDS A LOT OF SPACE.
OH...
HURRY UP, OR MADAM DOLLY WILL BE MAD.
SO...
...HERE WE ARE.

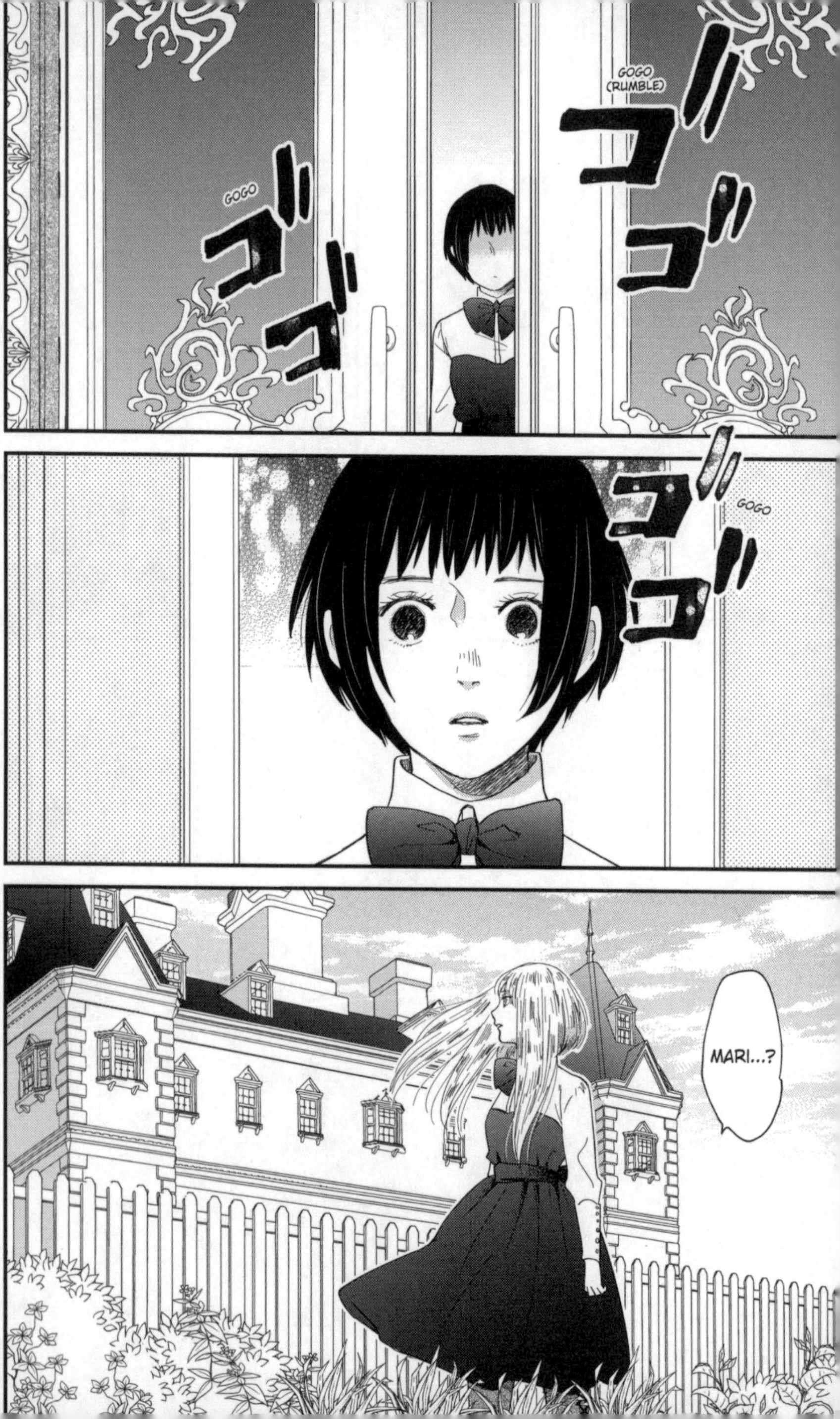
GOGO (RUMBLE)
GOGO
GOGO
MARI...?

A Witch's Love at the End of the World

A Witch's Love at the End of the World

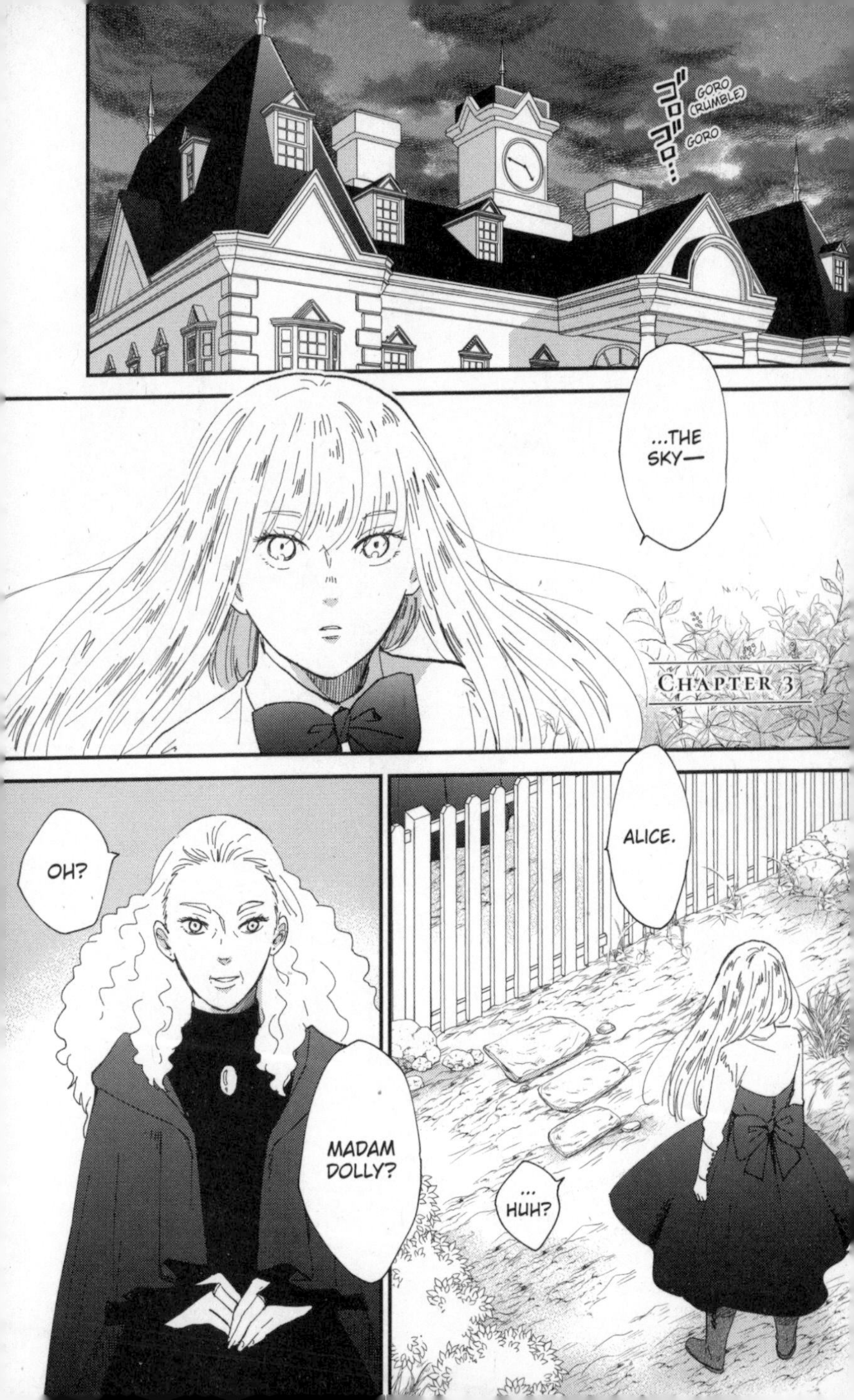
ゴロゴロ…
GORO (RUMBLE) GORO
...THE SKY—
CHAPTER 3
ALICE.
...HUH?
OH?
MADAM DOLLY?

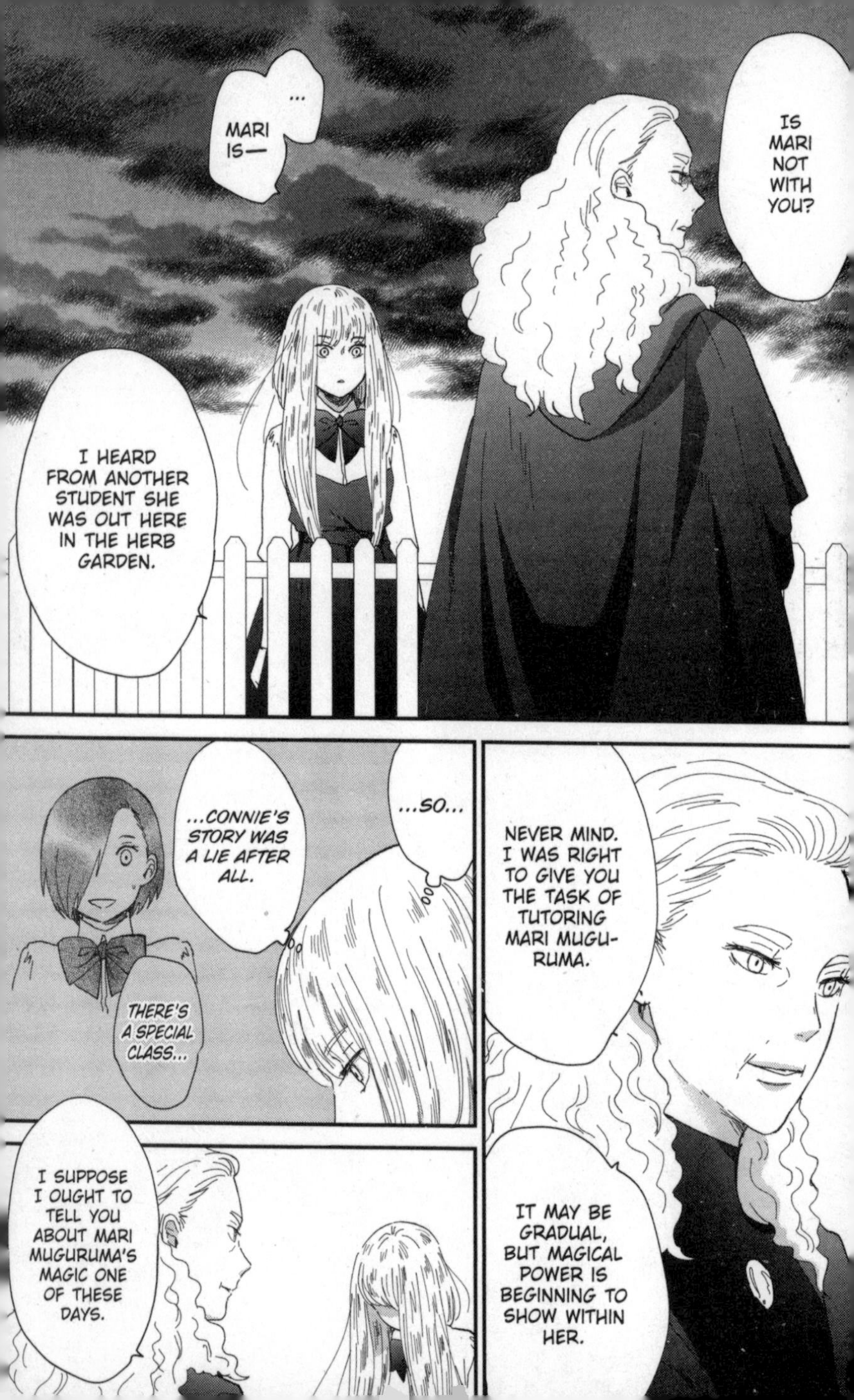
IS MARI NOT WITH YOU?
... MARI IS—
I HEARD FROM ANOTHER STUDENT SHE WAS OUT HERE IN THE HERB GARDEN.
NEVER MIND. I WAS RIGHT TO GIVE YOU THE TASK OF TUTORING MARI MUGU-RUMA.
IT MAY BE GRADUAL, BUT MAGICAL POWER IS BEGINNING TO SHOW WITHIN HER.
...SO...
...CONNIE'S STORY WAS A LIE AFTER ALL.
THERE'S A SPECIAL CLASS...
I SUPPOSE I OUGHT TO TELL YOU ABOUT MARI MUGURUMA'S MAGIC ONE OF THESE DAYS.

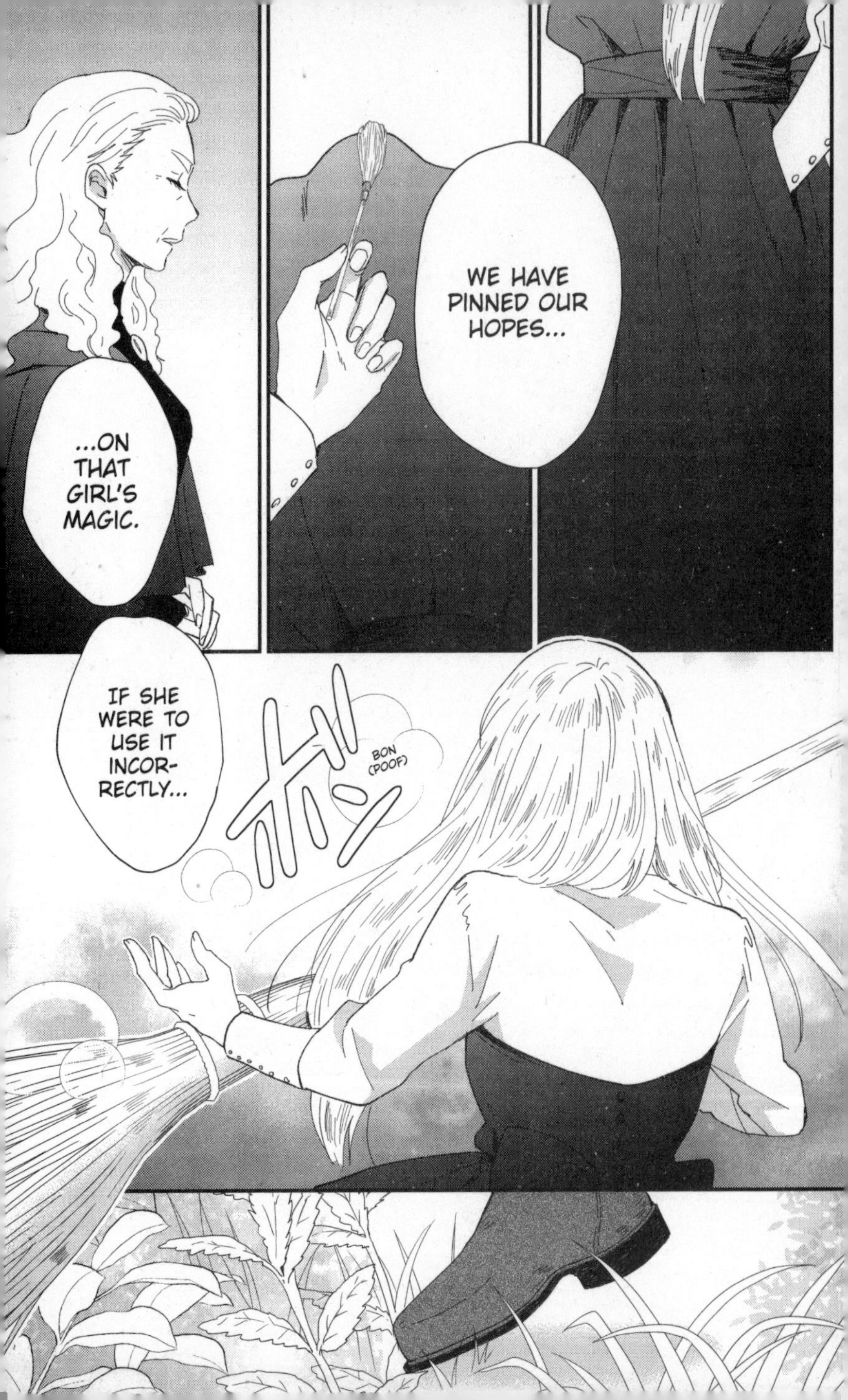
WE HAVE PINNED OUR HOPES...
...ON THAT GIRL'S MAGIC.
IF SHE WERE TO USE IT INCORRECTLY...
BON (POOF)

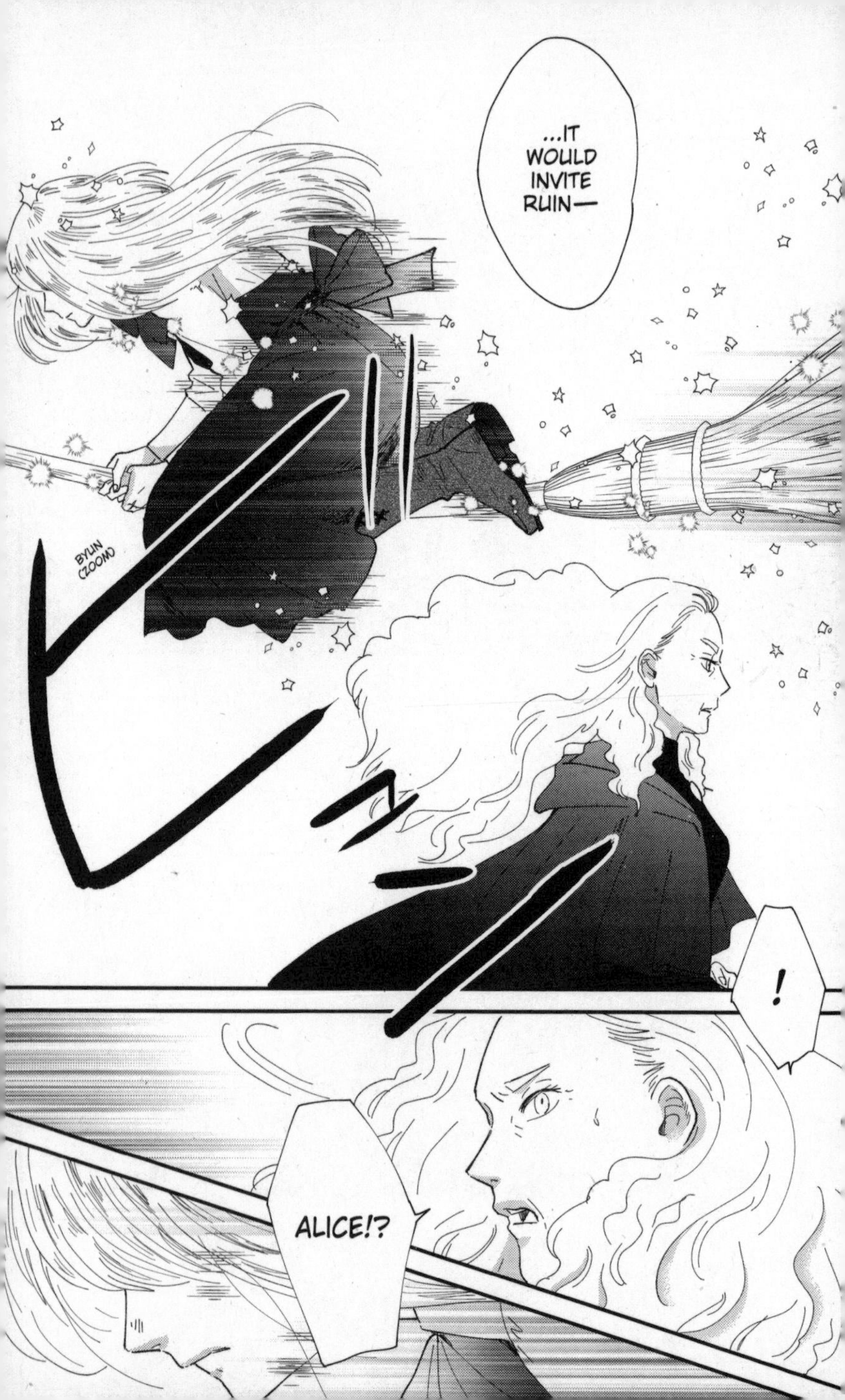
...IT WOULD INVITE RUIN—
BYUN (ZOOM)
!
ALICE!?

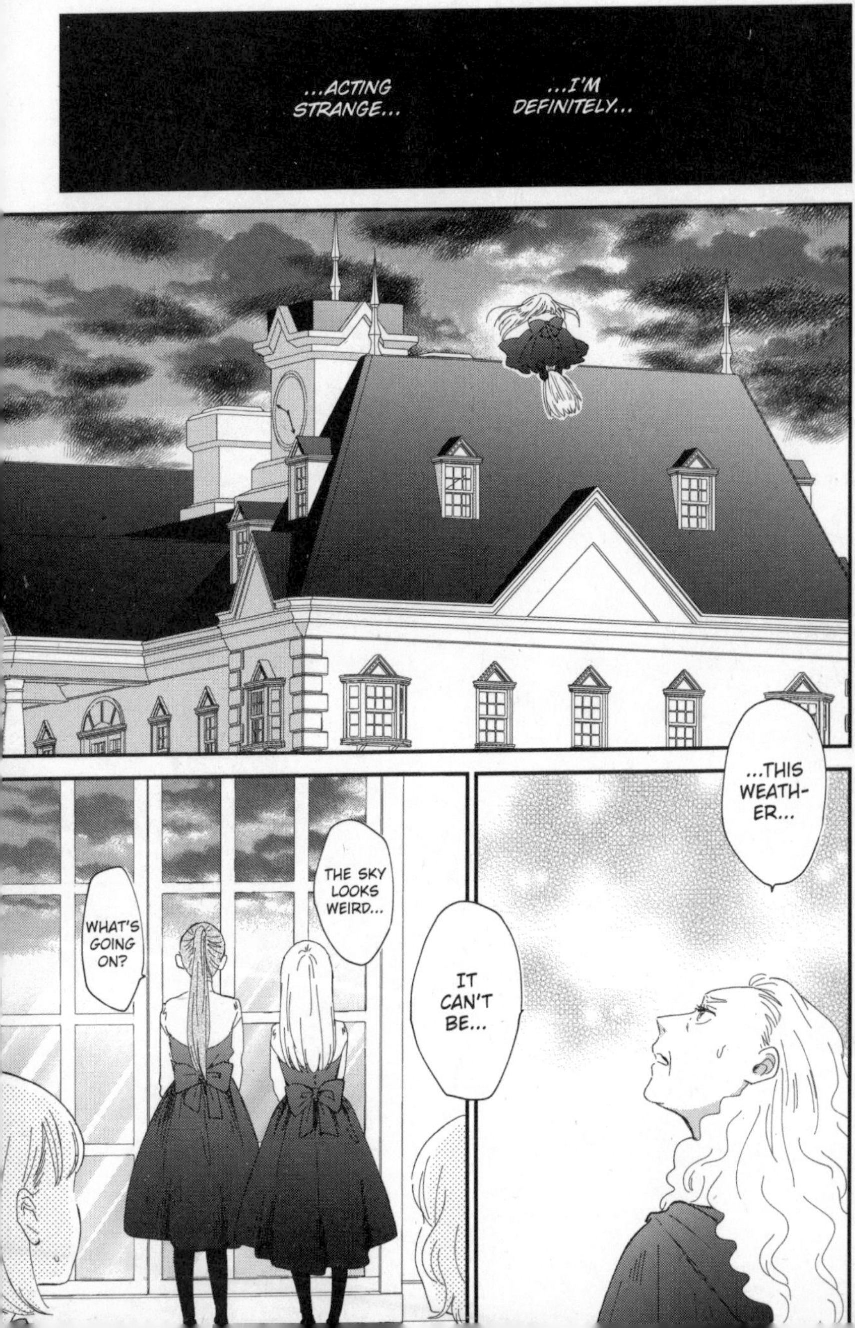
...I'M DEFINITELY...
...ACTING STRANGE...
...THIS WEATHER...
IT CAN'T BE...
THE SKY LOOKS WEIRD...
WHAT'S GOING ON?

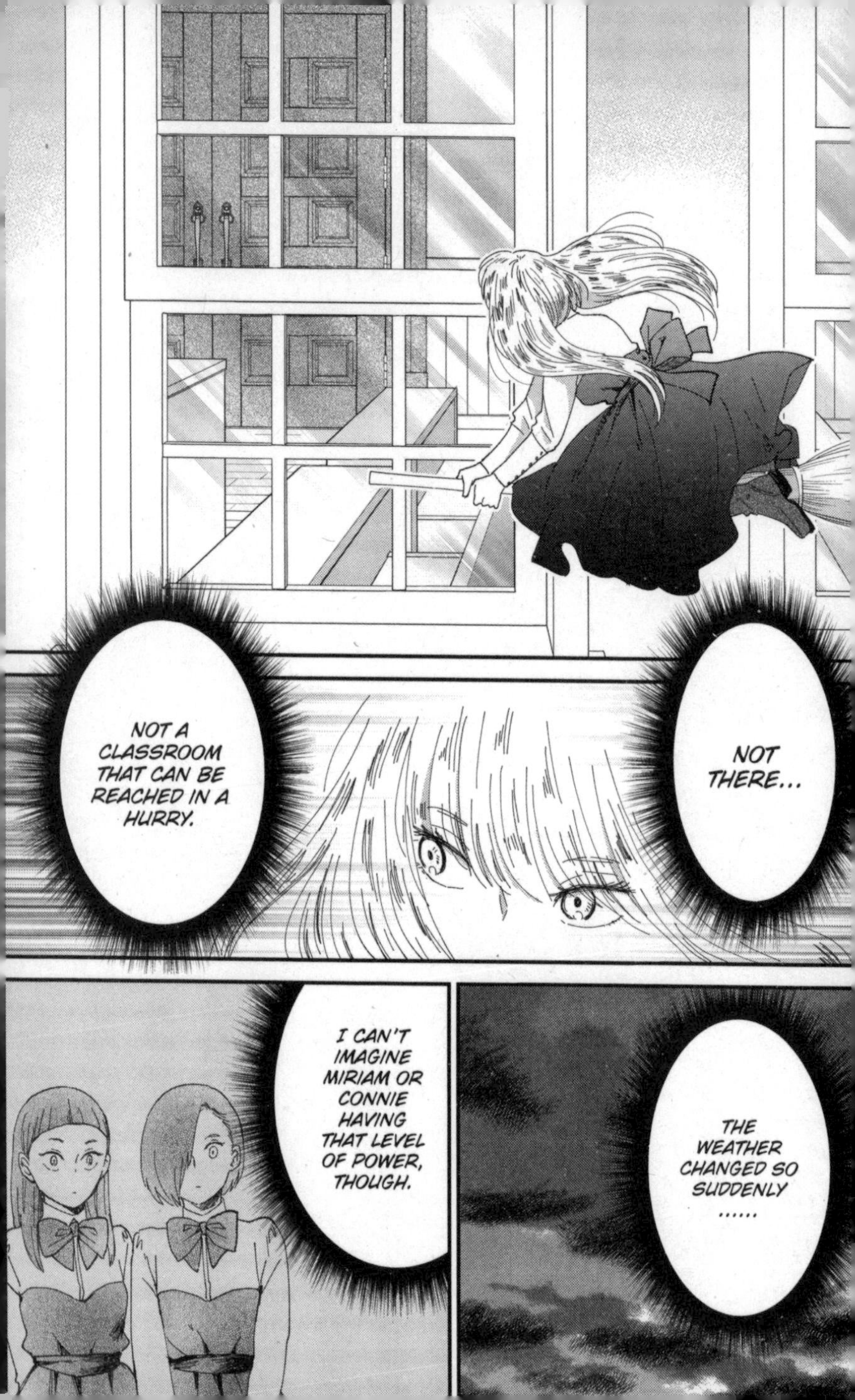
NOT THERE...
NOT A CLASSROOM THAT CAN BE REACHED IN A HURRY.
THE WEATHER CHANGED SO SUDDENLY ......
I CAN'T IMAGINE MIRIAM OR CONNIE HAVING THAT LEVEL OF POWER, THOUGH.

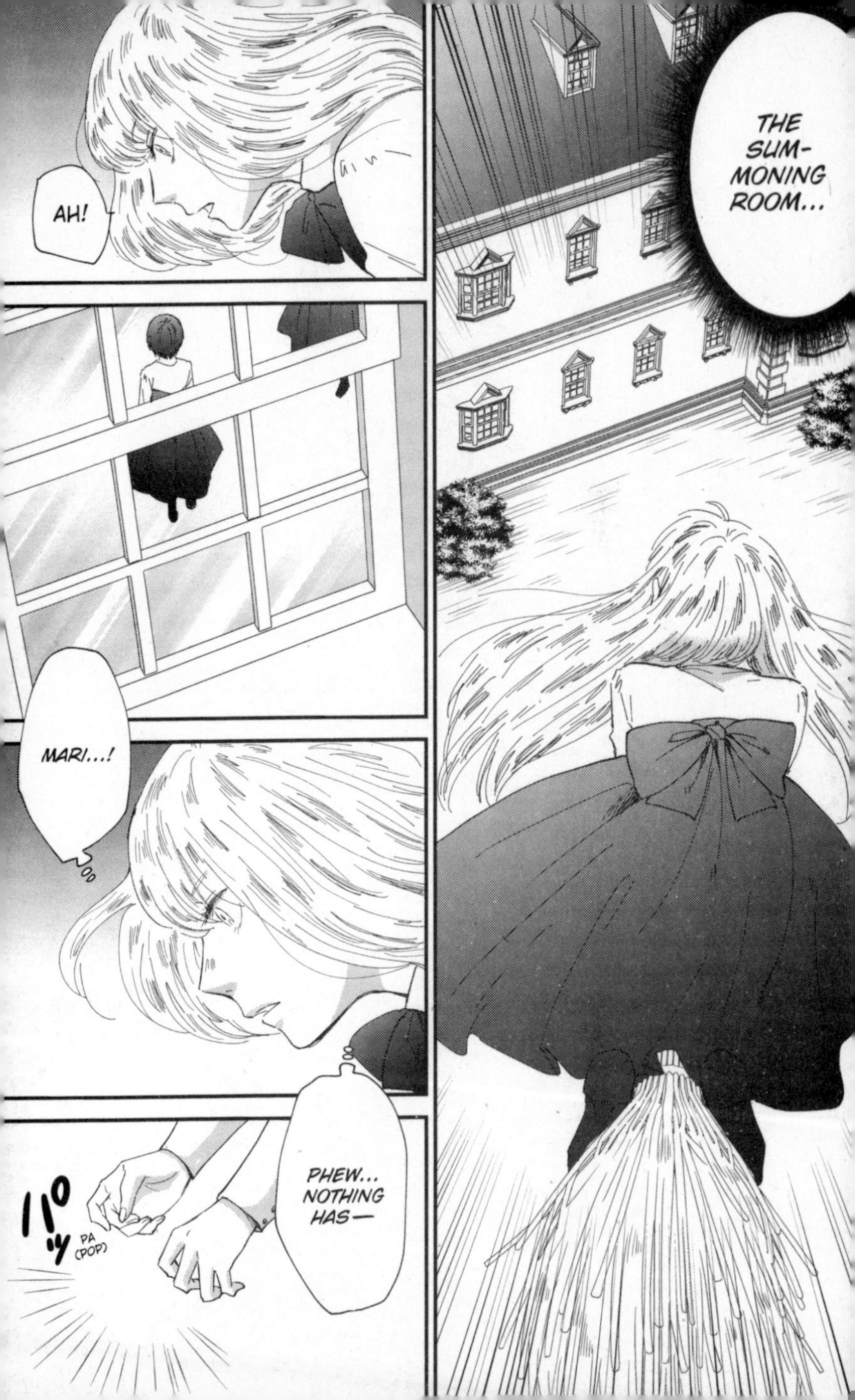
THE SUM-MONING ROOM...
AH!
MARI...!
PHEW... NOTHING HAS—
PA (POP)

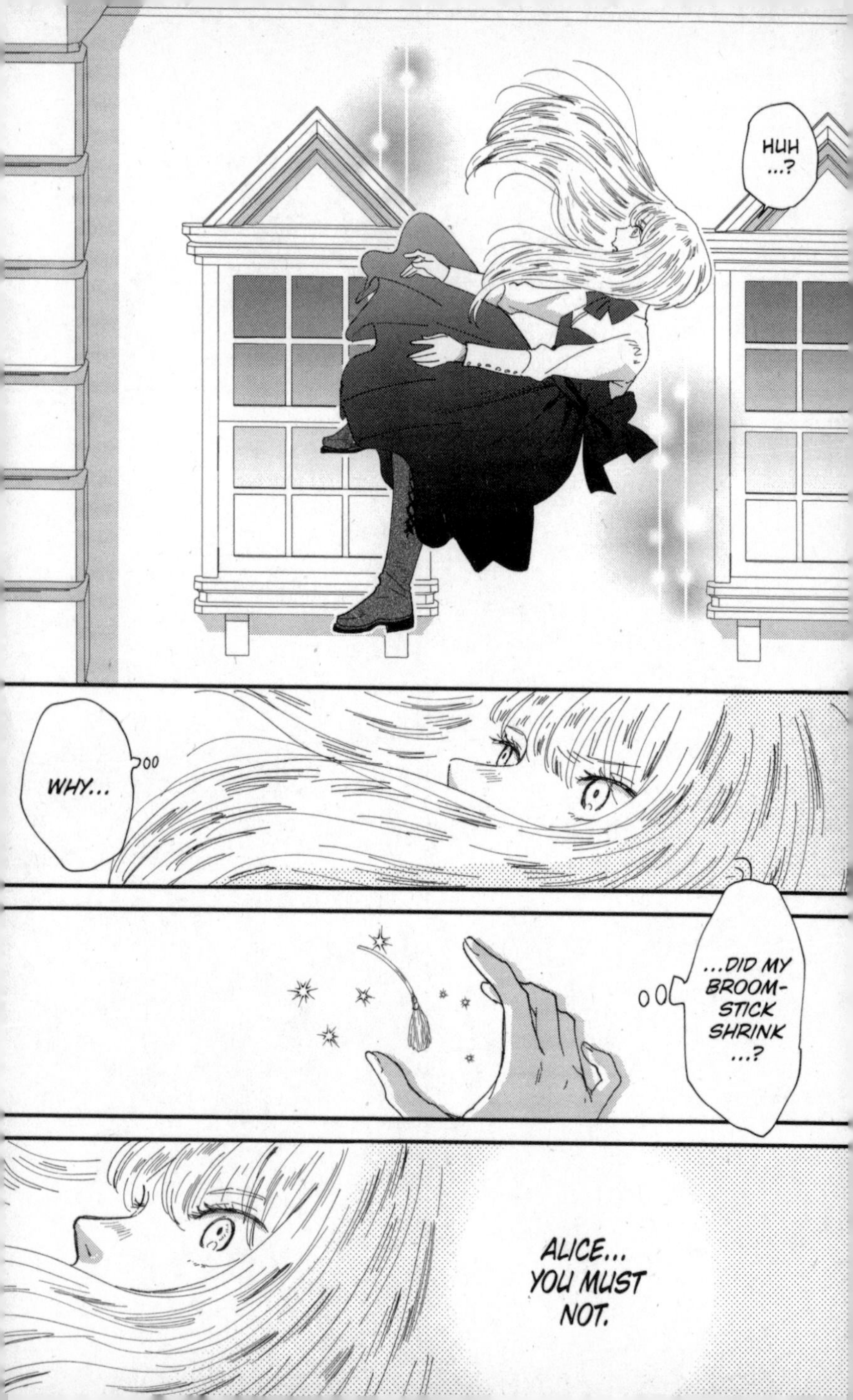
HUH ...?
WHY...
...DID MY BROOM-STICK SHRINK ...?
ALICE... YOU MUST NOT.

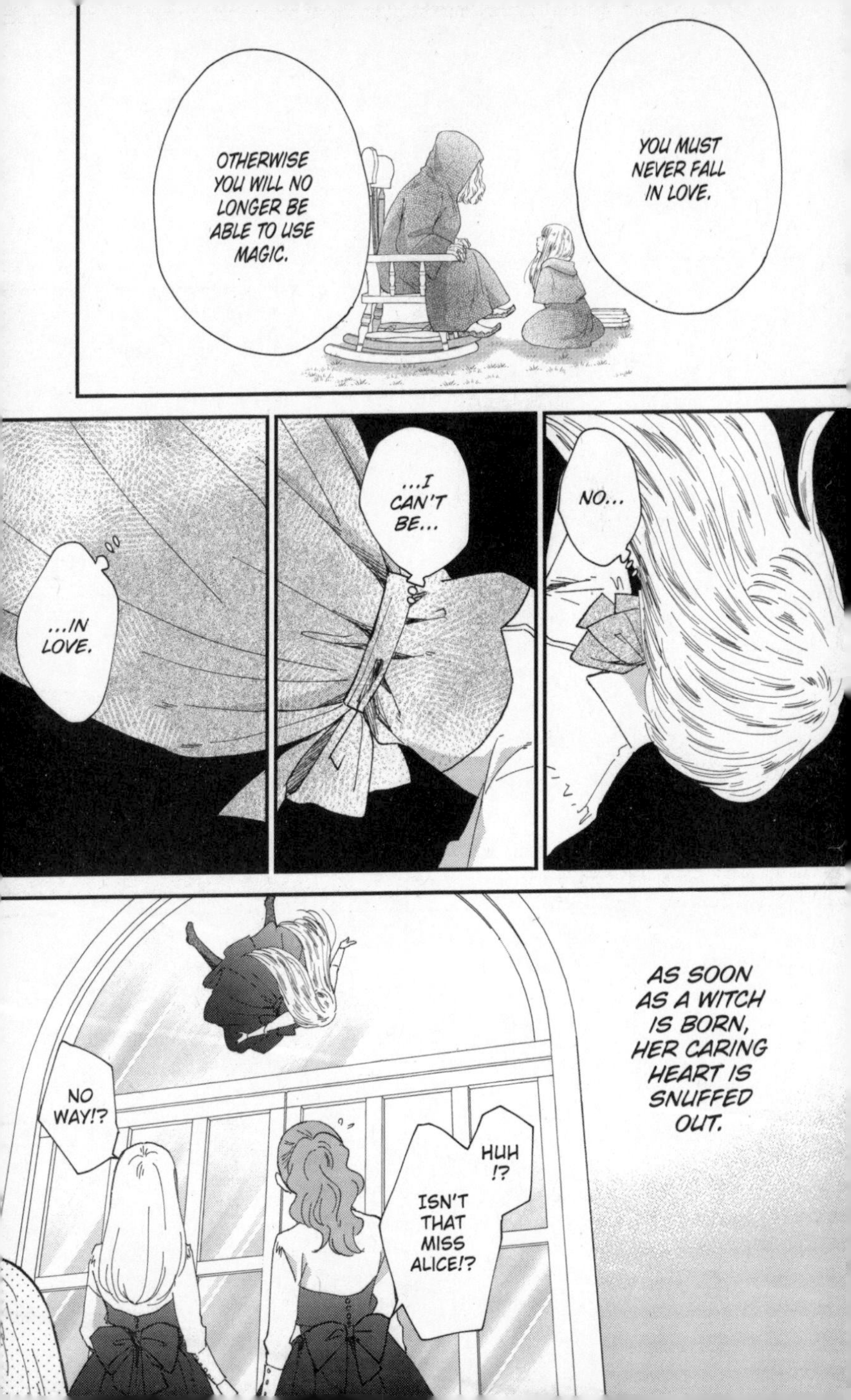
YOU MUST NEVER FALL IN LOVE.
OTHERWISE YOU WILL NO LONGER BE ABLE TO USE MAGIC.
NO...
...I CAN'T BE...
...IN LOVE.
AS SOON AS A WITCH IS BORN, HER CARING HEART IS SNUFFED OUT.
HUH!?
ISN'T THAT MISS ALICE!?
NO WAY!?

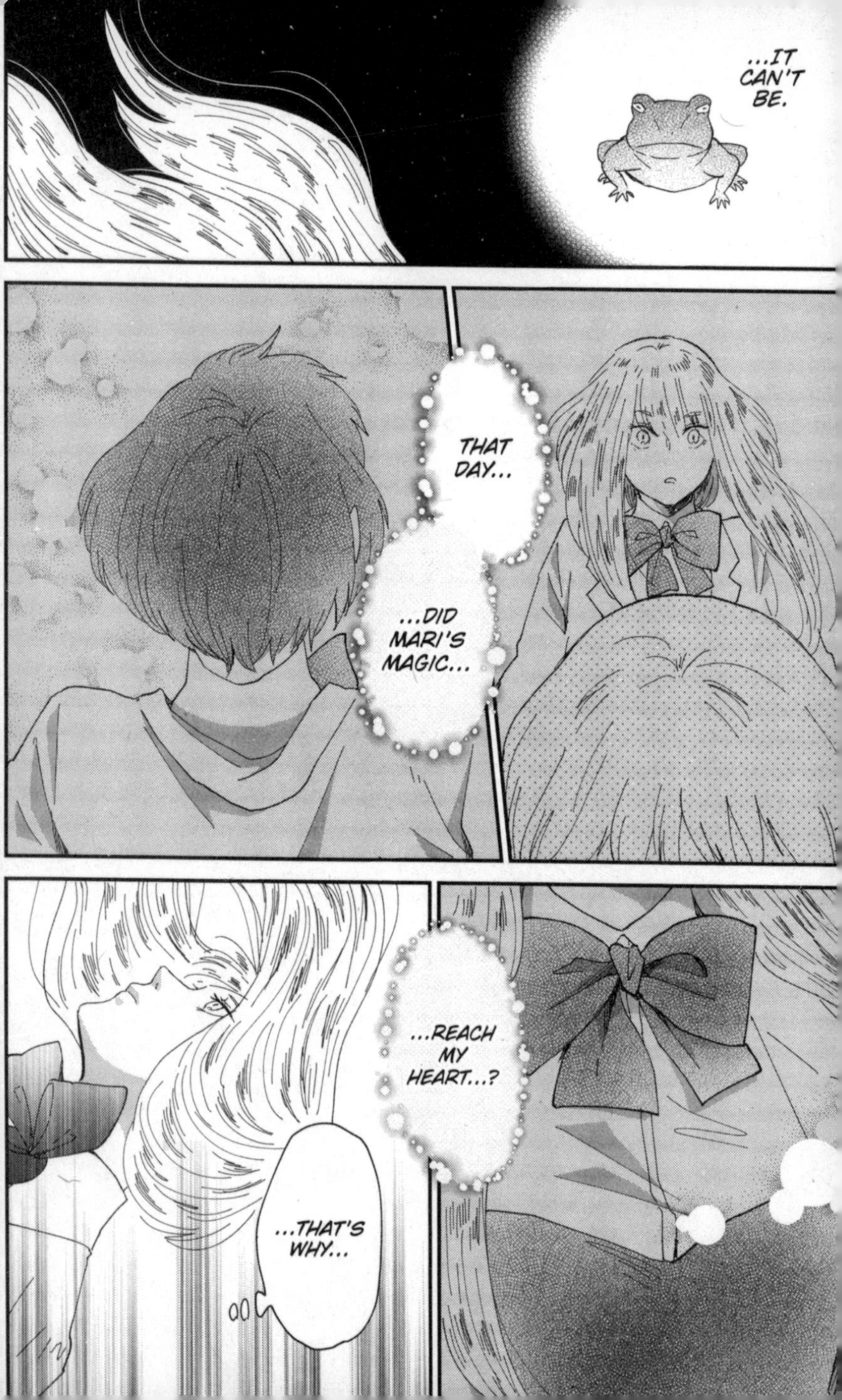
...IT CAN'T BE.
THAT DAY...
...DID MARI'S MAGIC...
...REACH MY HEART...?
...THAT'S WHY...

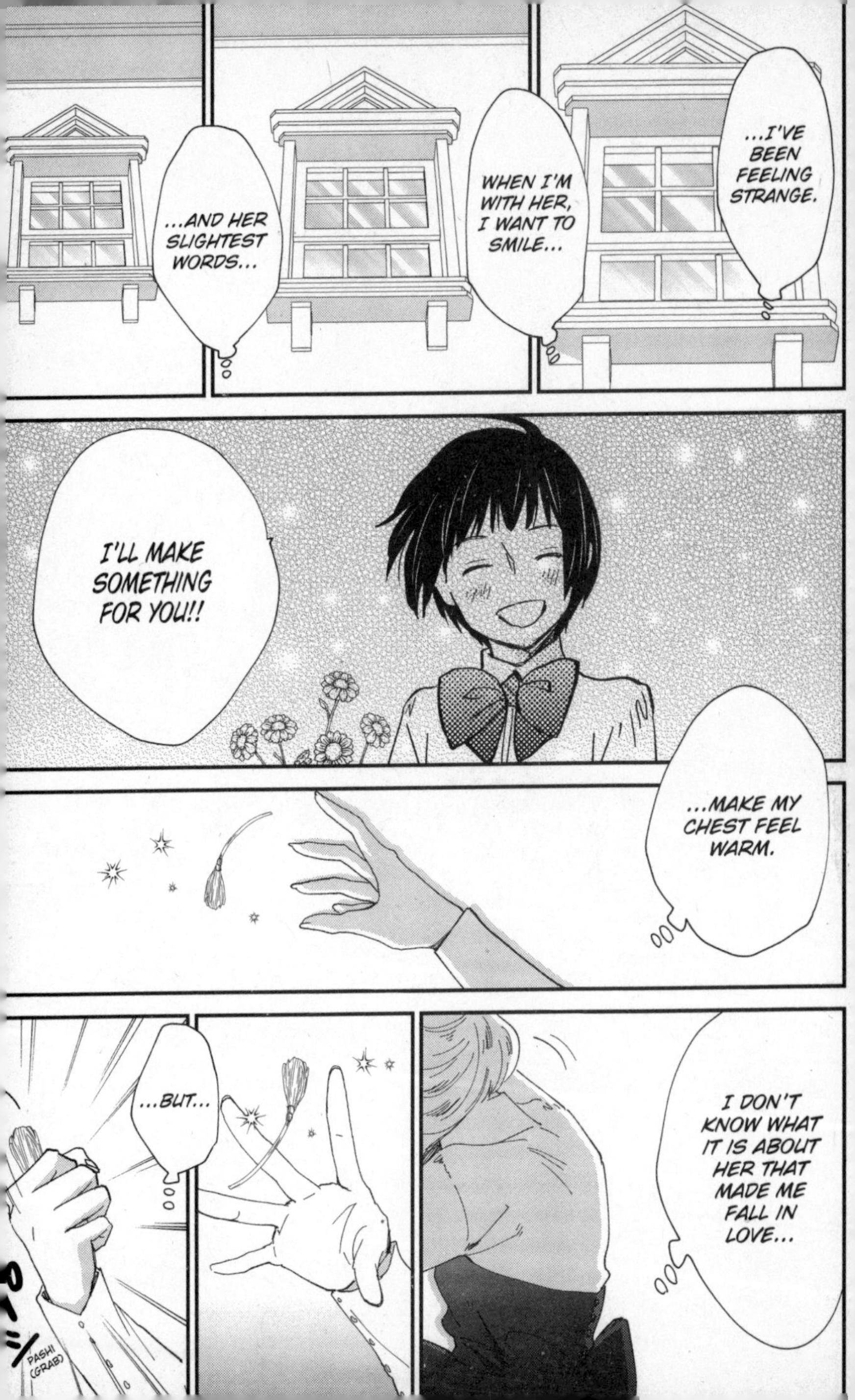
...I'VE BEEN FEELING STRANGE.
WHEN I'M WITH HER, I WANT TO SMILE...
...AND HER SLIGHTEST WORDS...
I'LL MAKE SOMETHING FOR YOU!!
...MAKE MY CHEST FEEL WARM.
I DON'T KNOW WHAT IT IS ABOUT HER THAT MADE ME FALL IN LOVE...
...BUT...
PASHI (GRAB)

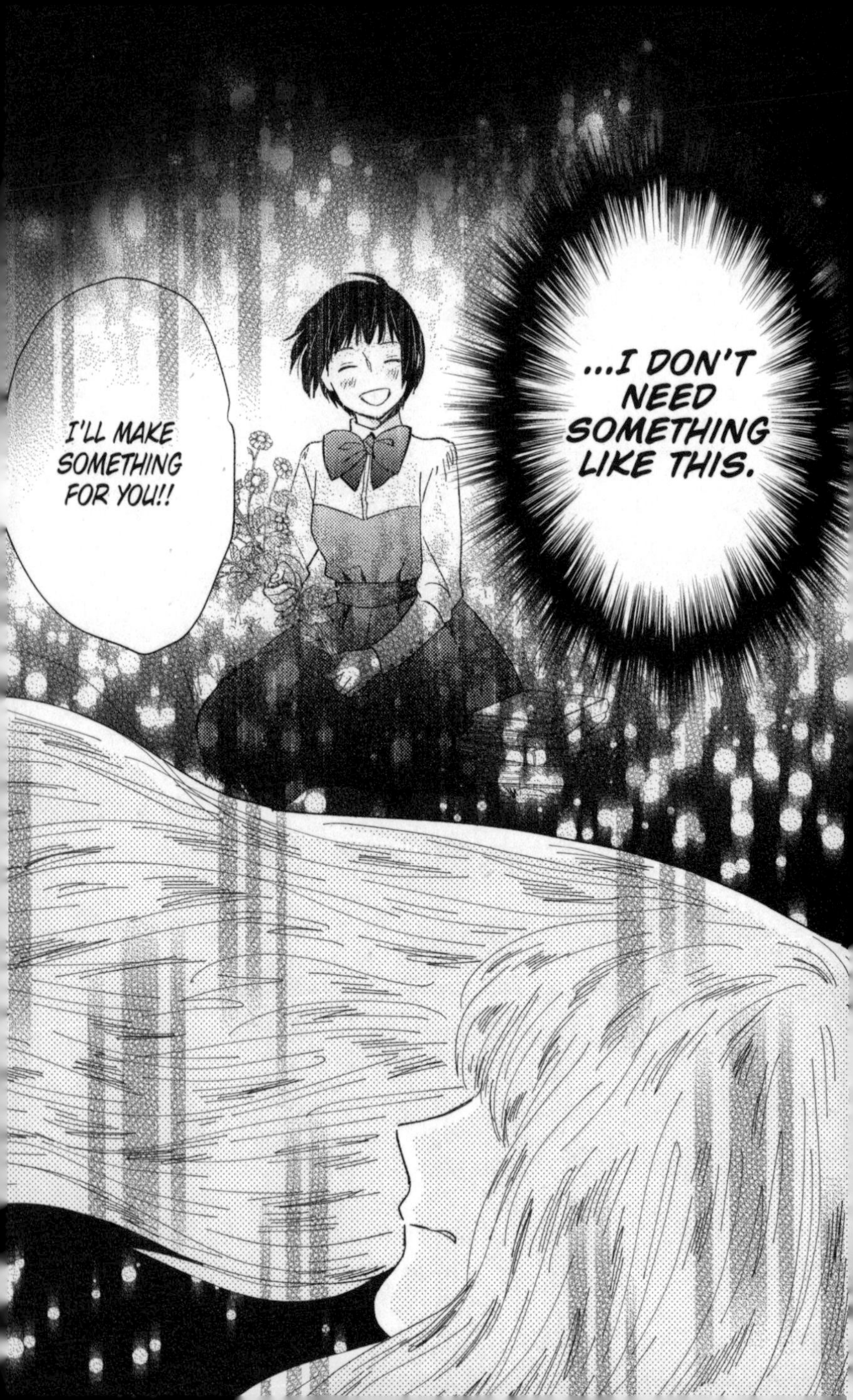
...I DON'T NEED SOMETHING LIKE THIS.
I'LL MAKE SOMETHING FOR YOU!!

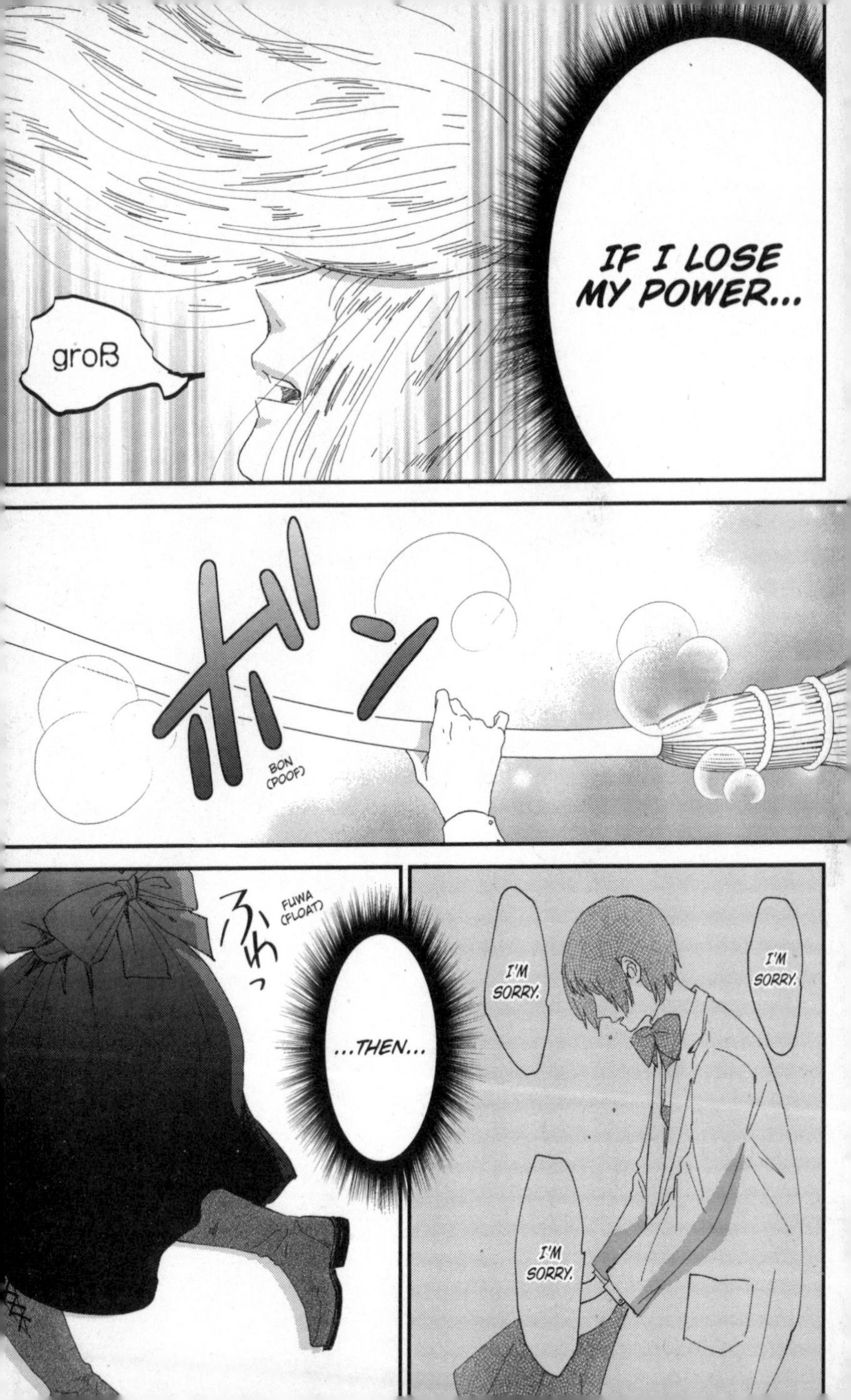
IF I LOSE MY POWER...
groß
ボン
BON (POOF)
I'M SORRY.
I'M SORRY.
I'M SORRY.
ふわっ
FUWA (FLOAT)
...THEN...

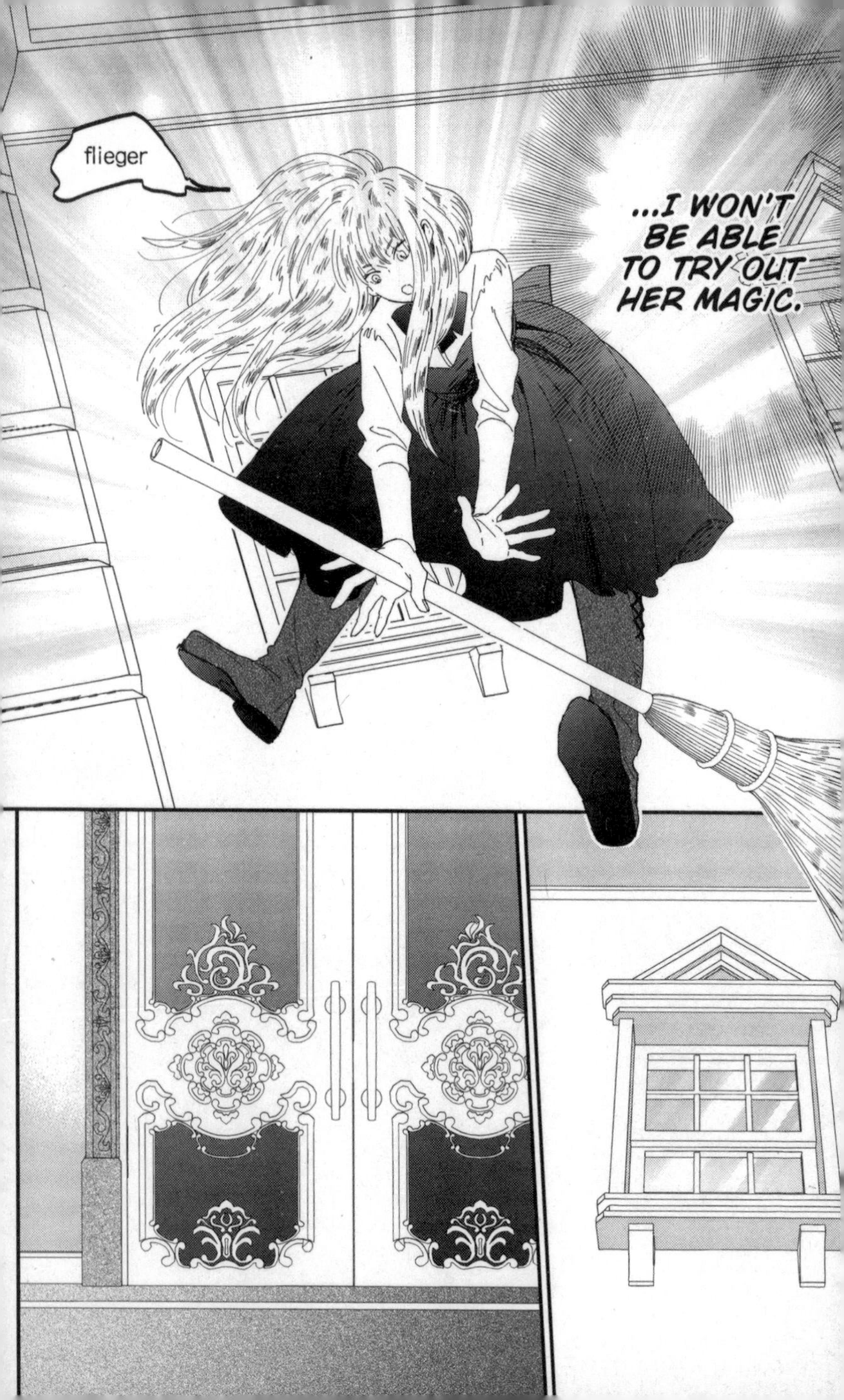
...I WON'T BE ABLE TO TRY OUT HER MAGIC.
flieger

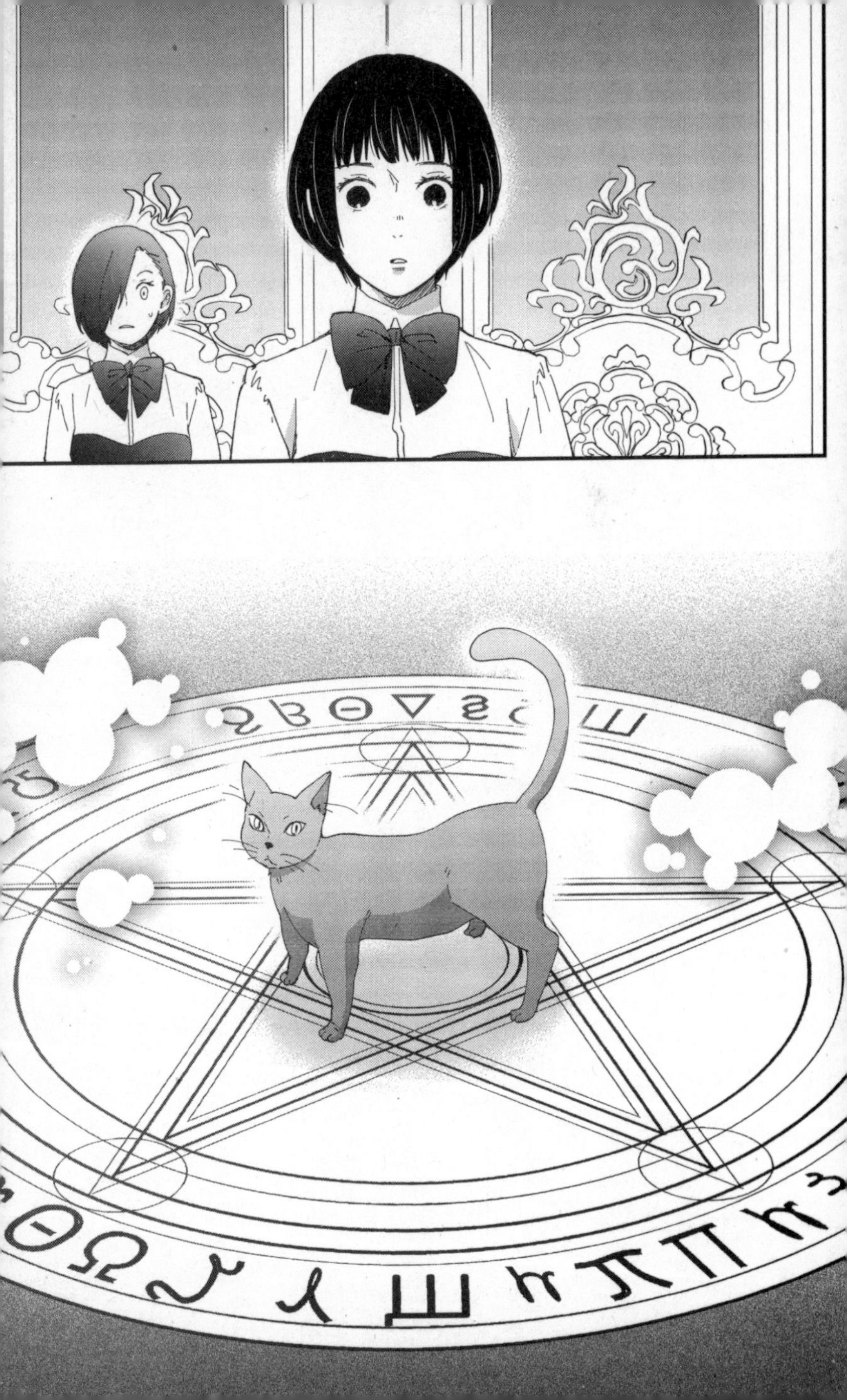

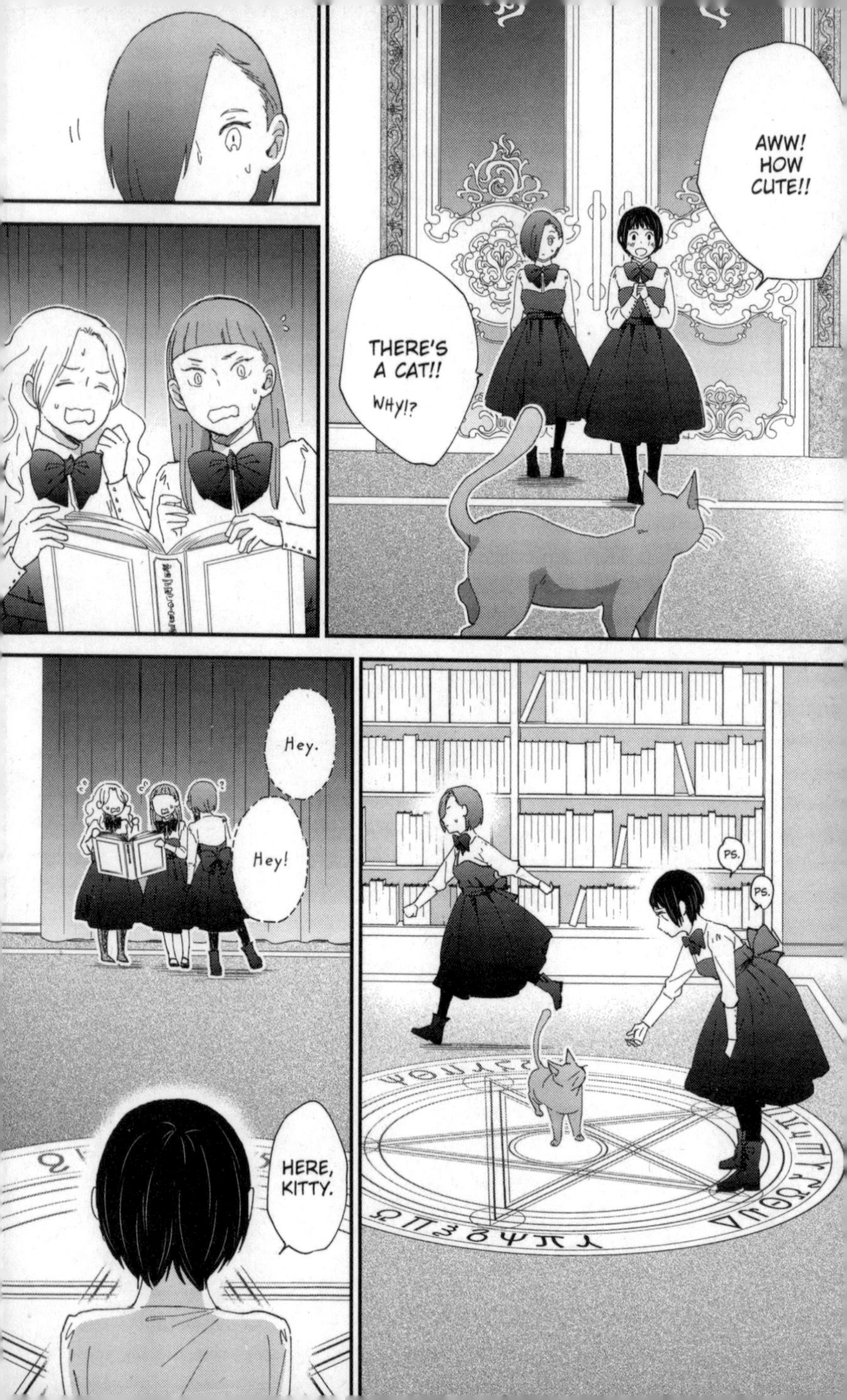
AWW! HOW CUTE!!
THERE'S A CAT!!
WHY!?
PS.
PS.
Hey.
Hey!
HERE, KITTY.

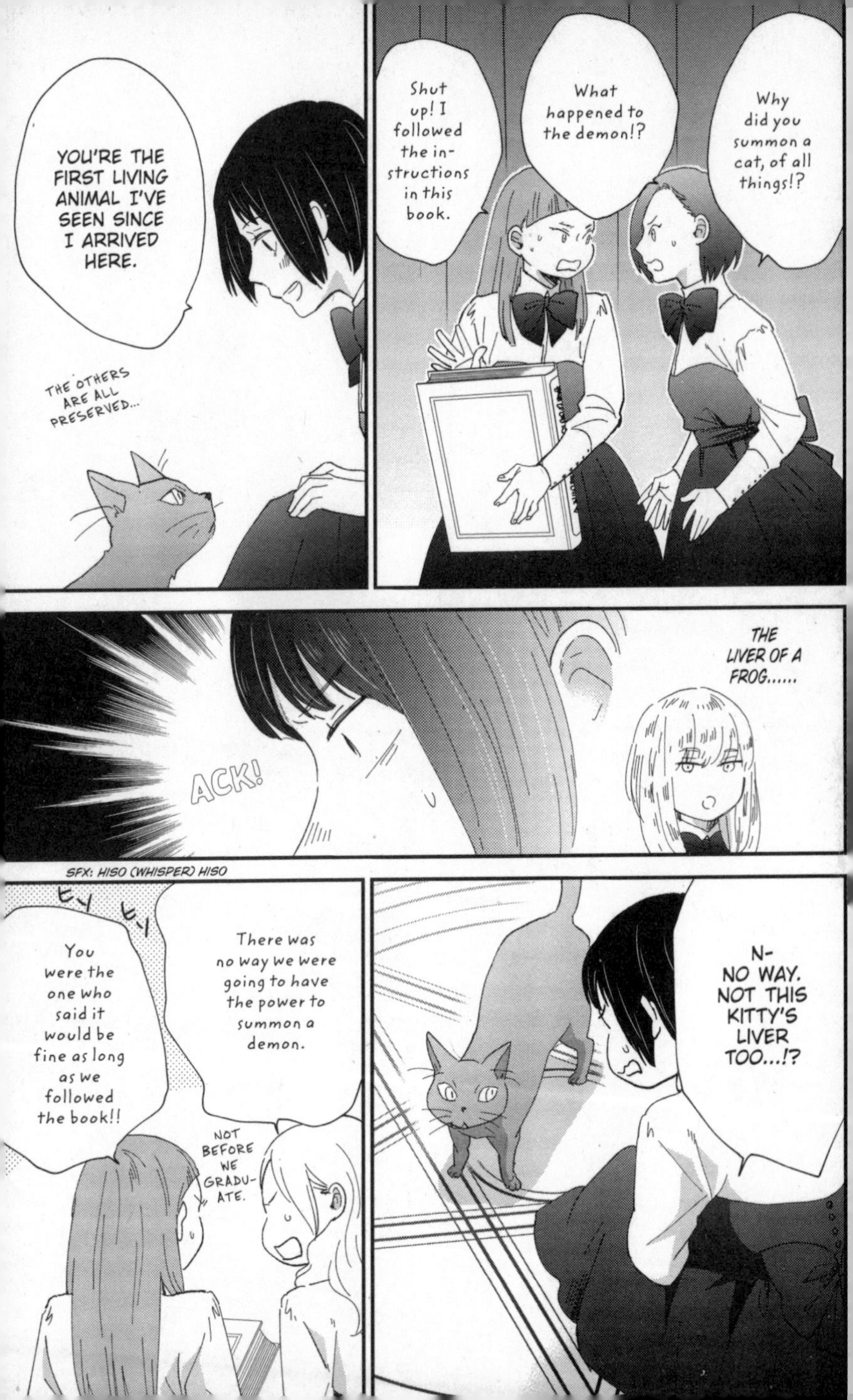
Why did you summon a cat, of all things!?
What happened to the demon!?
Shut up! I followed the instructions in this book.
YOU'RE THE FIRST LIVING ANIMAL I'VE SEEN SINCE I ARRIVED HERE.
THE OTHERS ARE ALL PRESERVED...
THE LIVER OF A FROG......
ACK!
SFX: HISO (WHISPER) HISO
N- NO WAY. NOT THIS KITTY'S LIVER TOO...!?
There was no way we were going to have the power to summon a demon.
ヒソ ヒソ
You were the one who said it would be fine as long as we followed the book!!
NOT BEFORE WE GRADUATE.

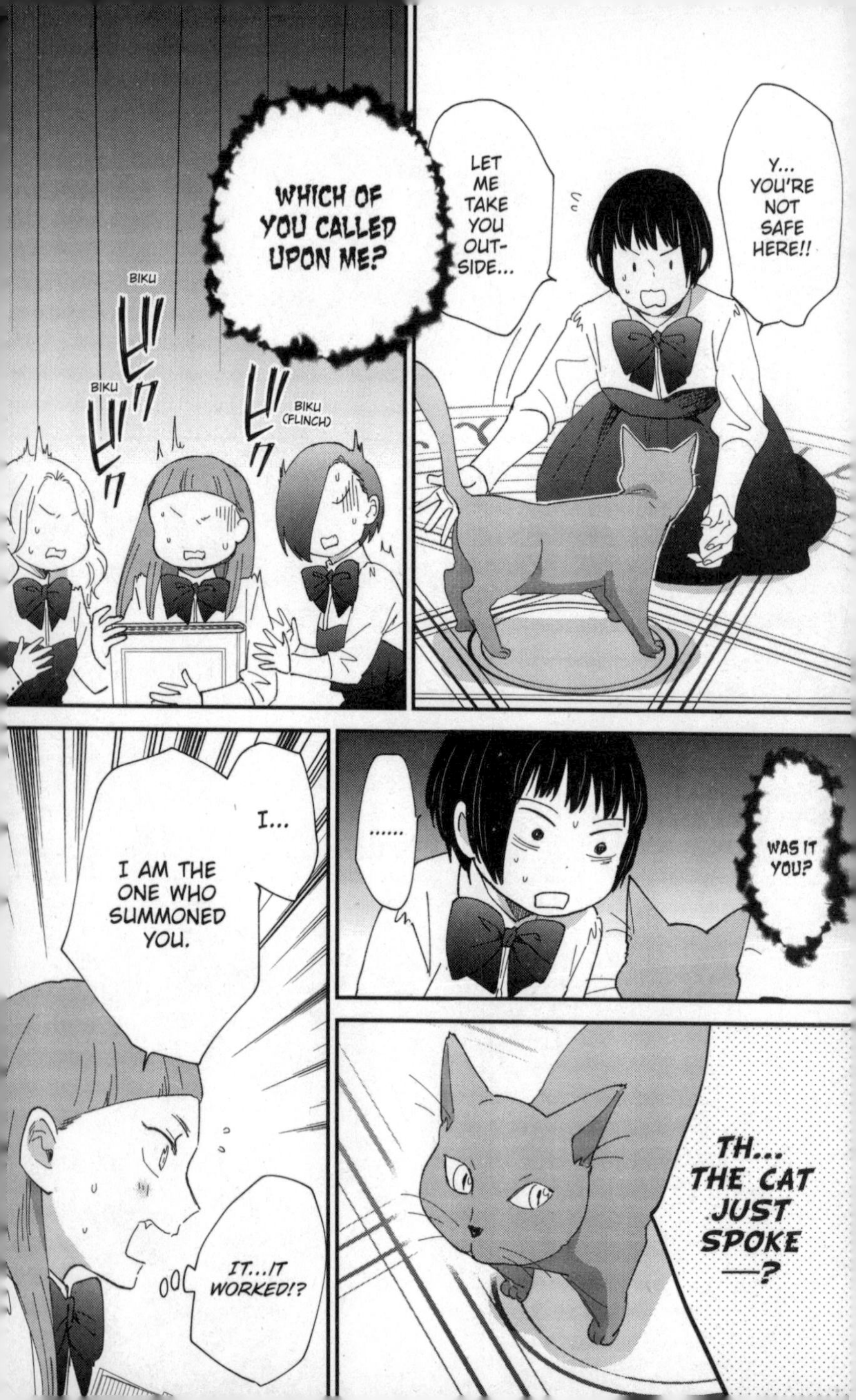
Y... YOU'RE NOT SAFE HERE!!
LET ME TAKE YOU OUT-SIDE...
WHICH OF YOU CALLED UPON ME?
BIKU
BIKU
BIKU (FLINCH)
WAS IT YOU?
......
TH... THE CAT JUST SPOKE —?
I...
I AM THE ONE WHO SUMMONED YOU.
IT...IT WORKED!?

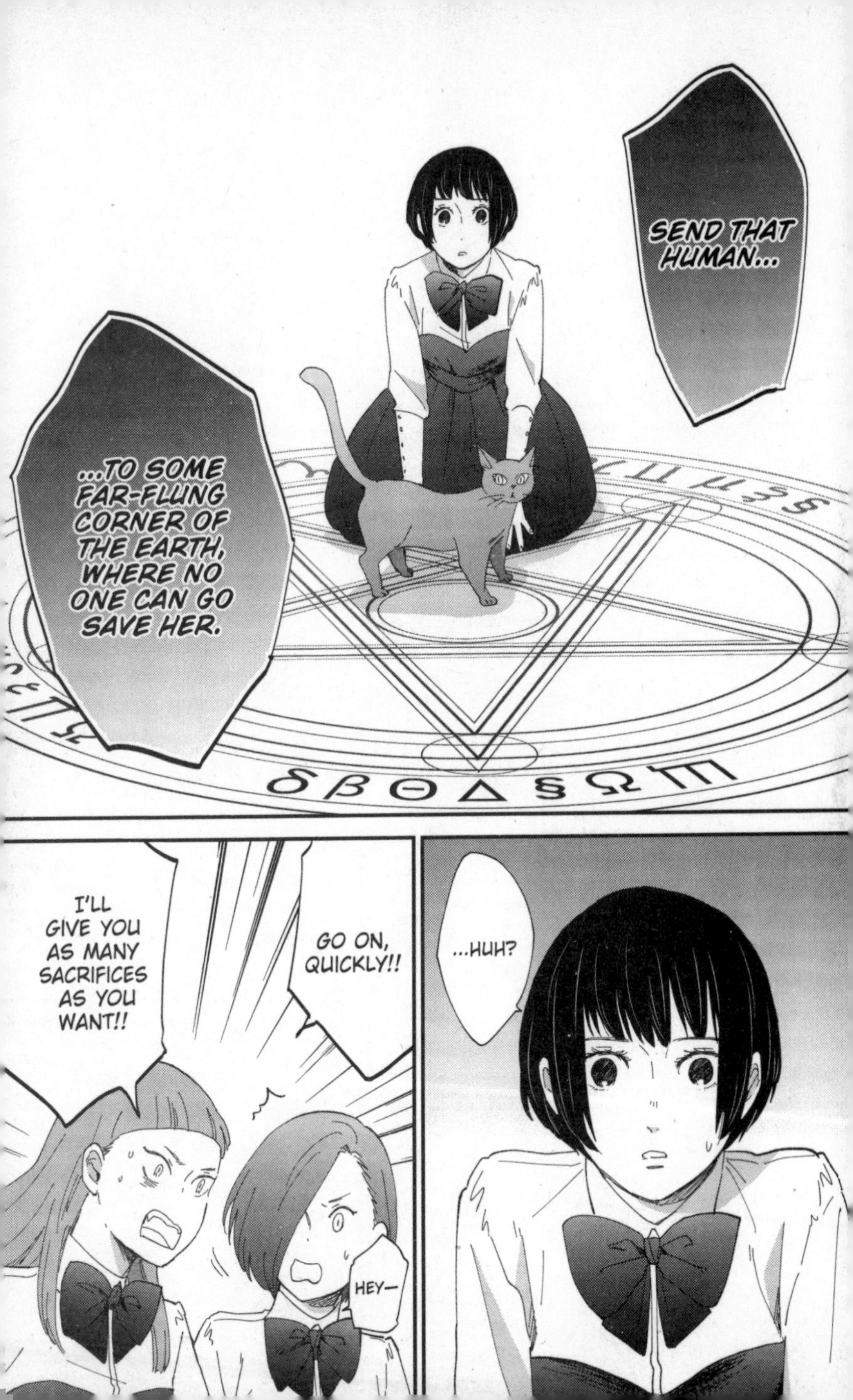
SEND THAT HUMAN...
...TO SOME FAR-FLUNG CORNER OF THE EARTH, WHERE NO ONE CAN GO SAVE HER.
...HUH?
GO ON, QUICKLY!!
I'LL GIVE YOU AS MANY SACRIFICES AS YOU WANT!!
HEY—

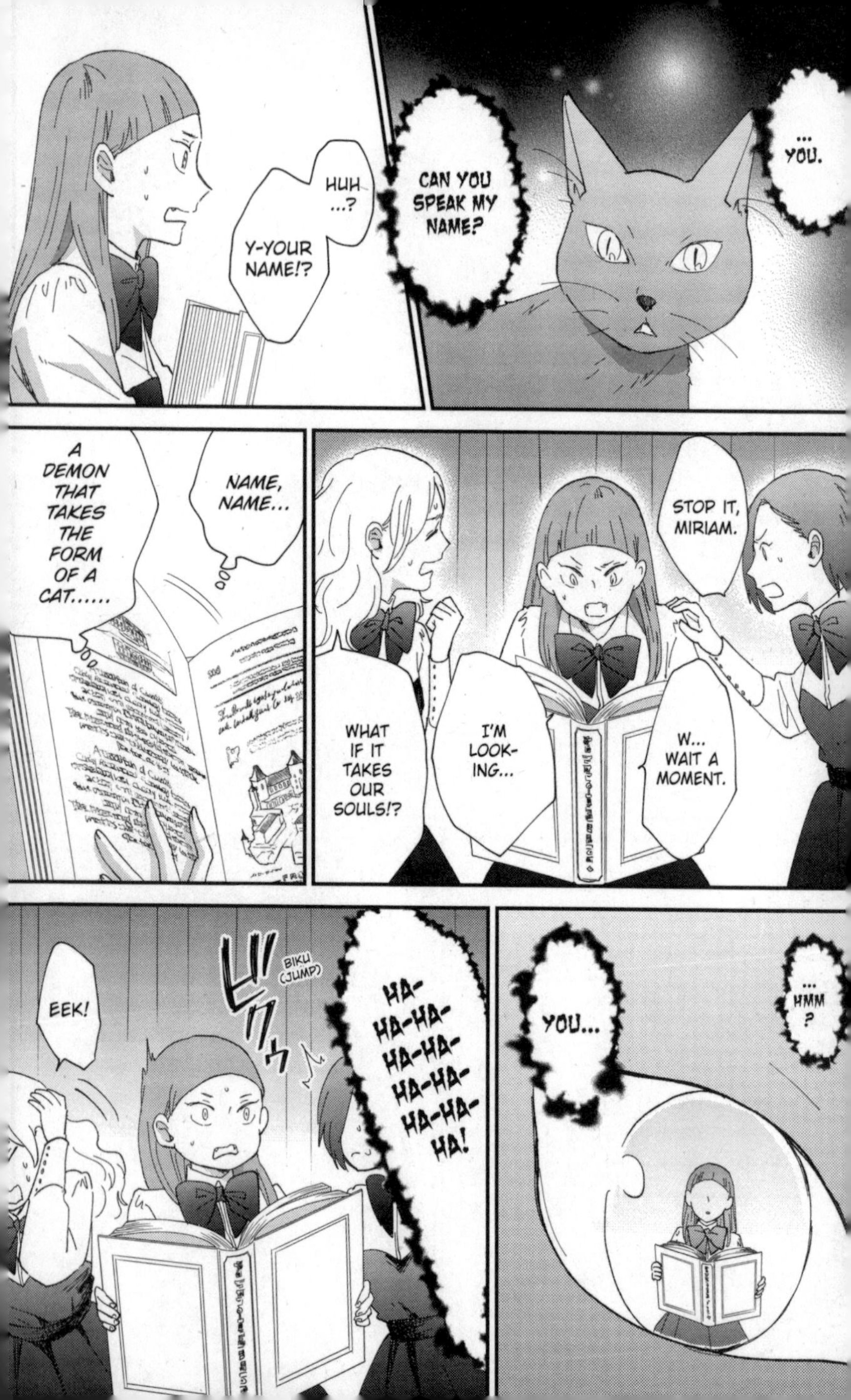
... YOU.
CAN YOU SPEAK MY NAME?
HUH ...?
Y-YOUR NAME!?
STOP IT, MIRIAM.
W... WAIT A MOMENT.
I'M LOOK-ING...
WHAT IF IT TAKES OUR SOULS!?
NAME, NAME...
A DEMON THAT TAKES THE FORM OF A CAT......
... HMM ?
YOU...
HA-HA-HA-HA-HA-HA-HA-HA-HA-HA-HA-HA!
BIKU (JUMP)
EEK!

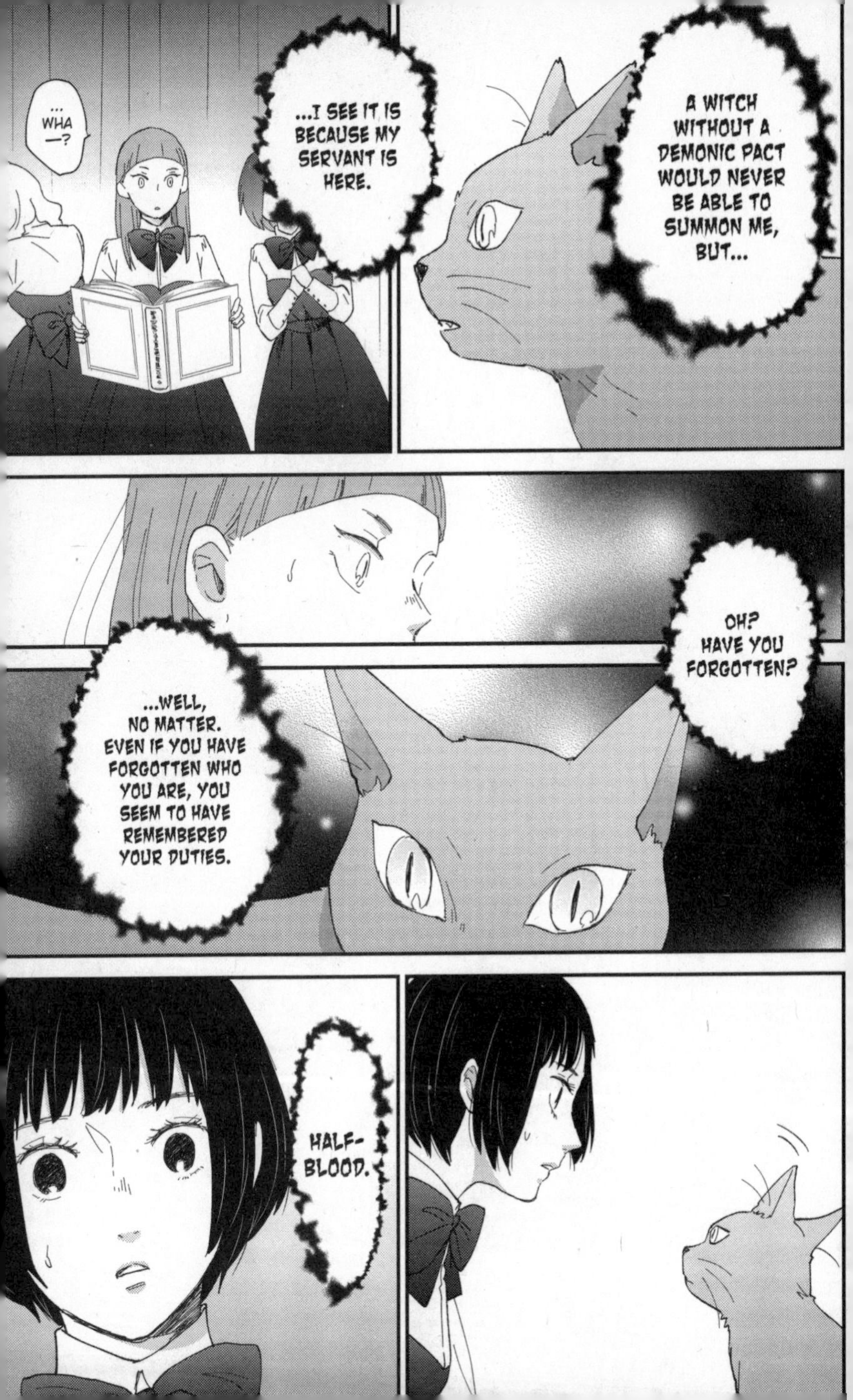
A WITCH WITHOUT A DEMONIC PACT WOULD NEVER BE ABLE TO SUMMON ME, BUT...
...I SEE IT IS BECAUSE MY SERVANT IS HERE.
...WHA—?
OH? HAVE YOU FORGOTTEN?
...WELL, NO MATTER. EVEN IF YOU HAVE FORGOTTEN WHO YOU ARE, YOU SEEM TO HAVE REMEMBERED YOUR DUTIES.
HALF-BLOOD.

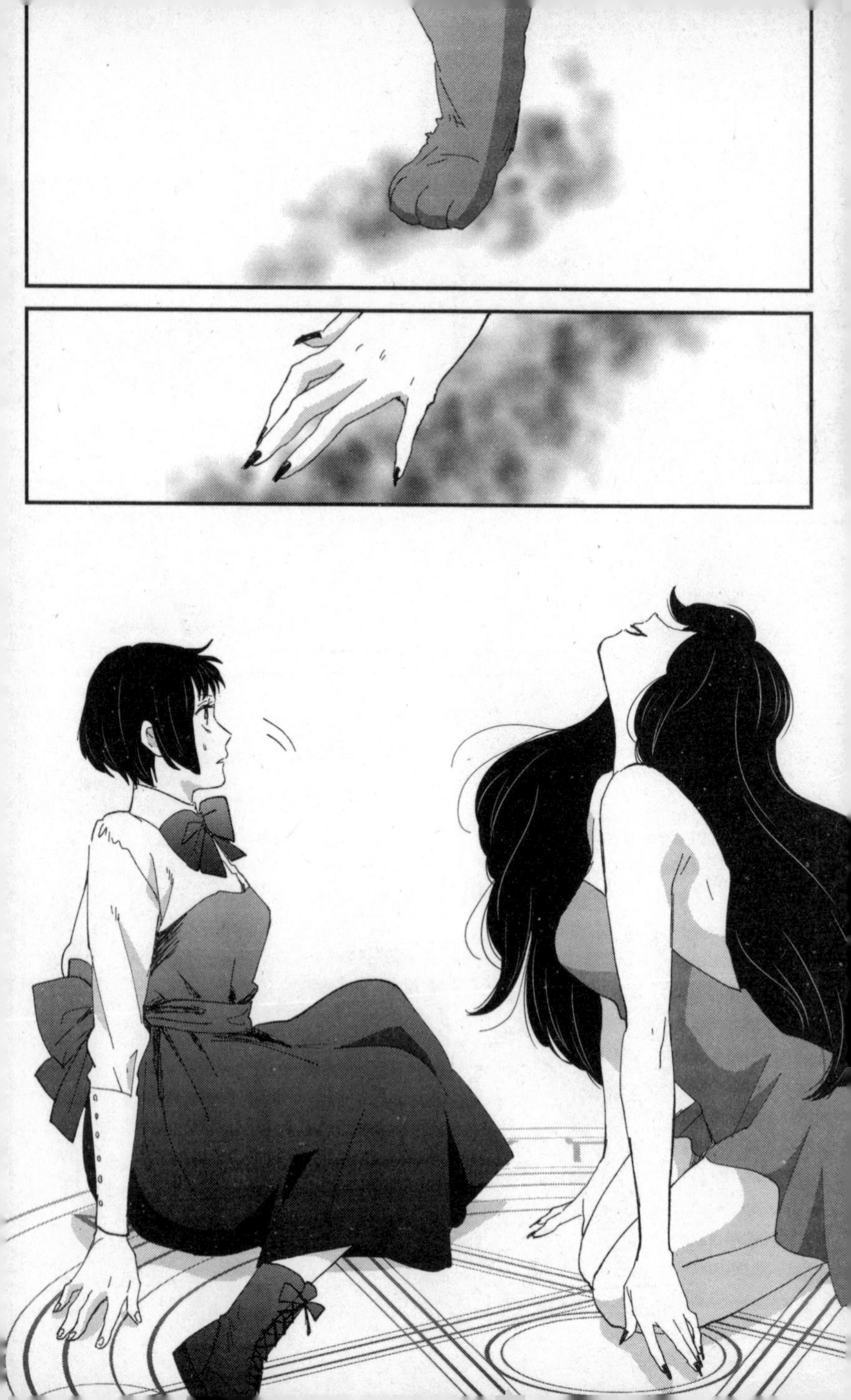

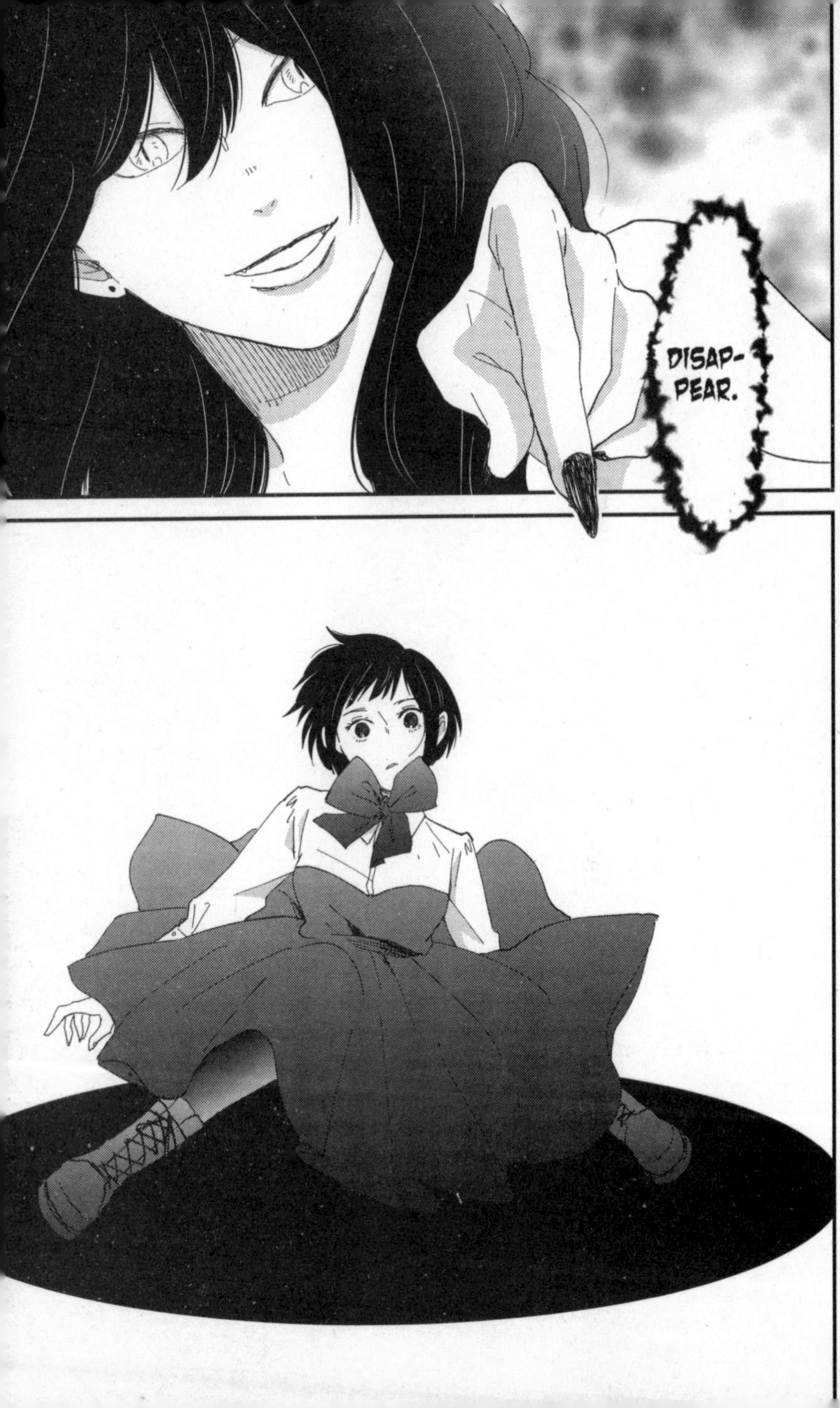
DISAP-
PEAR.

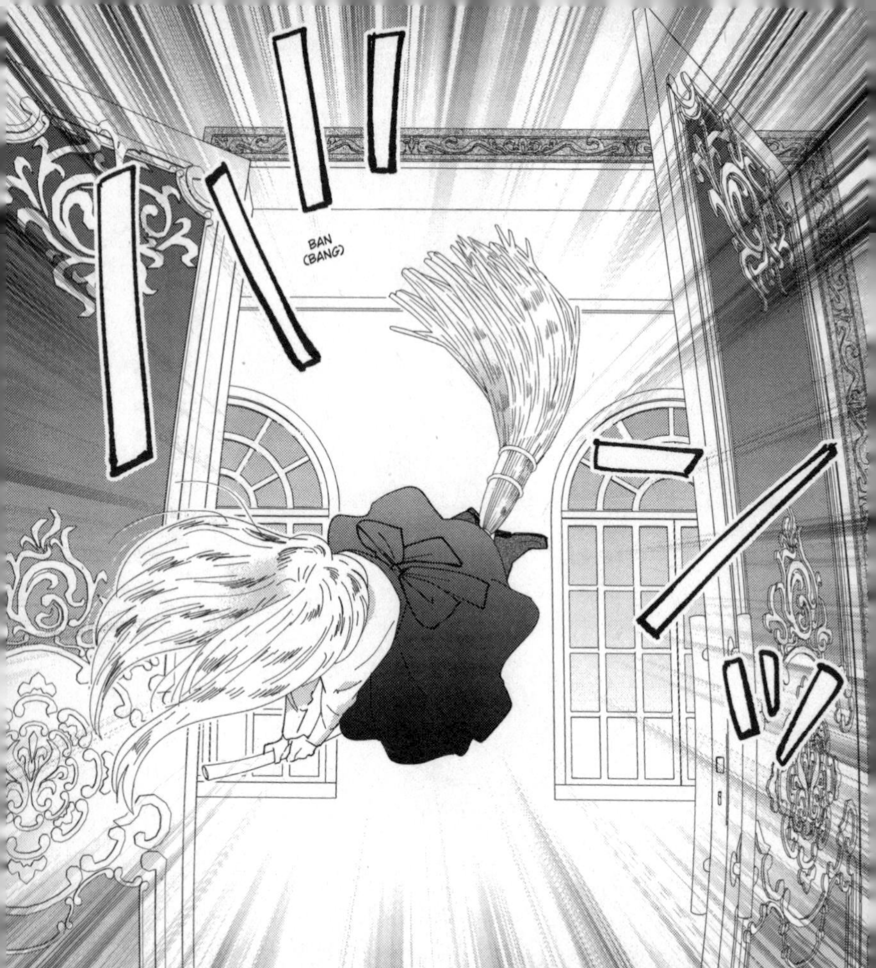
BAN
(BANG)
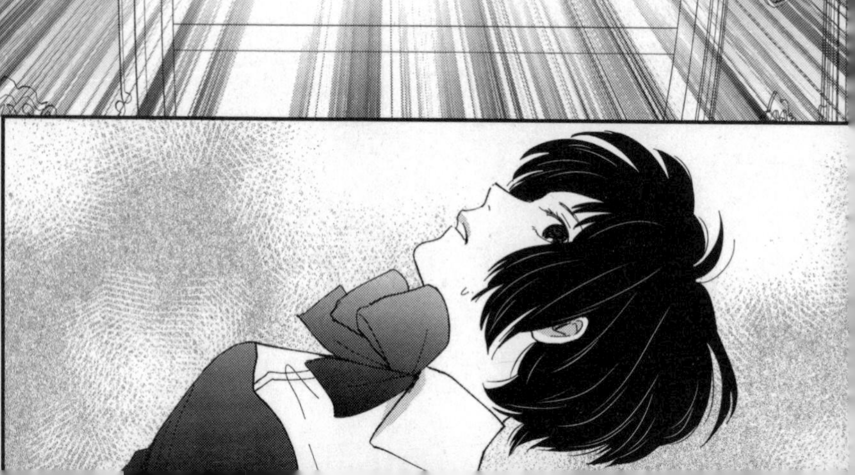

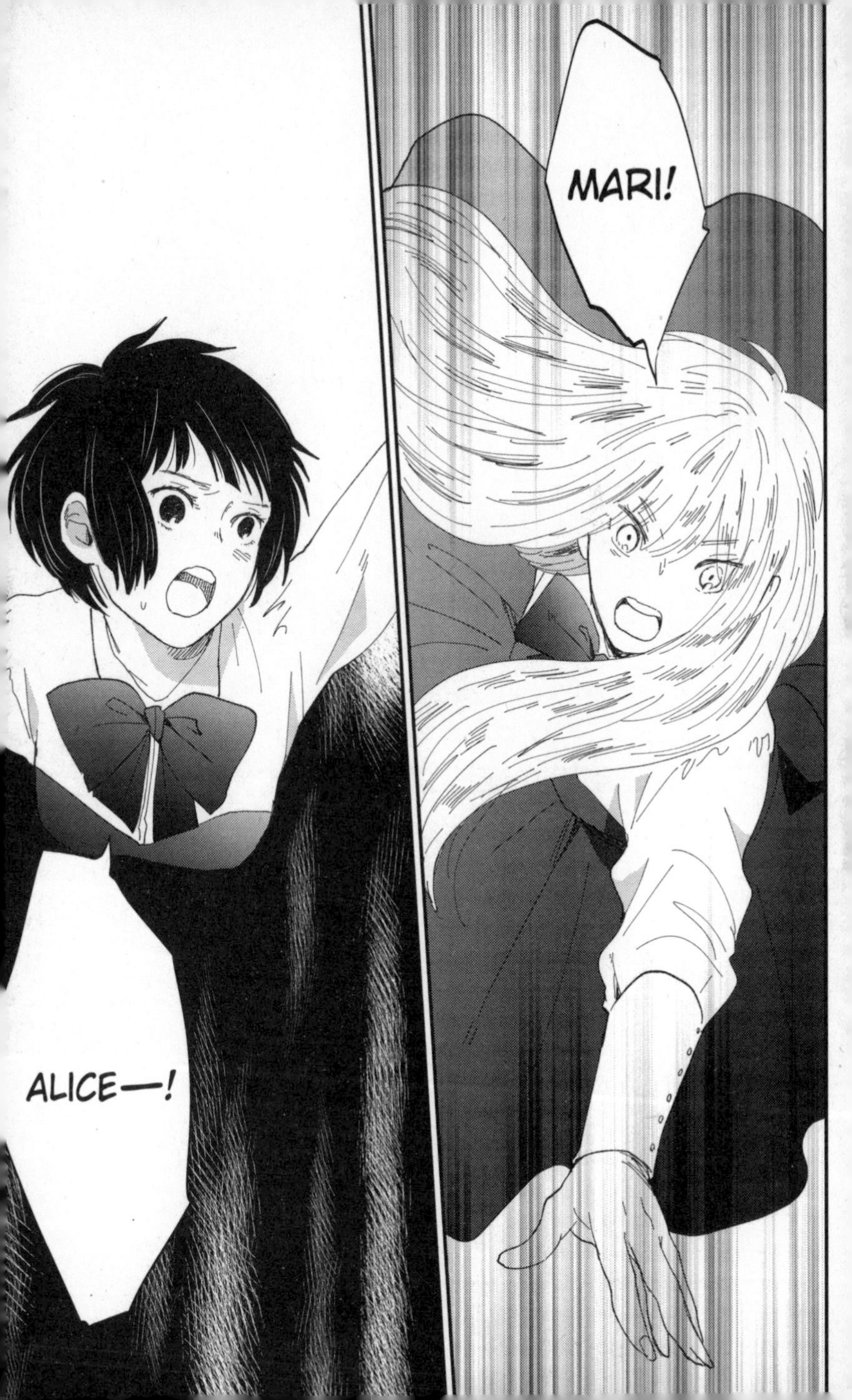
MARI!
ALICE—!

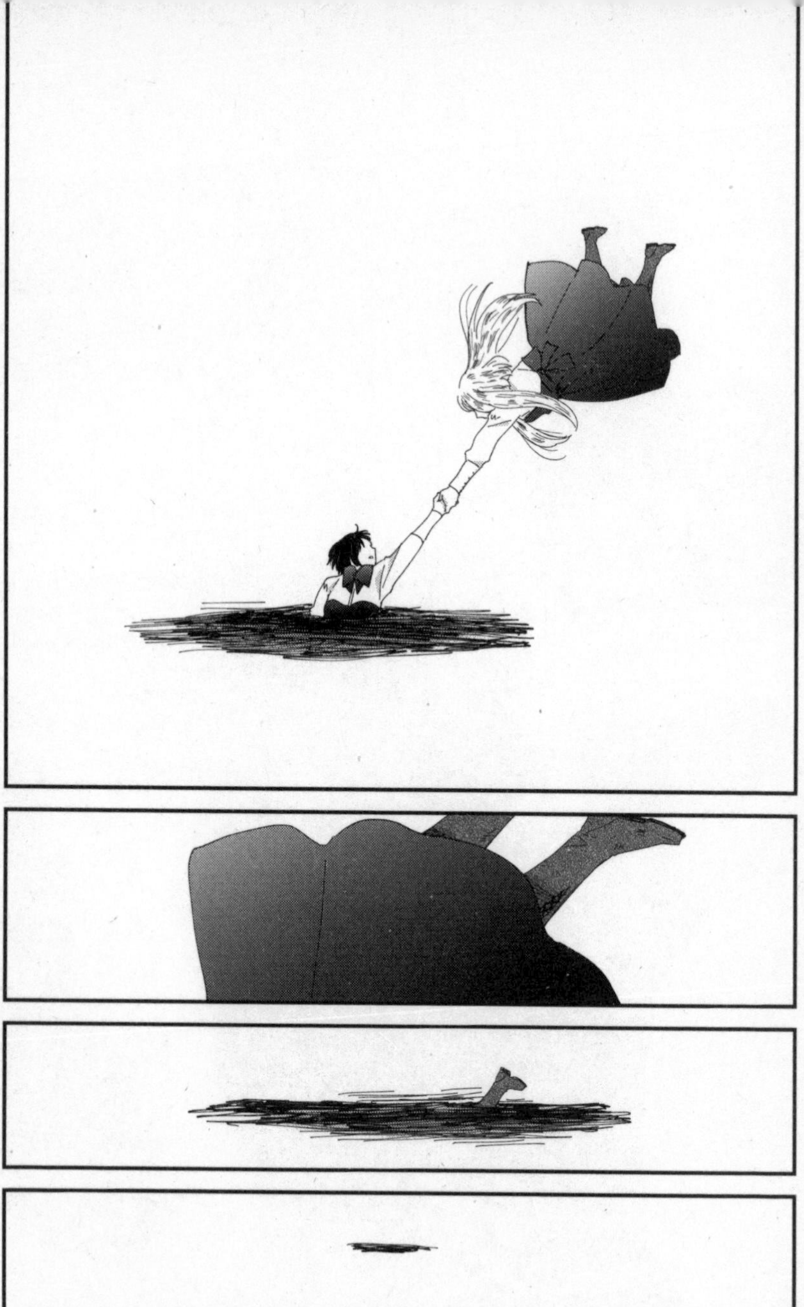

A Witch's Love at the End of the World

A Witch's Love at the End of the World

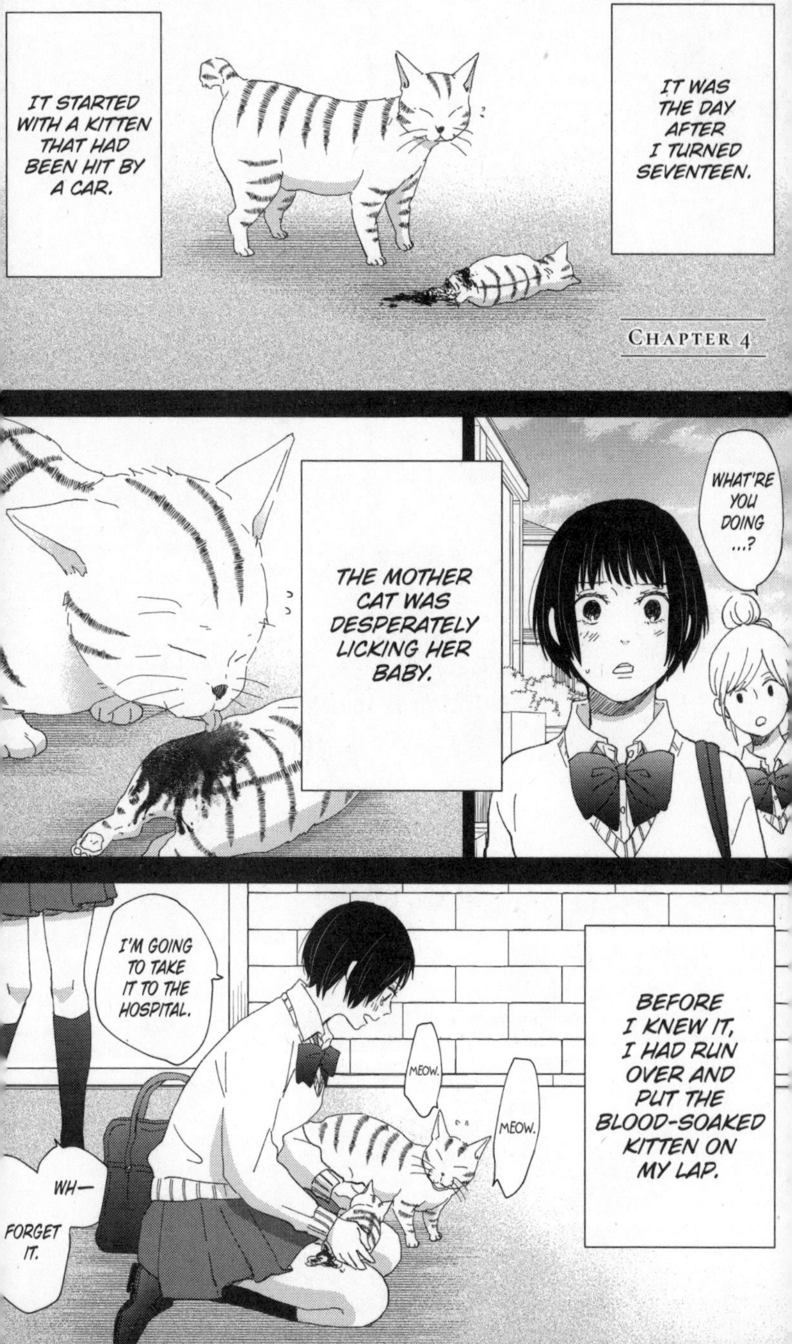
IT WAS THE DAY AFTER I TURNED SEVENTEEN.
IT STARTED WITH A KITTEN THAT HAD BEEN HIT BY A CAR.
CHAPTER 4
WHAT'RE YOU DOING ...?
THE MOTHER CAT WAS DESPERATELY LICKING HER BABY.
BEFORE I KNEW IT, I HAD RUN OVER AND PUT THE BLOOD-SOAKED KITTEN ON MY LAP.
MEOW.
MEOW.
I'M GOING TO TAKE IT TO THE HOSPITAL.
WH—
FORGET IT.

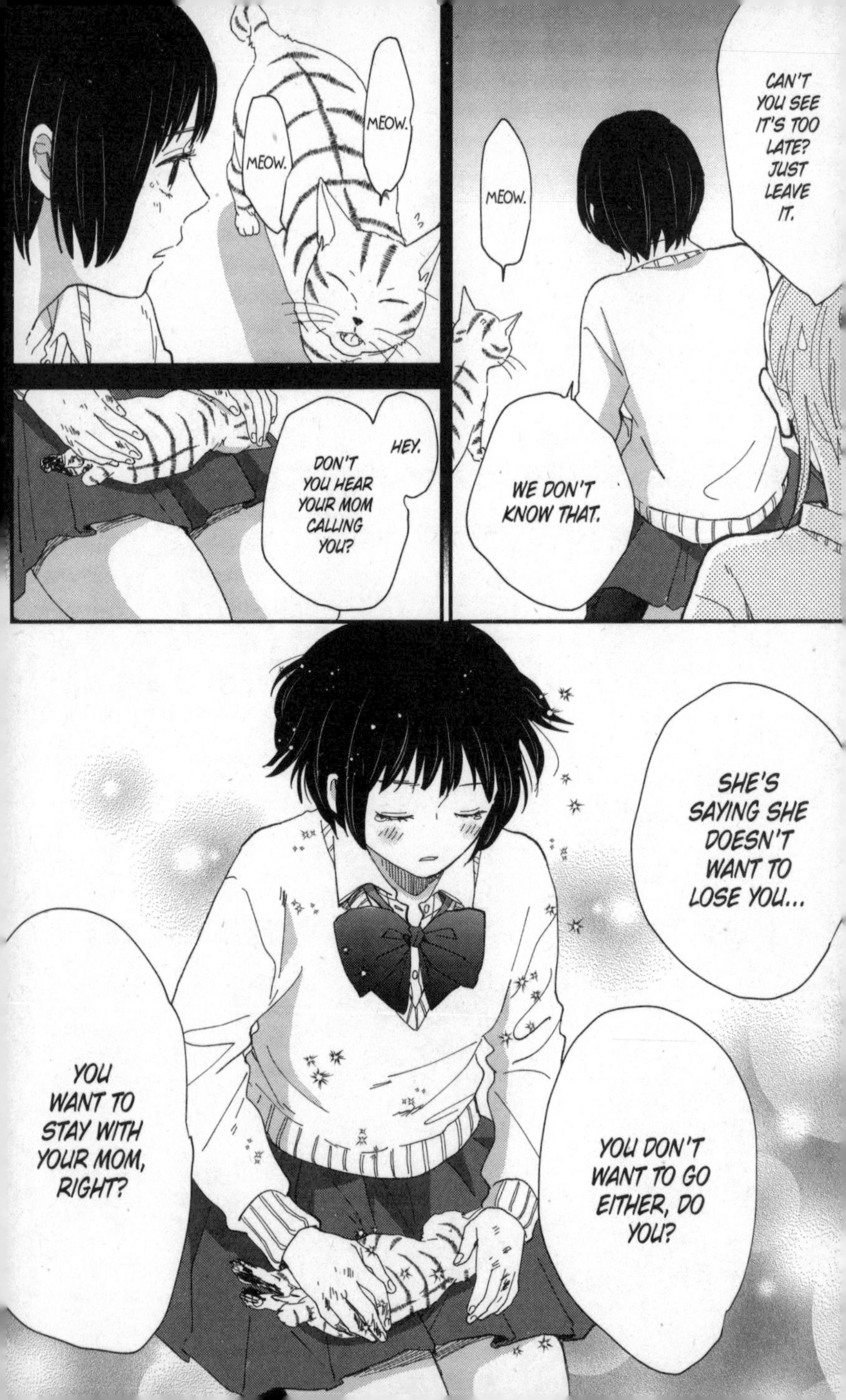
CAN'T YOU SEE IT'S TOO LATE? JUST LEAVE IT.
MEOW.
WE DON'T KNOW THAT.
MEOW.
MEOW.
HEY.
DON'T YOU HEAR YOUR MOM CALLING YOU?
SHE'S SAYING SHE DOESN'T WANT TO LOSE YOU...
YOU DON'T WANT TO GO EITHER, DO YOU?
YOU WANT TO STAY WITH YOUR MOM, RIGHT?

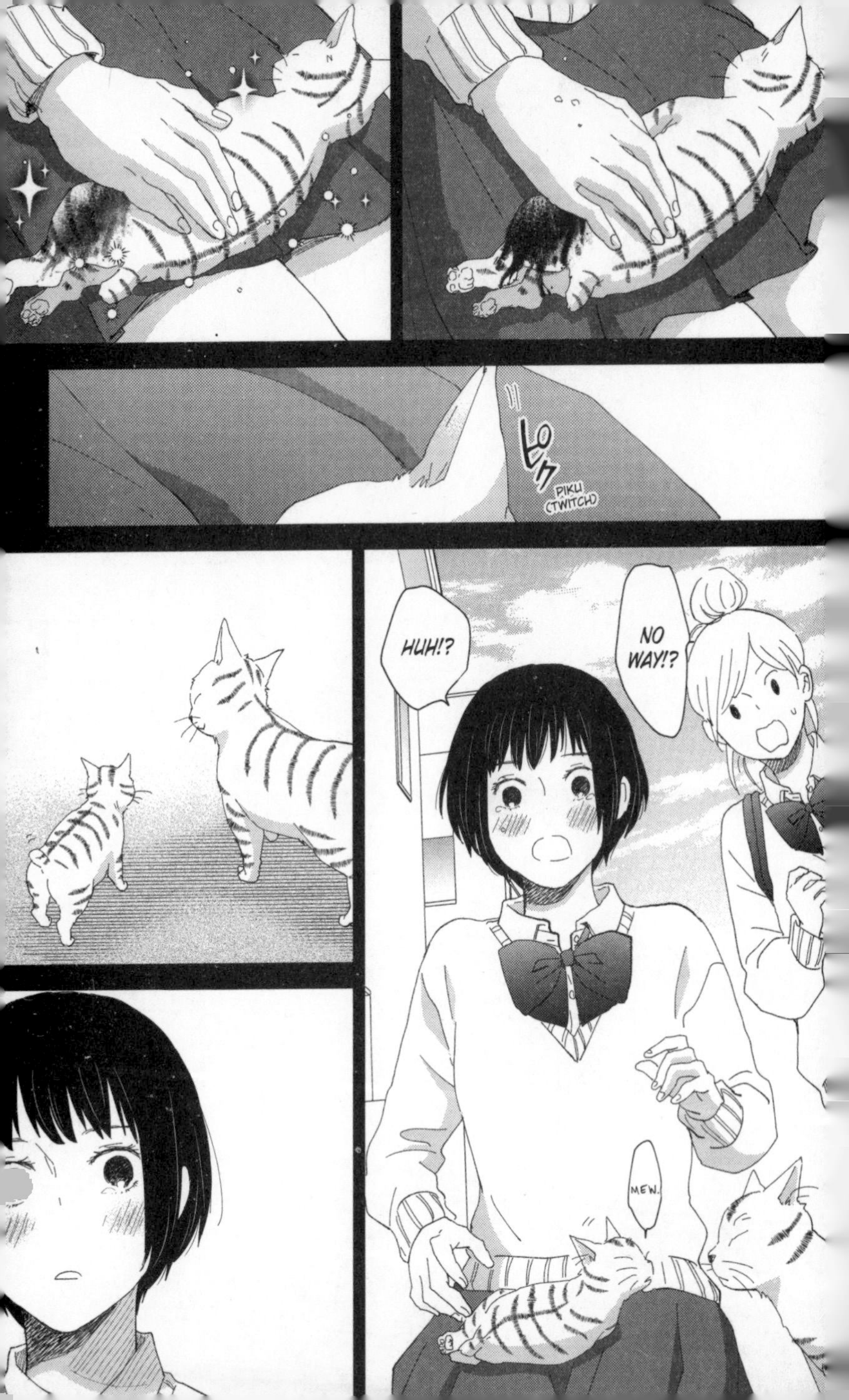
ピク
PIKU (TWITCH)
NO WAY!?
HUH!?
MEW.

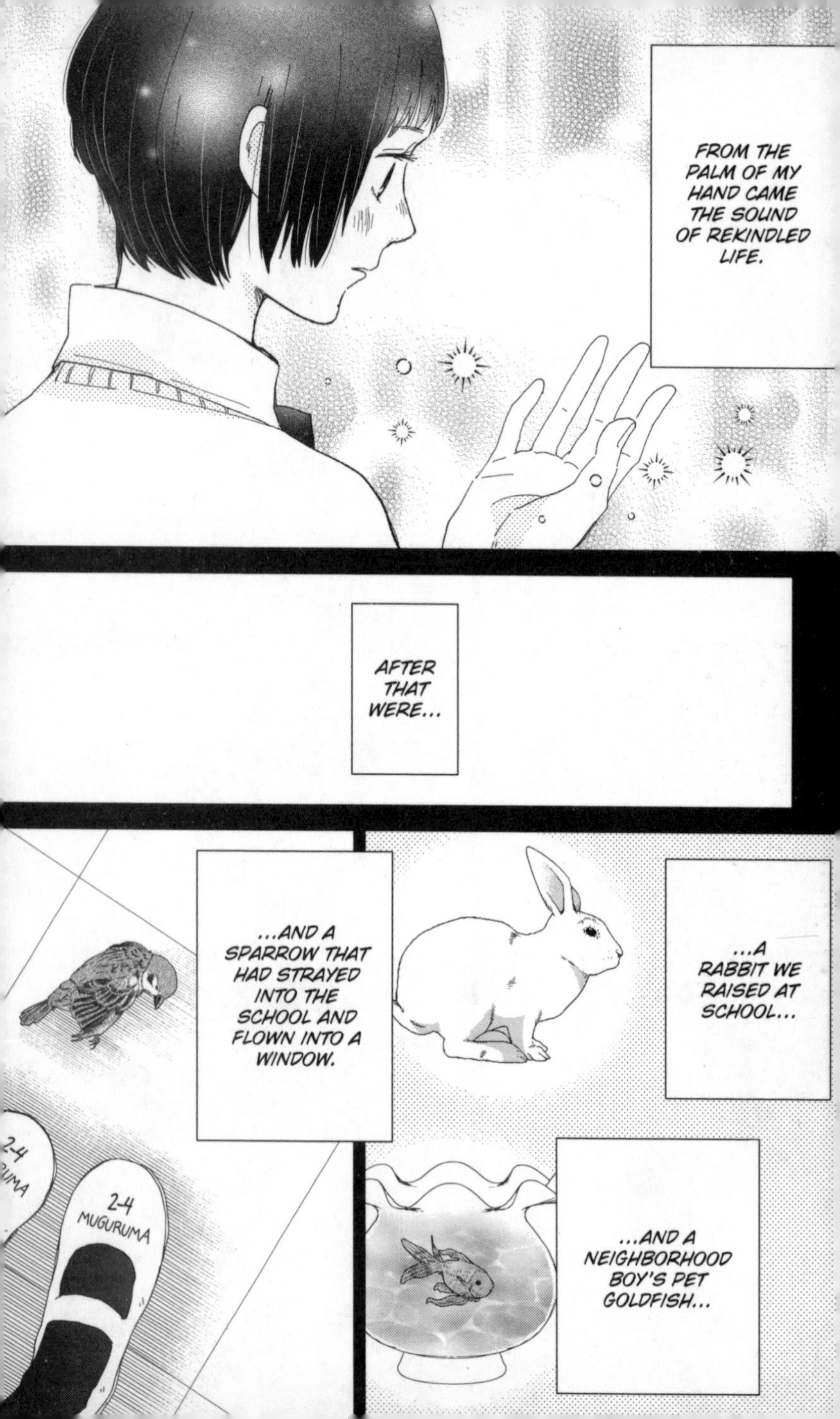
FROM THE PALM OF MY HAND CAME THE SOUND OF REKINDLED LIFE.
AFTER THAT WERE...
...A RABBIT WE RAISED AT SCHOOL...
...AND A NEIGHBORHOOD BOY'S PET GOLDFISH...
...AND A SPARROW THAT HAD STRAYED INTO THE SCHOOL AND FLOWN INTO A WINDOW.
2-4 MUGURUMA

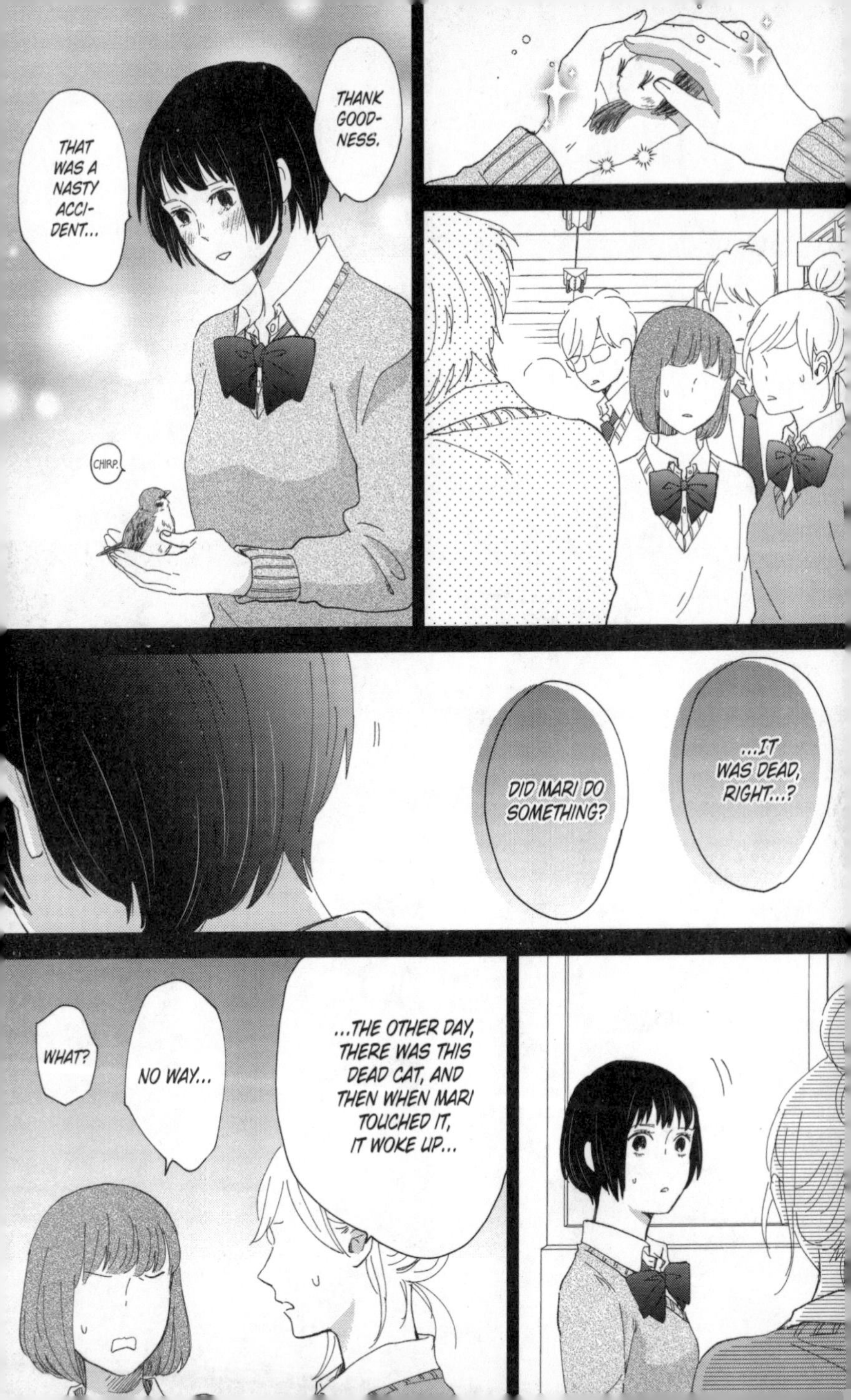
THANK GOODNESS.
THAT WAS A NASTY ACCIDENT...
CHIRP.
...IT WAS DEAD, RIGHT...?
DID MARI DO SOMETHING?
...THE OTHER DAY, THERE WAS THIS DEAD CAT, AND THEN WHEN MARI TOUCHED IT, IT WOKE UP...
NO WAY...
WHAT?

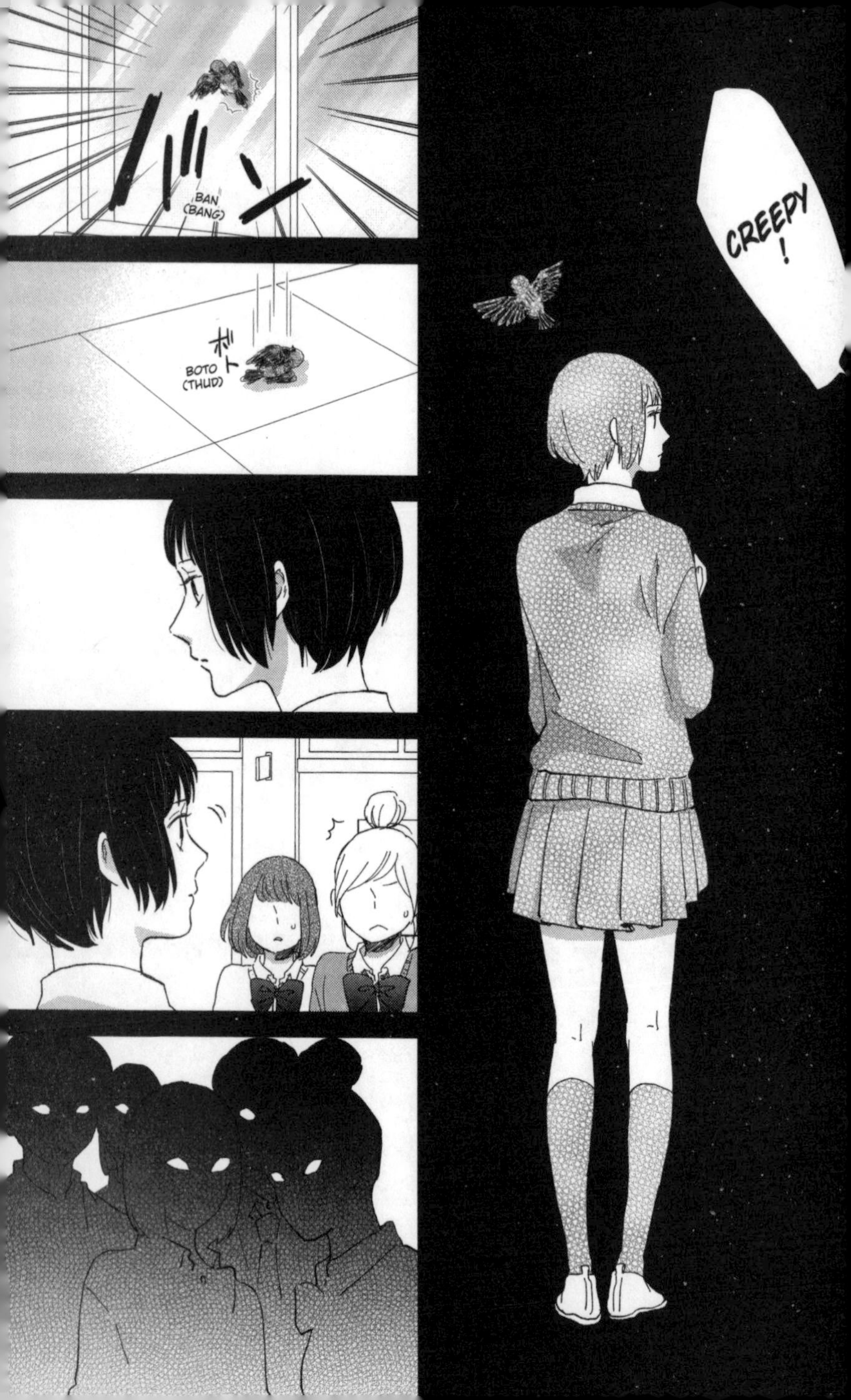
CREEPY!
BAN
(BANG)
ボト
BOTO
(THUD)

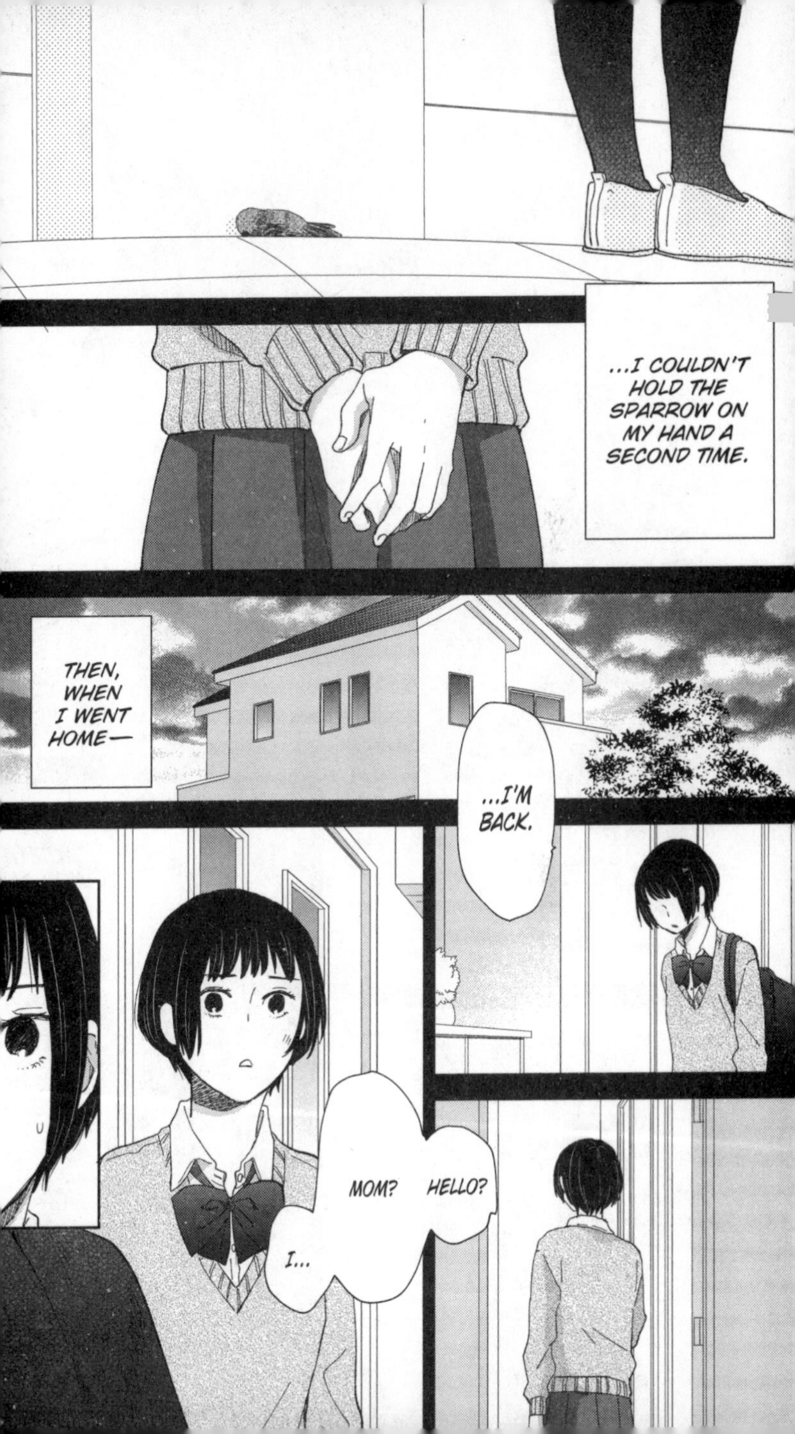
...I COULDN'T HOLD THE SPARROW ON MY HAND A SECOND TIME.
THEN, WHEN I WENT HOME—
...I'M BACK.
MOM? HELLO?
I...

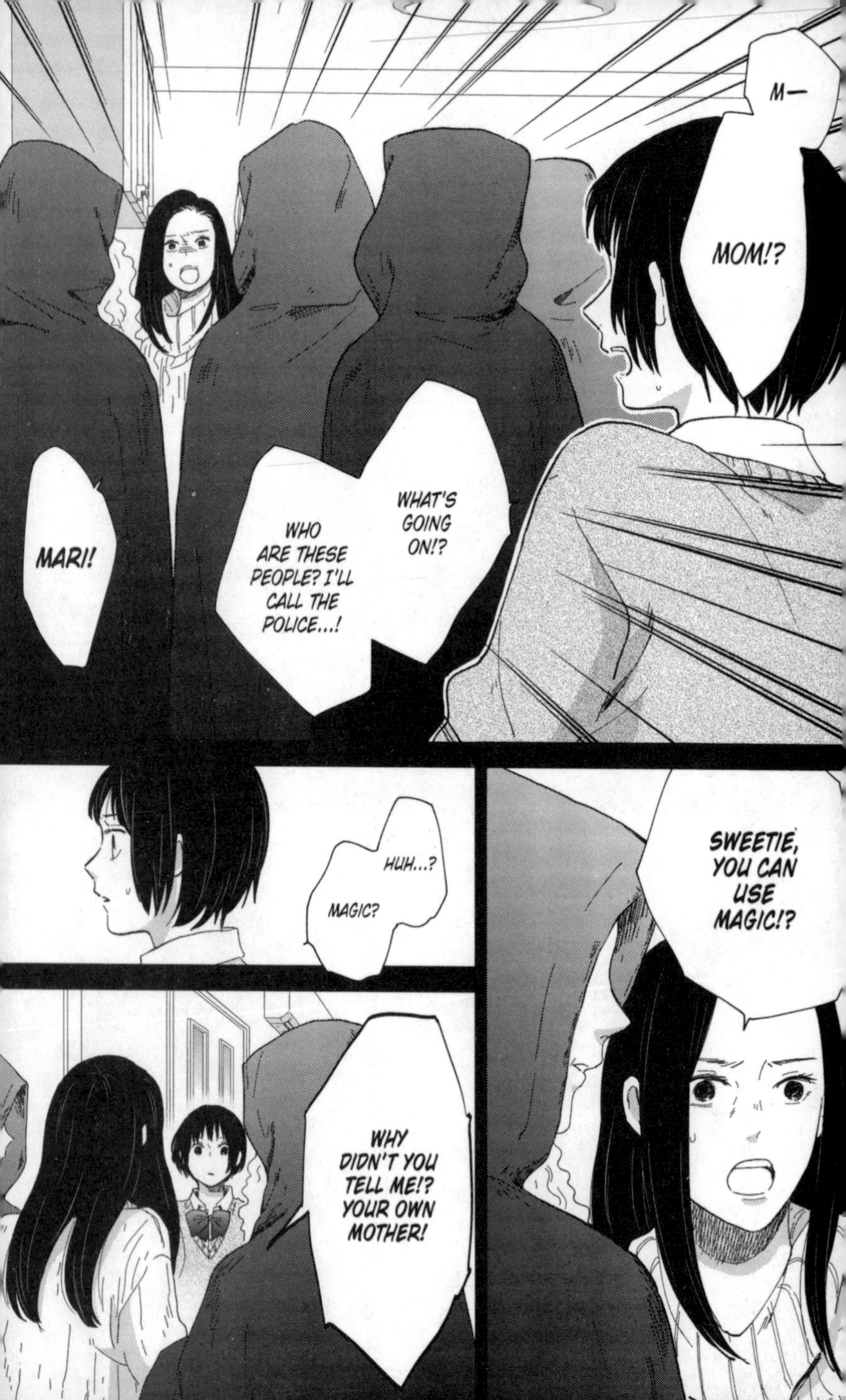
M—
MOM!?
WHAT'S GOING ON!?
WHO ARE THESE PEOPLE? I'LL CALL THE POLICE...!
MARI!
SWEETIE, YOU CAN USE MAGIC!?
HUH...?
MAGIC?
WHY DIDN'T YOU TELL ME!? YOUR OWN MOTHER!

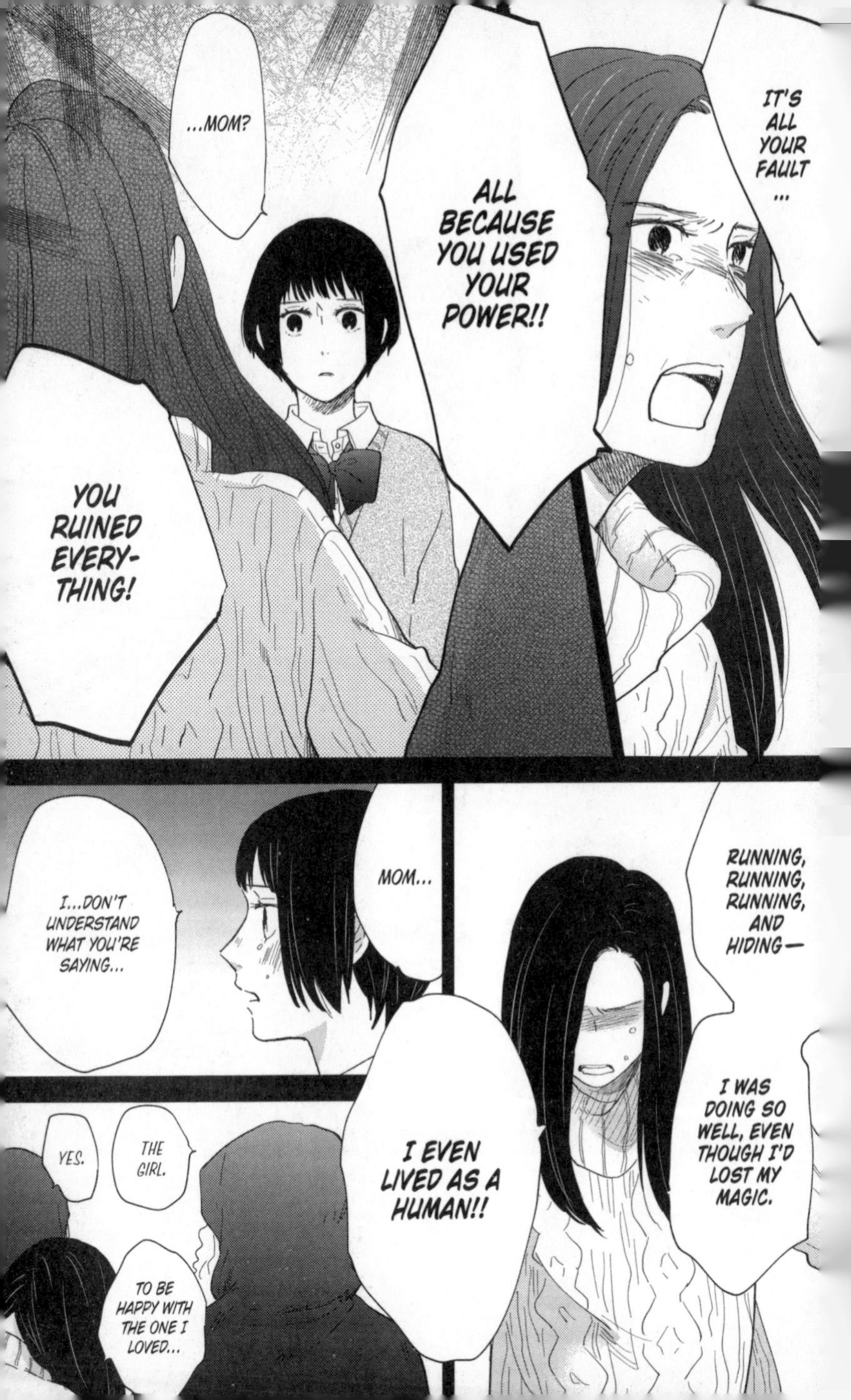
IT'S ALL YOUR FAULT...
ALL BECAUSE YOU USED YOUR POWER!!
...MOM?
YOU RUINED EVERY-THING!
RUNNING, RUNNING, RUNNING, AND HIDING—
I WAS DOING SO WELL, EVEN THOUGH I'D LOST MY MAGIC.
I EVEN LIVED AS A HUMAN!!
MOM...
I...DON'T UNDERSTAND WHAT YOU'RE SAYING...
THE GIRL.
YES.
TO BE HAPPY WITH THE ONE I LOVED...

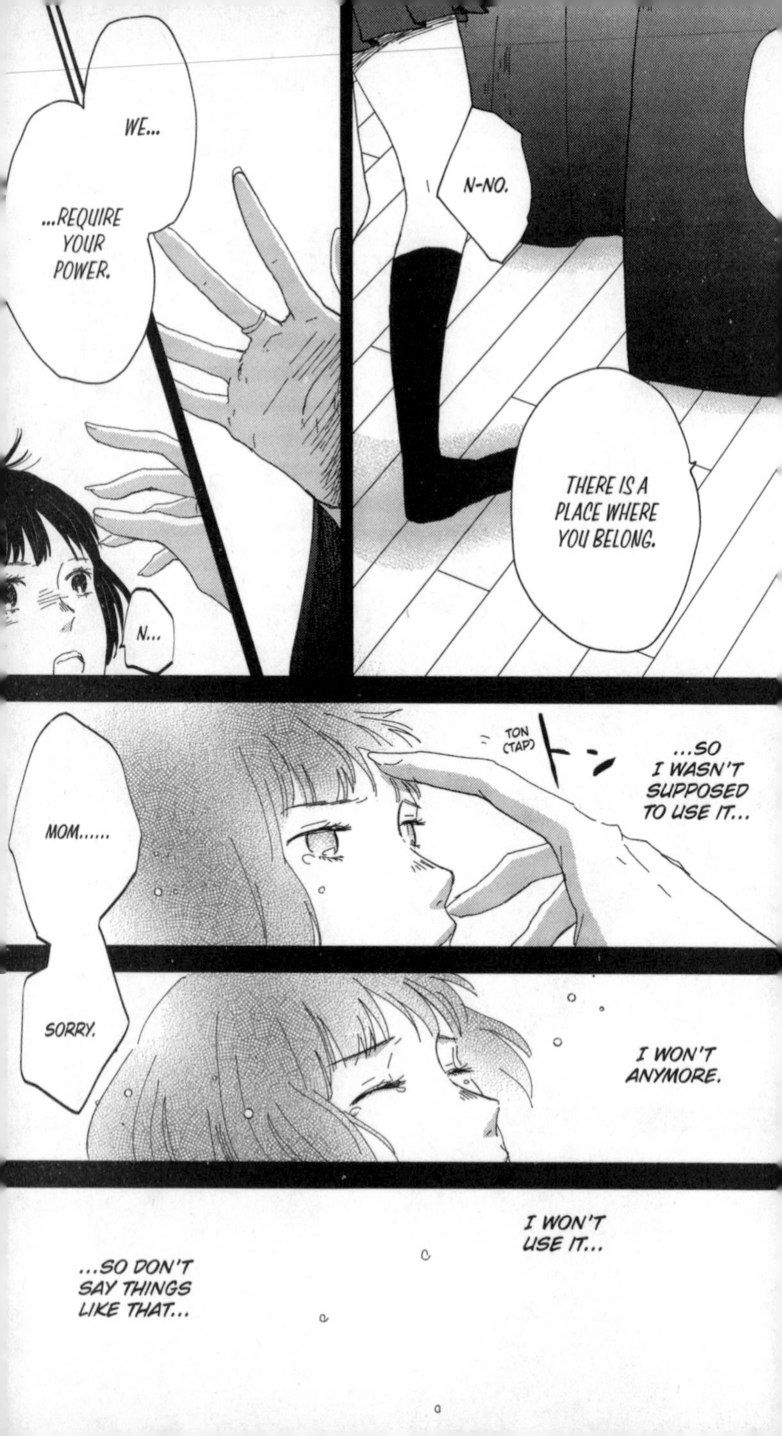
N-NO.
THERE IS A PLACE WHERE YOU BELONG.
WE...
...REQUIRE YOUR POWER.
N...
TON (TAP)
...SO I WASN'T SUPPOSED TO USE IT...
MOM......
I WON'T ANYMORE.
SORRY.
I WON'T USE IT...
...SO DON'T SAY THINGS LIKE THAT...

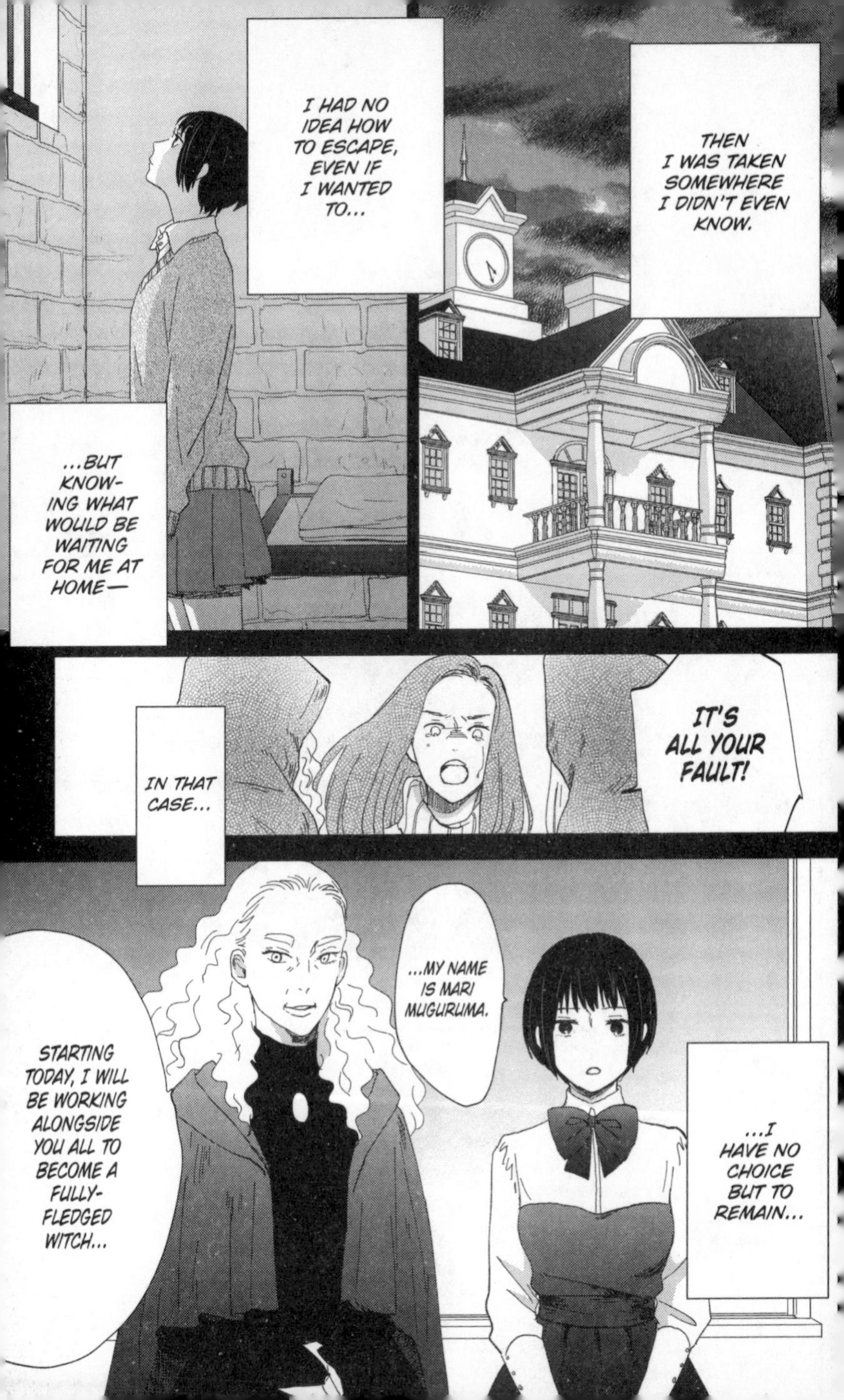
THEN I WAS TAKEN SOMEWHERE I DIDN'T EVEN KNOW.
I HAD NO IDEA HOW TO ESCAPE, EVEN IF I WANTED TO...
...BUT KNOWING WHAT WOULD BE WAITING FOR ME AT HOME—
IT'S ALL YOUR FAULT!
IN THAT CASE...
...I HAVE NO CHOICE BUT TO REMAIN...
...MY NAME IS MARI MUGURUMA.
STARTING TODAY, I WILL BE WORKING ALONGSIDE YOU ALL TO BECOME A FULLY-FLEDGED WITCH...

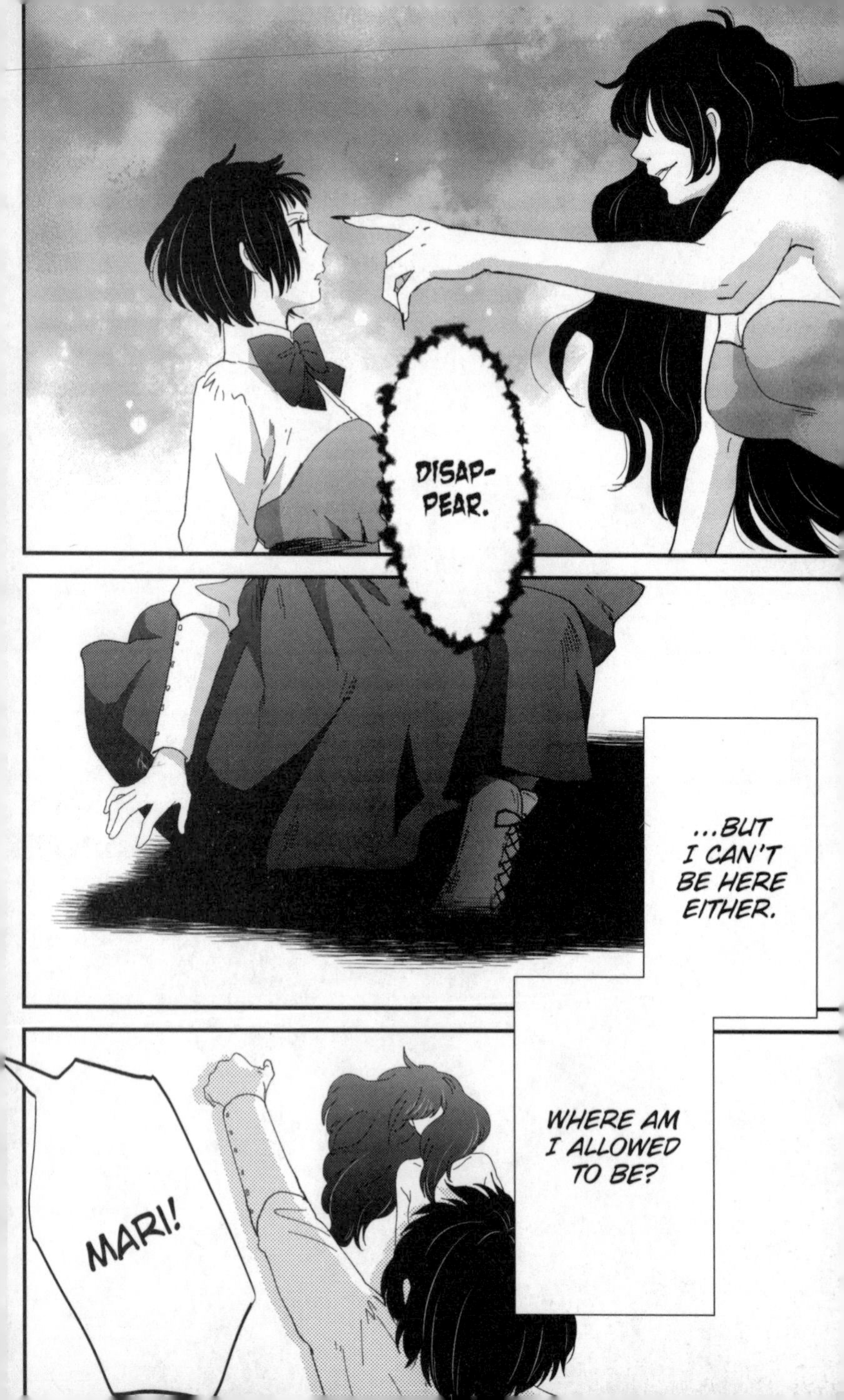
DISAP-PEAR.
...BUT I CAN'T BE HERE EITHER.
WHERE AM I ALLOWED TO BE?
MARI!

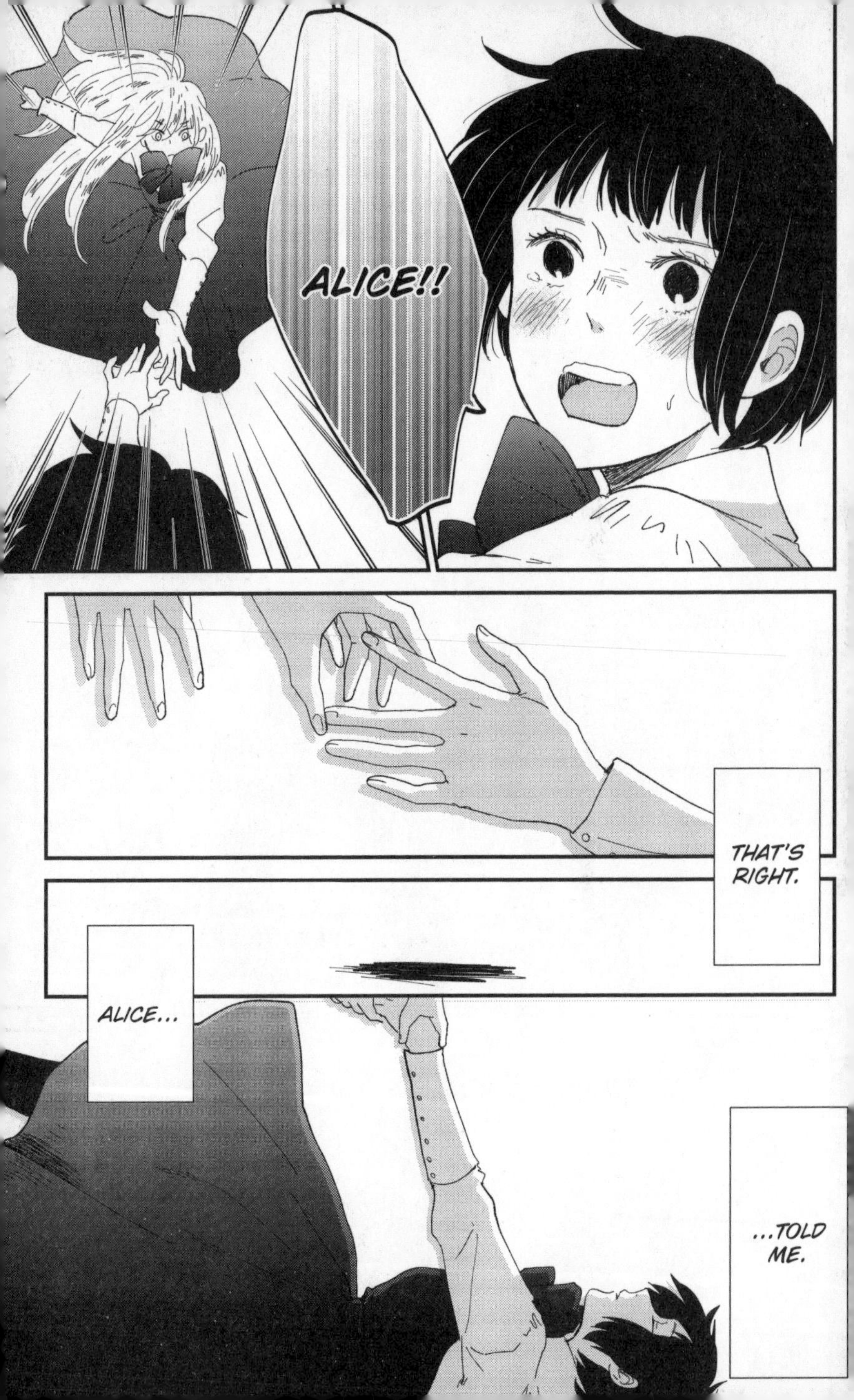
ALICE!!
THAT'S RIGHT.
ALICE...
...TOLD ME.

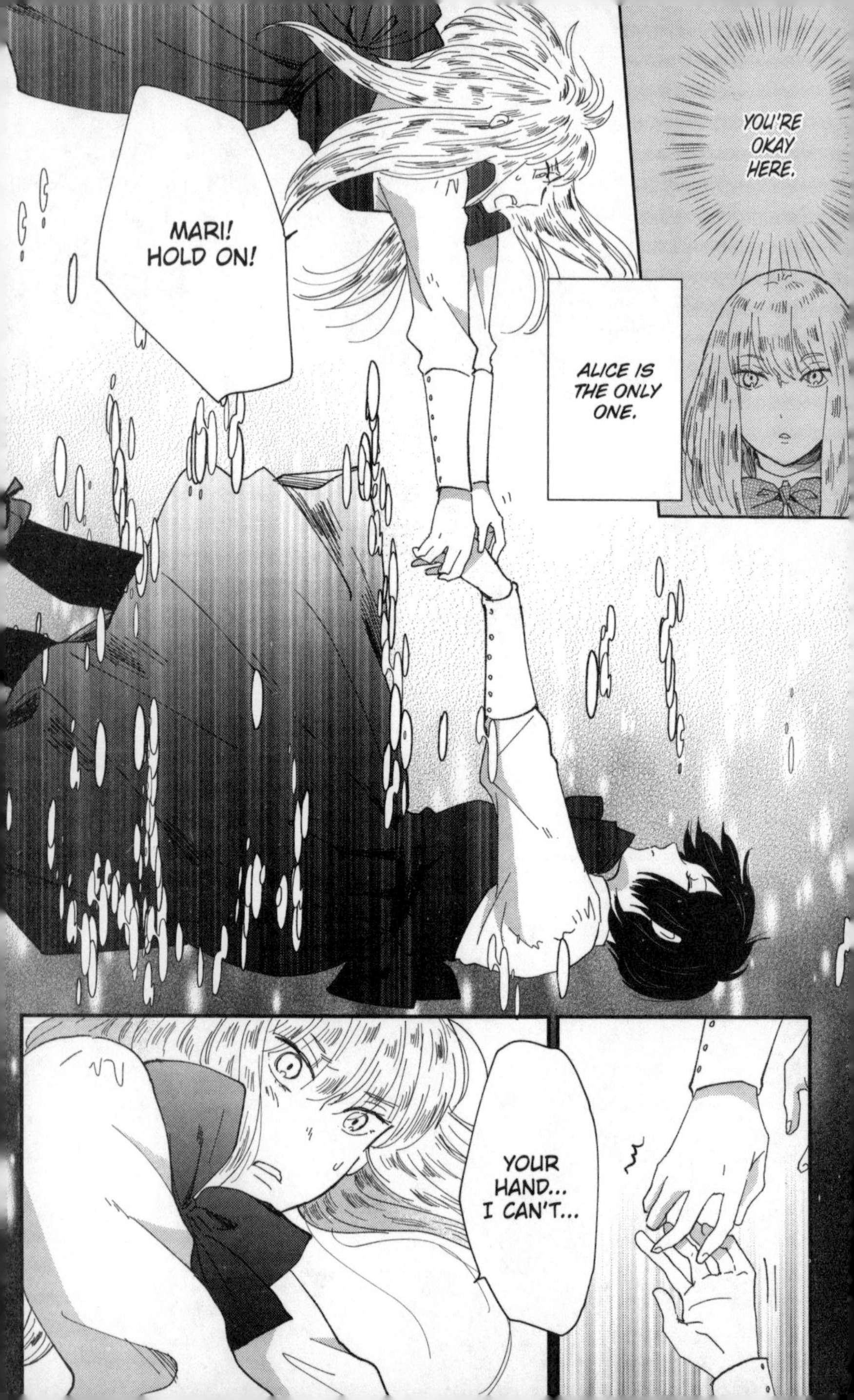
YOU'RE OKAY HERE.
ALICE IS THE ONLY ONE.
MARI! HOLD ON!
YOUR HAND... I CAN'T...

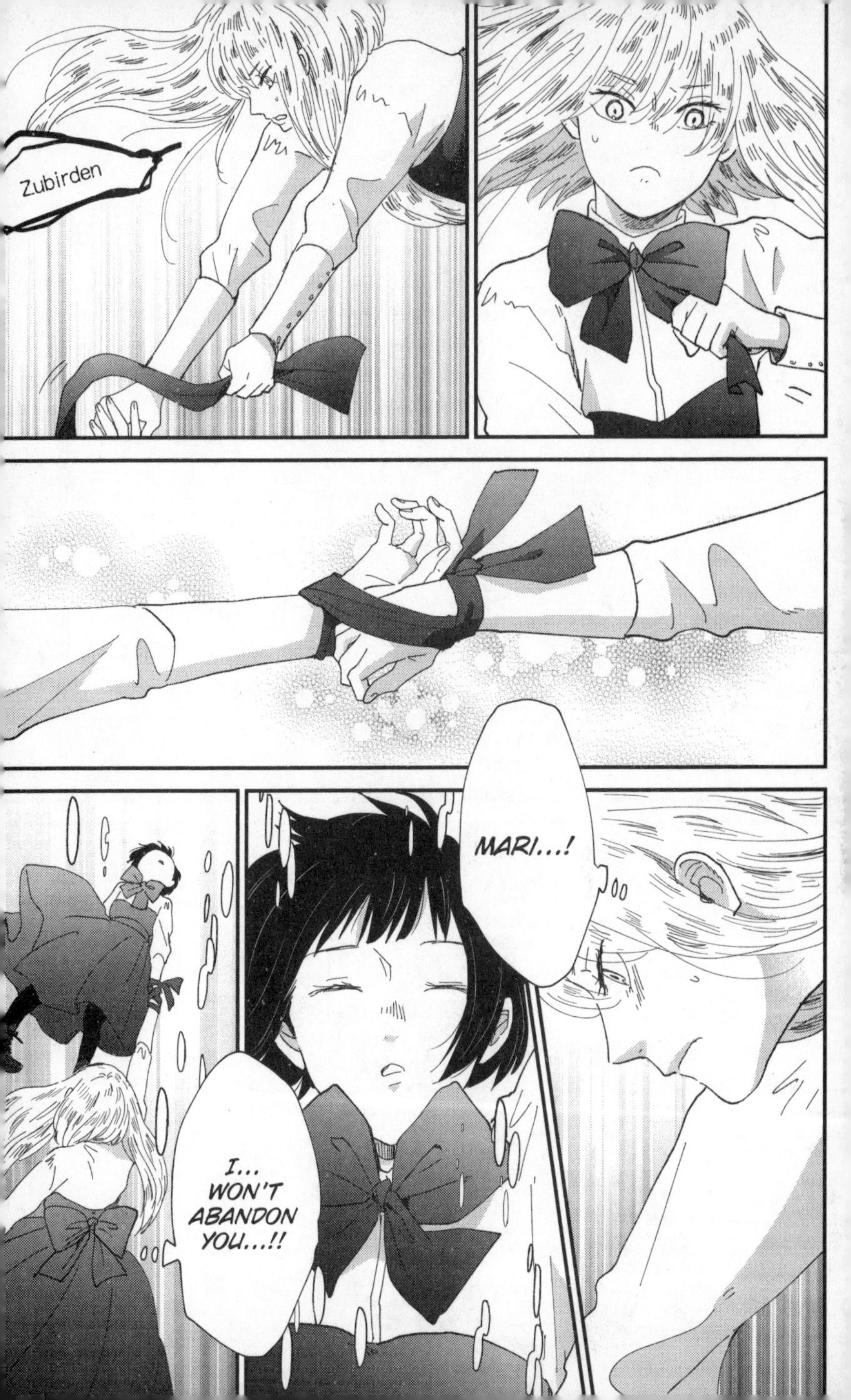
Zubirden
MARI...!
I... WON'T ABANDON YOU...!!

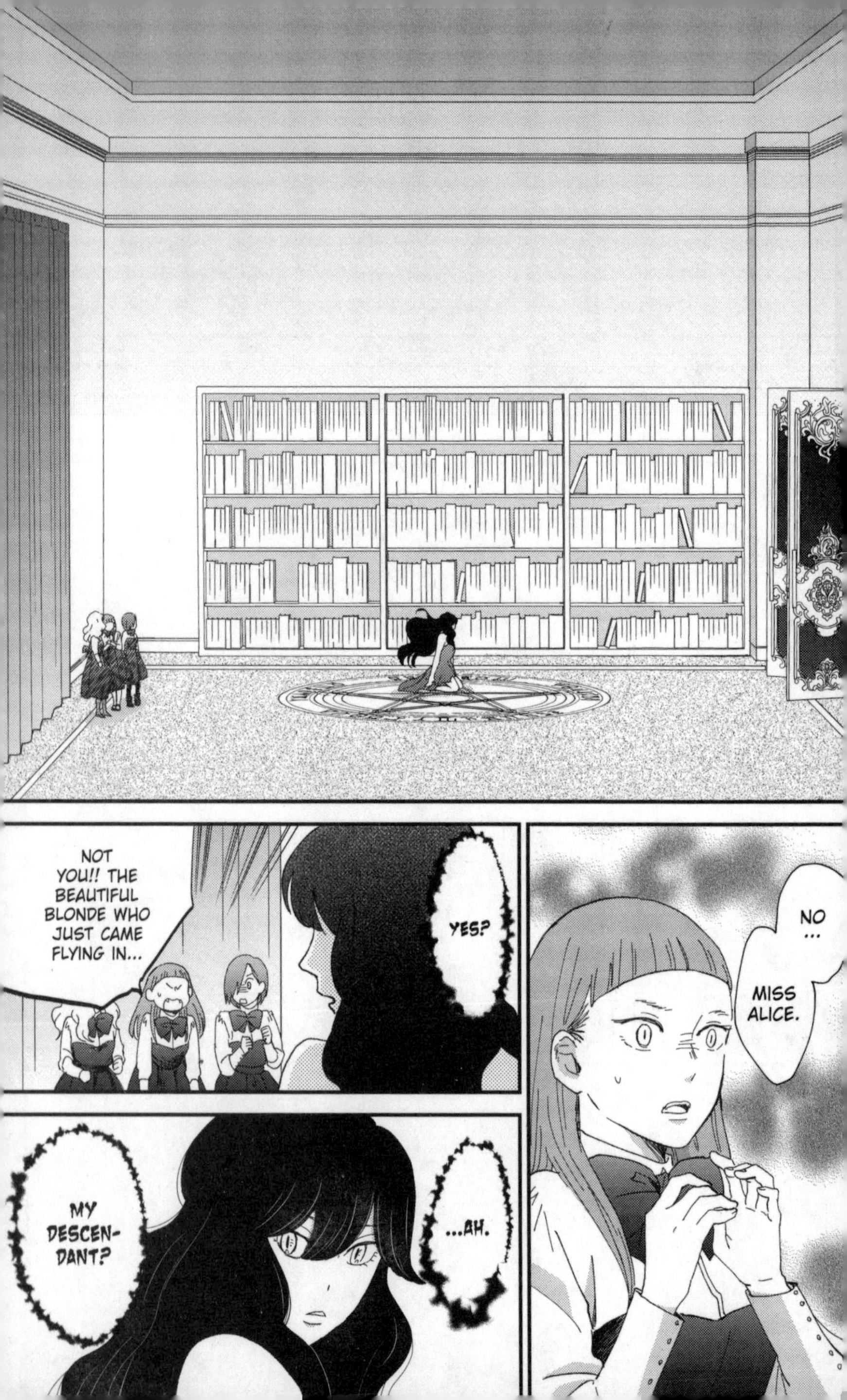
NO ... MISS ALICE.
YES?
NOT YOU!! THE BEAUTIFUL BLONDE WHO JUST CAME FLYING IN...
...AH.
MY DESCEN-DANT?

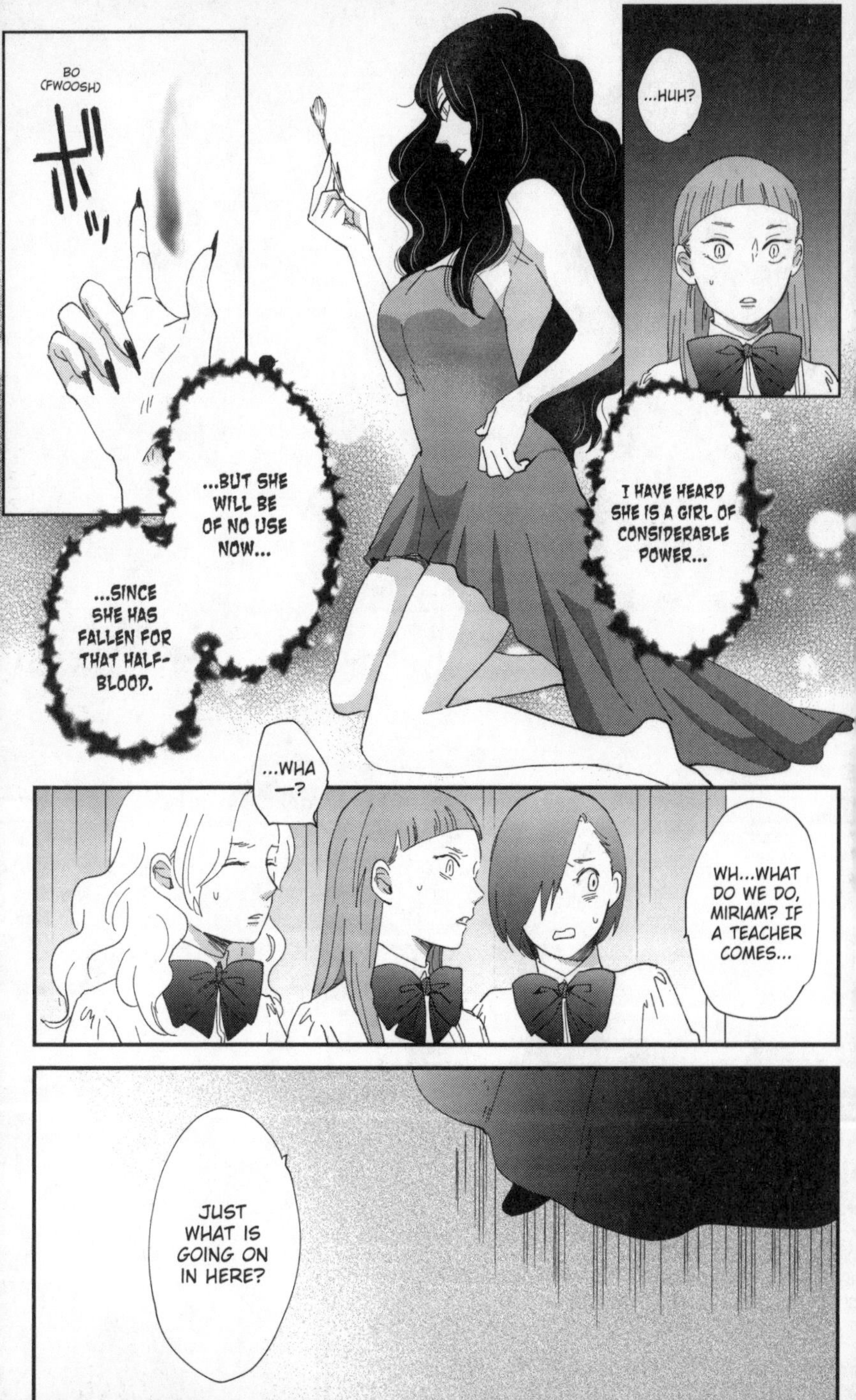
...HUH?
BO (FWOOSH)
I HAVE HEARD SHE IS A GIRL OF CONSIDERABLE POWER...
...BUT SHE WILL BE OF NO USE NOW...
...SINCE SHE HAS FALLEN FOR THAT HALF-BLOOD.
...WHA—?
WH...WHAT DO WE DO, MIRIAM? IF A TEACHER COMES...
JUST WHAT IS GOING ON IN HERE?

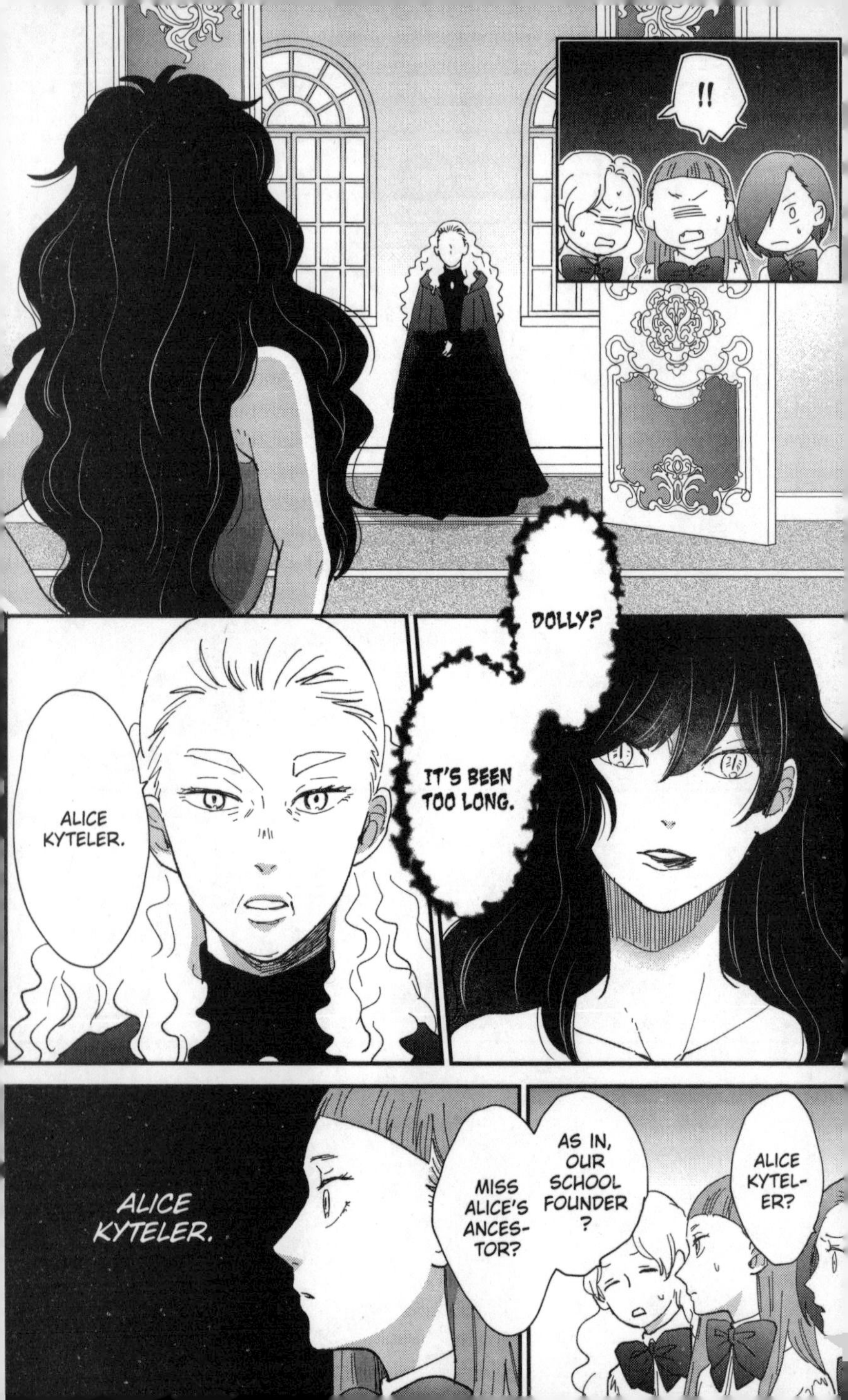
!!
DOLLY?
IT'S BEEN TOO LONG.
ALICE KYTELER.
ALICE KYTELER?
AS IN, OUR SCHOOL FOUNDER?
MISS ALICE'S ANCESTOR?
ALICE KYTELER.

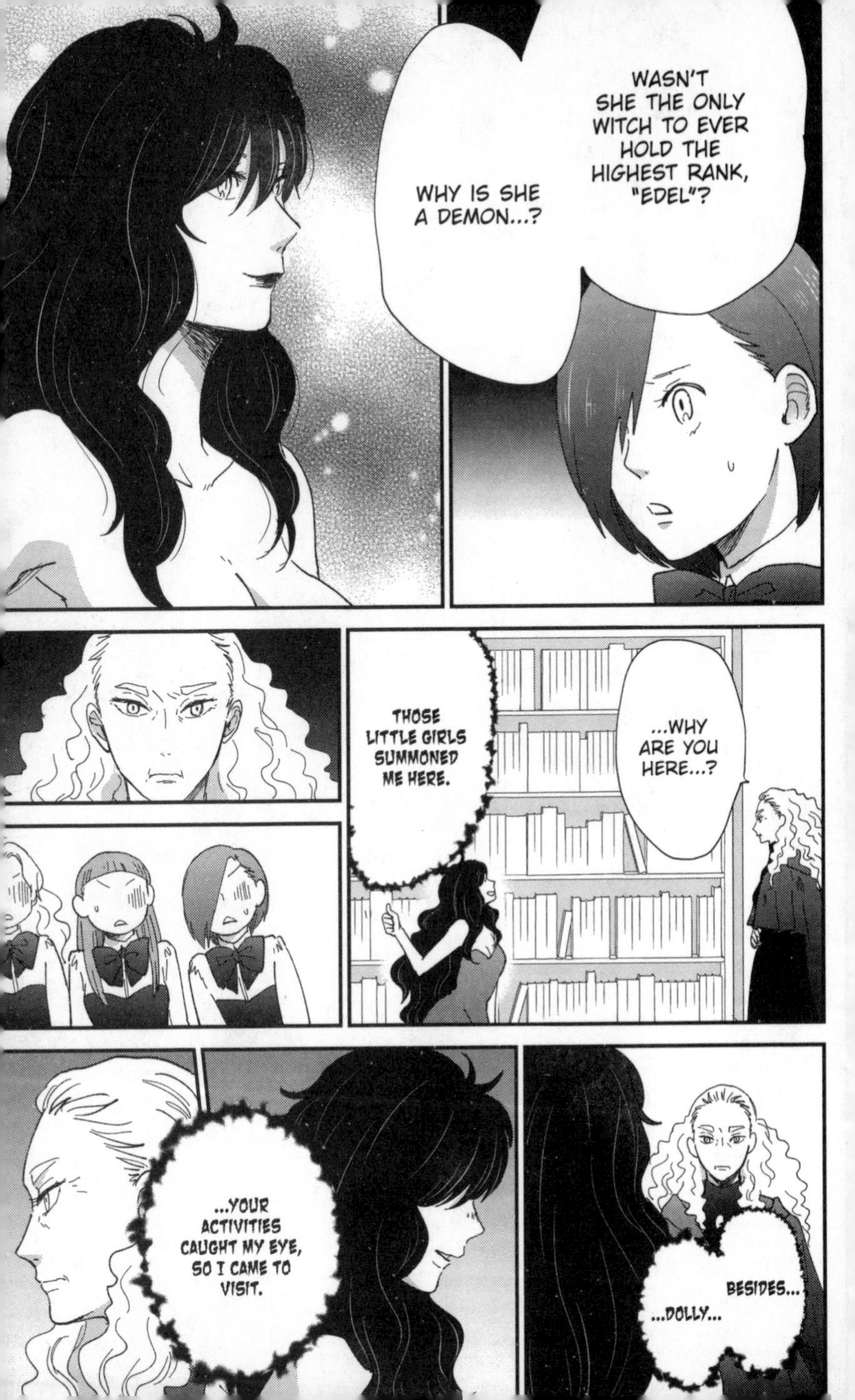
WASN'T SHE THE ONLY WITCH TO EVER HOLD THE HIGHEST RANK, "EDEL"?
WHY IS SHE A DEMON...?
...WHY ARE YOU HERE...?
THOSE LITTLE GIRLS SUMMONED ME HERE.
BESIDES...
...DOLLY...
...YOUR ACTIVITIES CAUGHT MY EYE, SO I CAME TO VISIT.

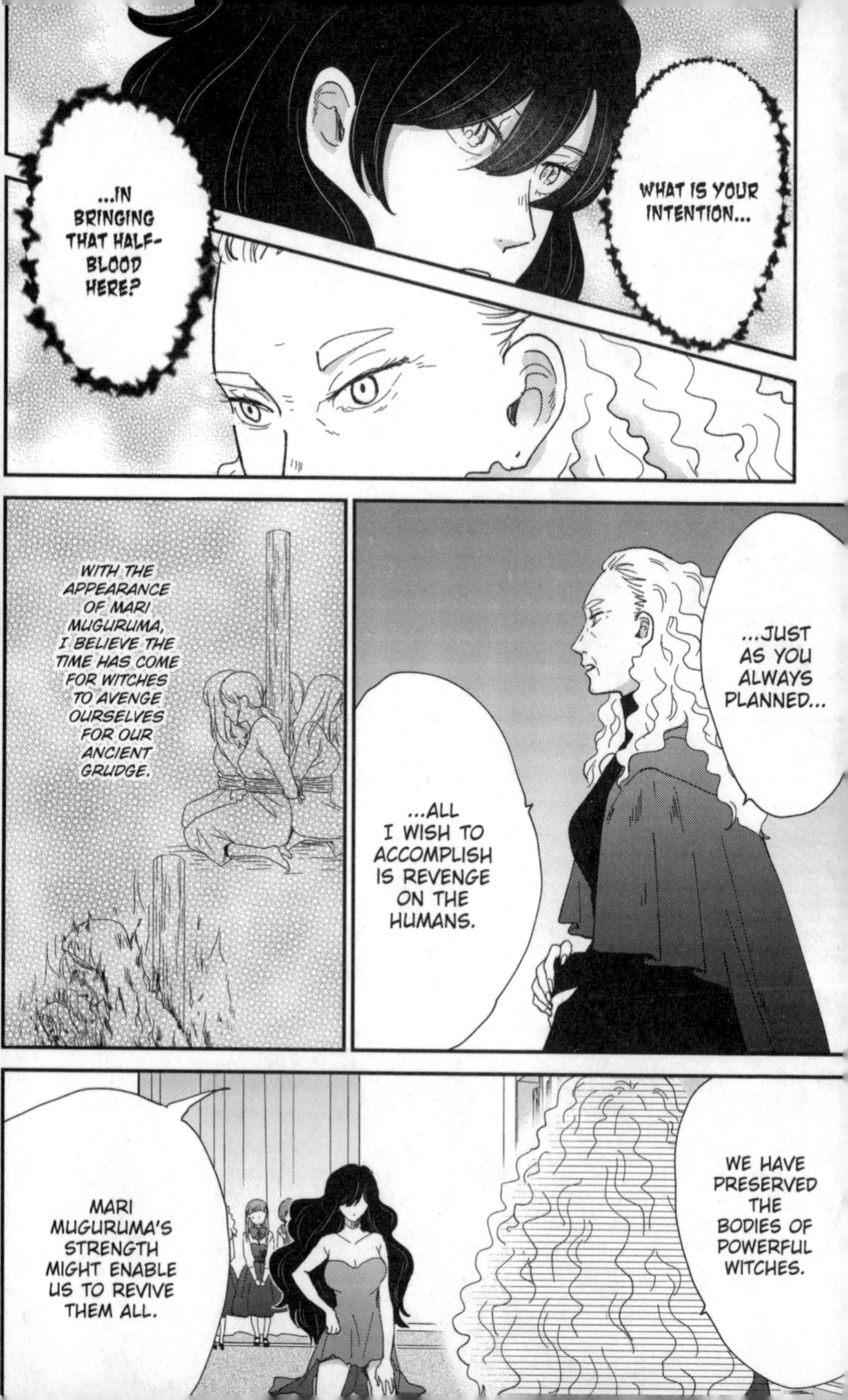
WHAT IS YOUR INTENTION...
...IN BRINGING THAT HALF-BLOOD HERE?
...JUST AS YOU ALWAYS PLANNED...
...ALL I WISH TO ACCOMPLISH IS REVENGE ON THE HUMANS.
WITH THE APPEARANCE OF MARI MUGURUMA, I BELIEVE THE TIME HAS COME FOR WITCHES TO AVENGE OURSELVES FOR OUR ANCIENT GRUDGE.
WE HAVE PRESERVED THE BODIES OF POWERFUL WITCHES.
MARI MUGURUMA'S STRENGTH MIGHT ENABLE US TO REVIVE THEM ALL.

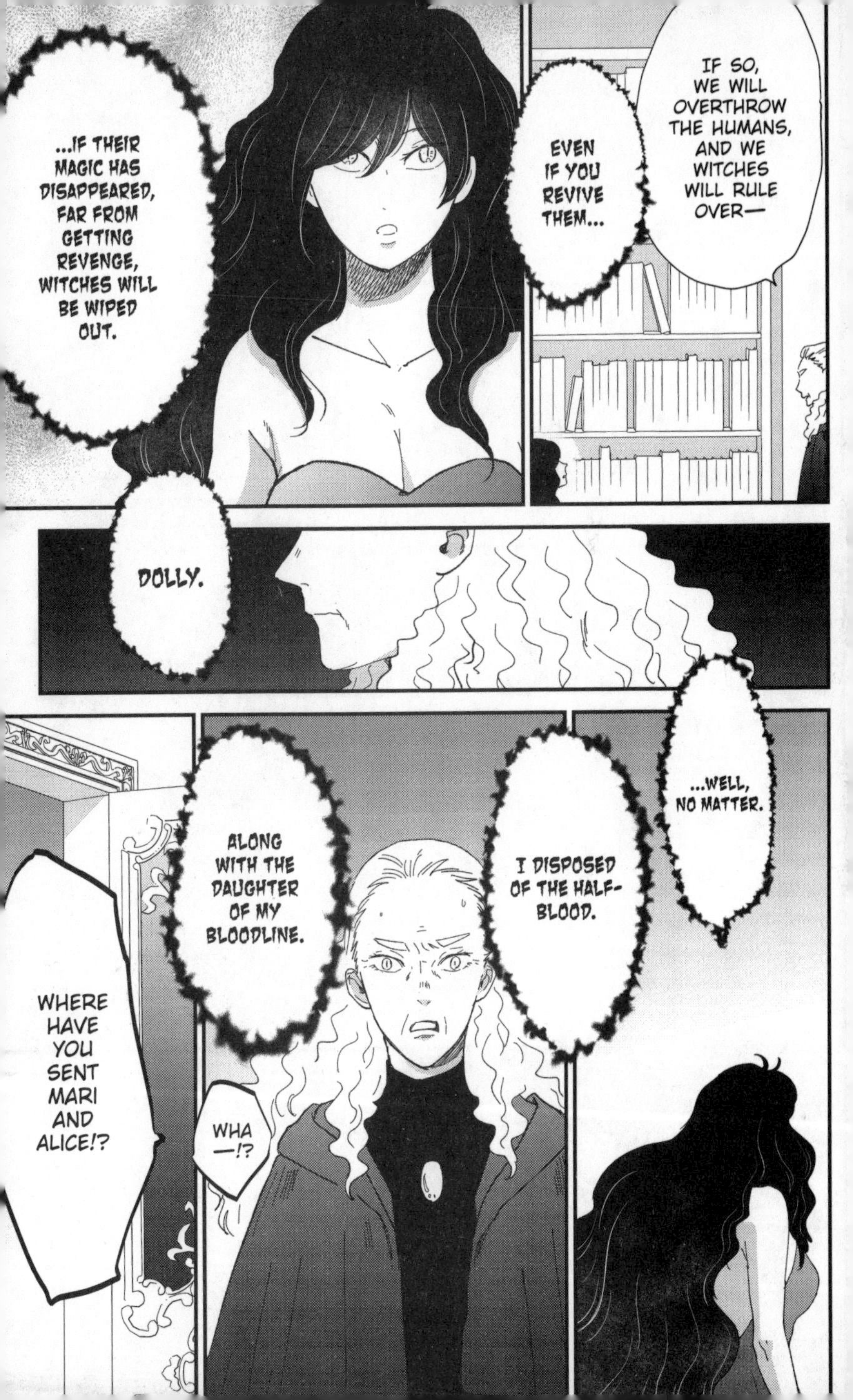
IF SO, WE WILL OVERTHROW THE HUMANS, AND WE WITCHES WILL RULE OVER—
EVEN IF YOU REVIVE THEM...
...IF THEIR MAGIC HAS DISAPPEARED, FAR FROM GETTING REVENGE, WITCHES WILL BE WIPED OUT.
DOLLY.
...WELL, NO MATTER.
I DISPOSED OF THE HALF-BLOOD.
ALONG WITH THE DAUGHTER OF MY BLOODLINE.
WHA—!?
WHERE HAVE YOU SENT MARI AND ALICE!?

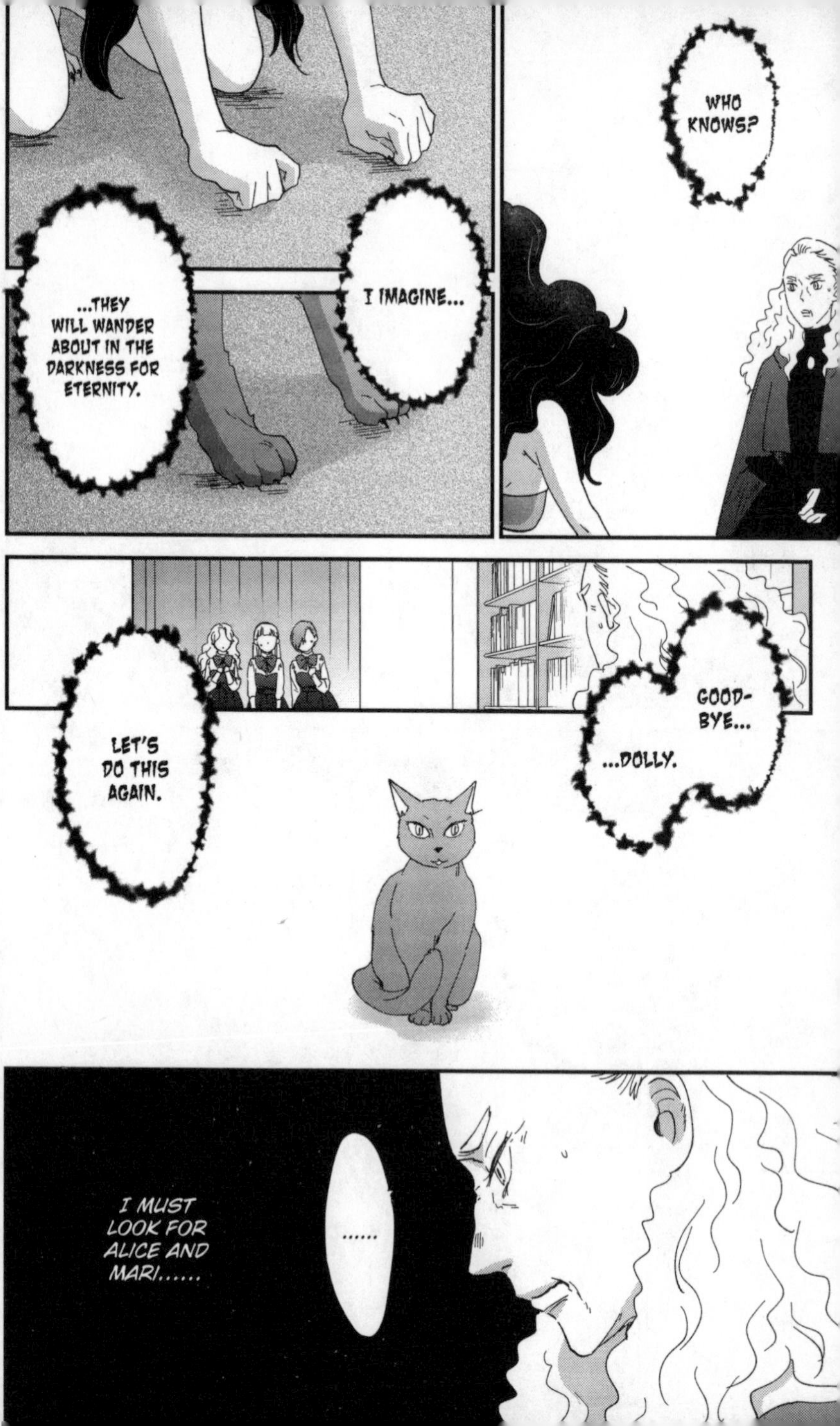
WHO KNOWS?
I IMAGINE...
...THEY WILL WANDER ABOUT IN THE DARKNESS FOR ETERNITY.
GOOD-BYE...
...DOLLY.
LET'S DO THIS AGAIN.
......
I MUST LOOK FOR ALICE AND MARI......

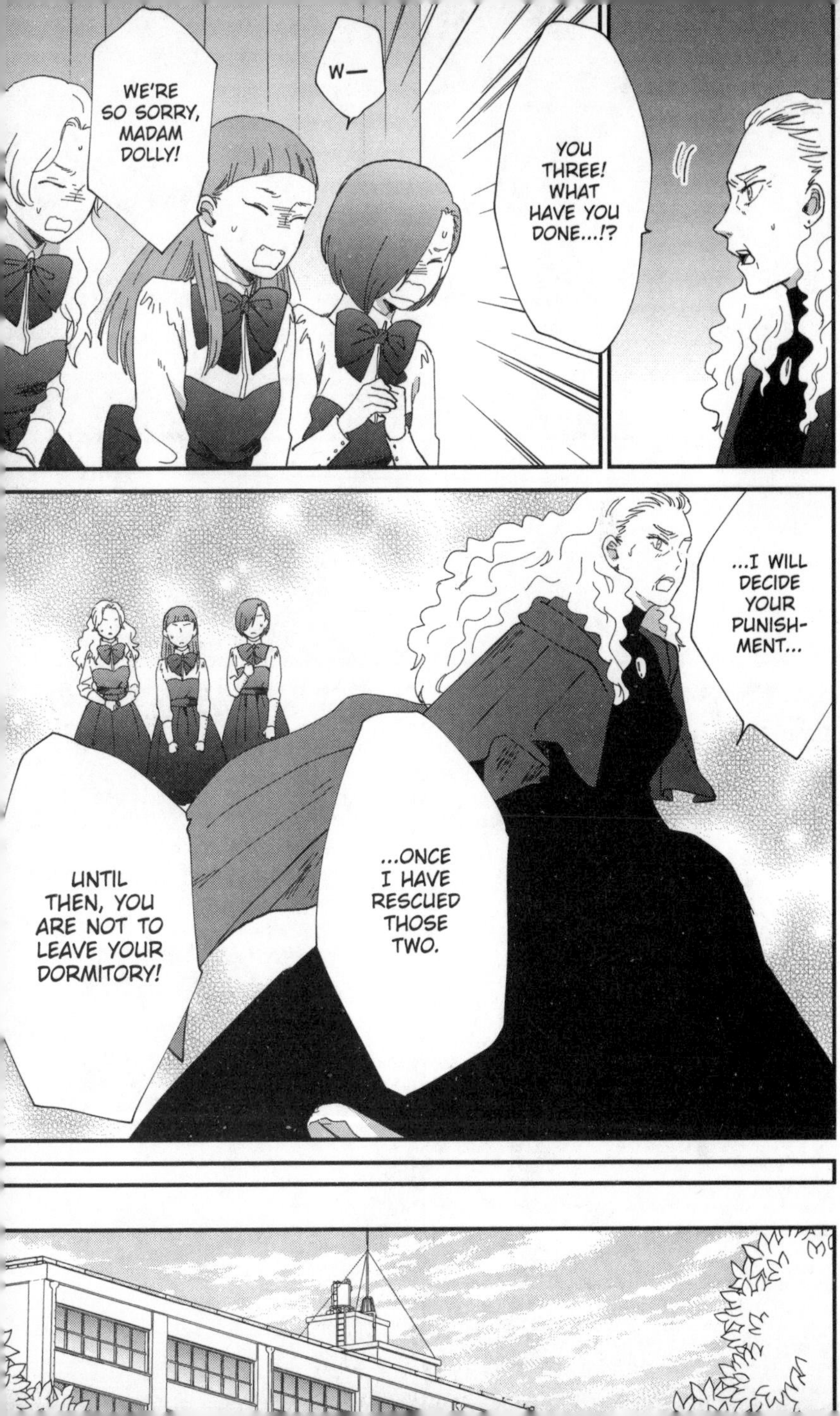
YOU THREE! WHAT HAVE YOU DONE...!?
W—
WE'RE SO SORRY, MADAM DOLLY!
...I WILL DECIDE YOUR PUNISH-MENT...
...ONCE I HAVE RESCUED THOSE TWO.
UNTIL THEN, YOU ARE NOT TO LEAVE YOUR DORMITORY!

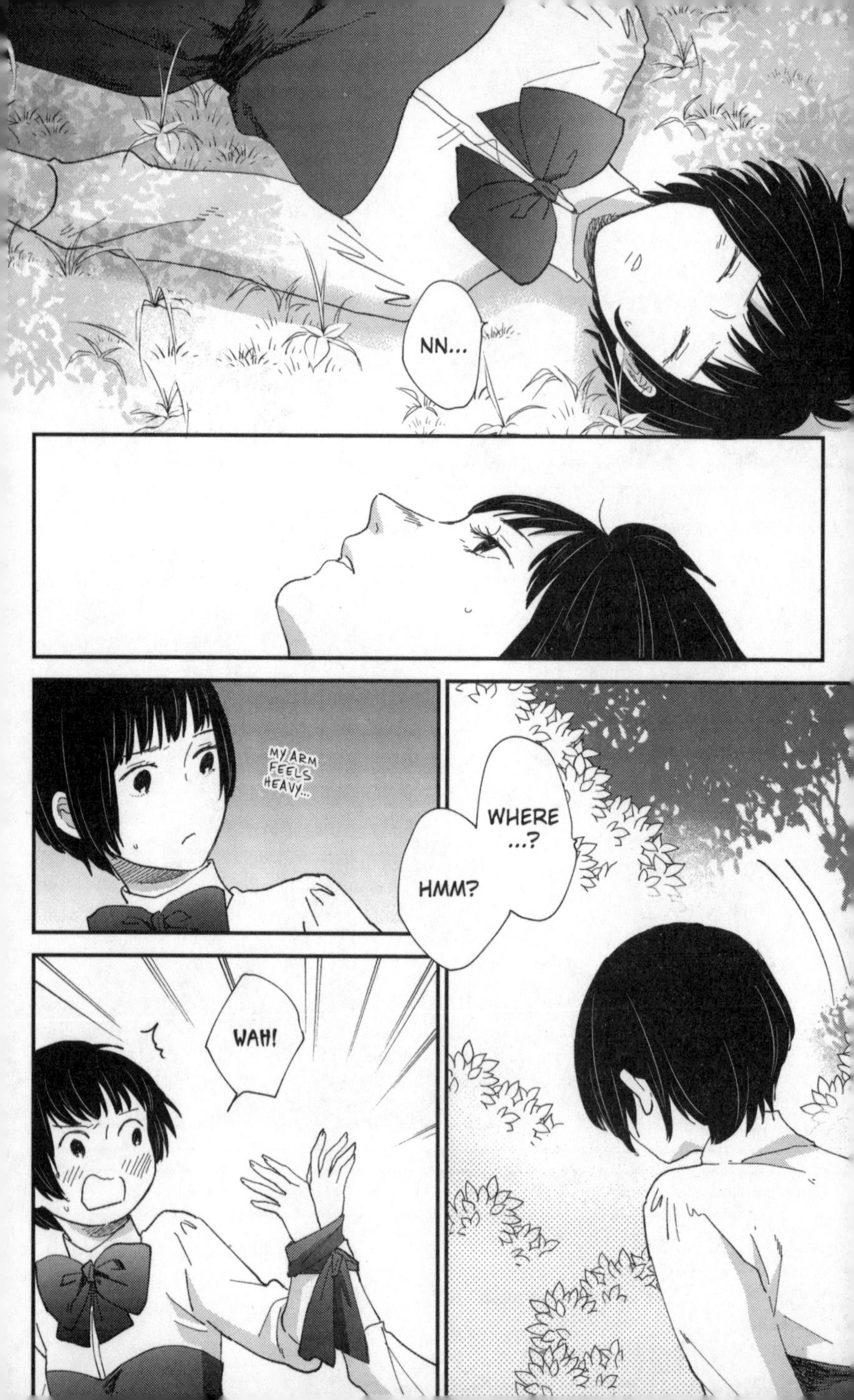
NN...
WHERE ...?
HMM?
MY ARM FEELS HEAVY...
WAH!

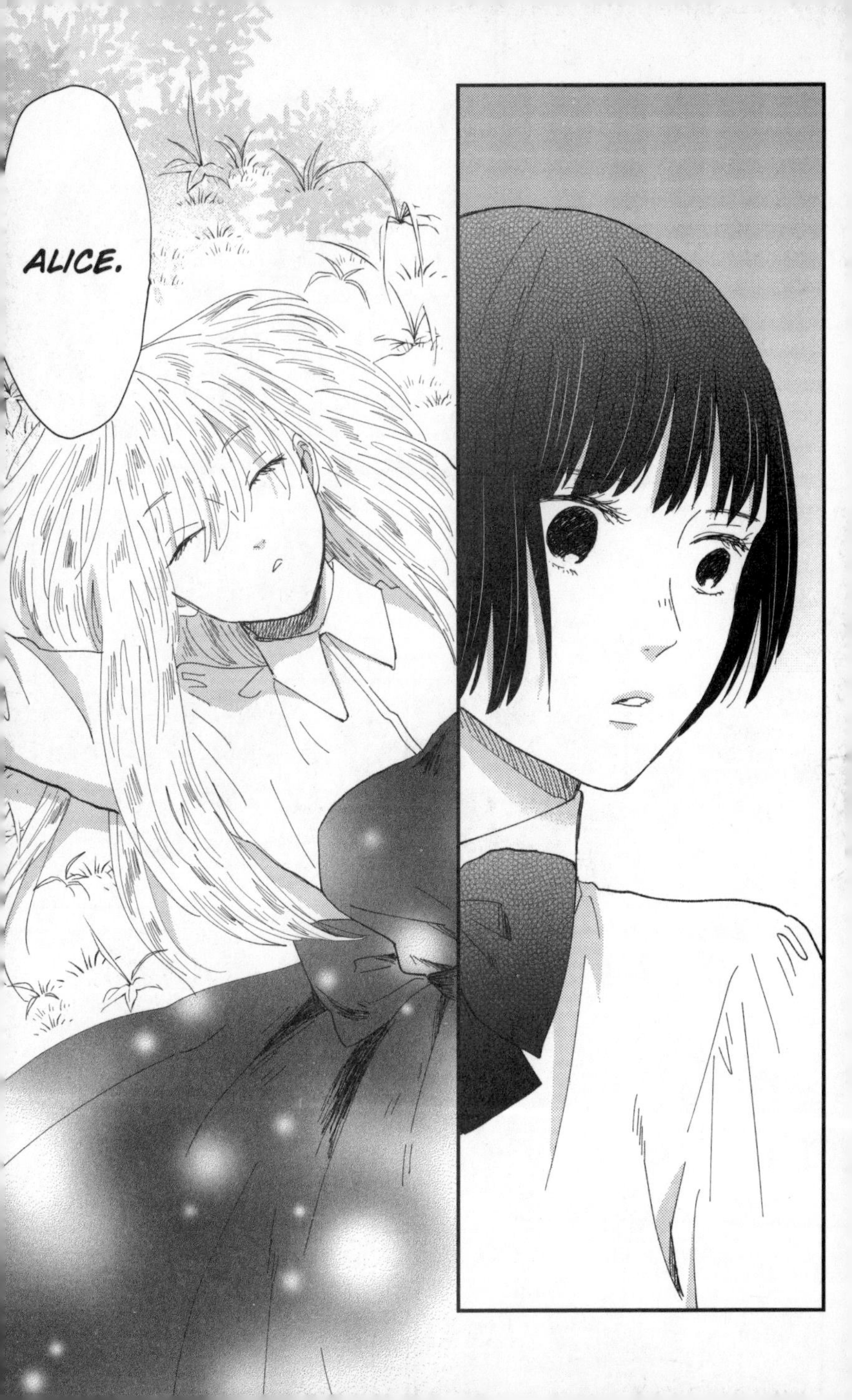
ALICE.

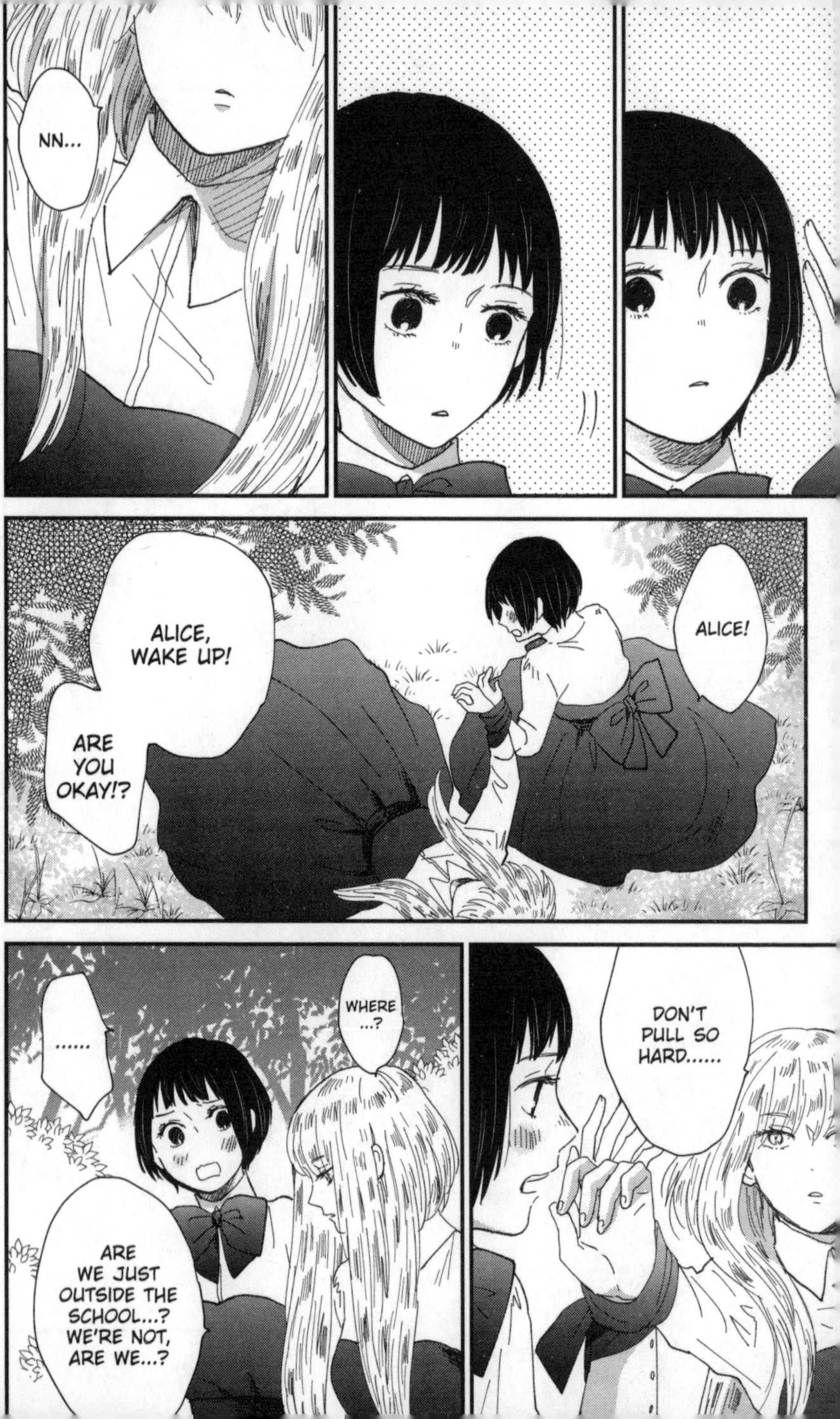
NN...
ALICE!
ALICE, WAKE UP! ARE YOU OKAY!?
DON'T PULL SO HARD......
WHERE ...?
......
ARE WE JUST OUTSIDE THE SCHOOL...? WE'RE NOT, ARE WE...?

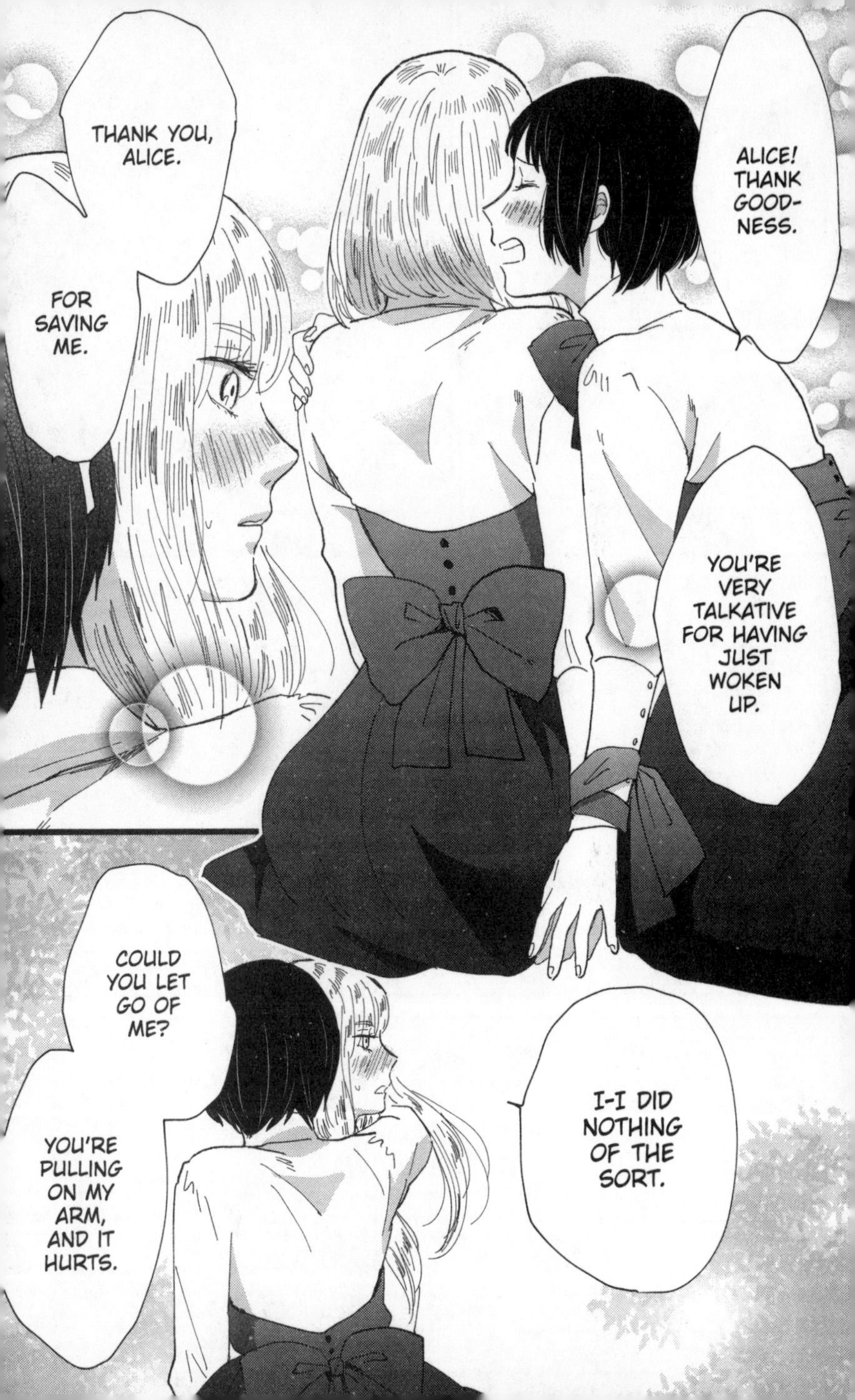
ALICE! THANK GOODNESS.
THANK YOU, ALICE.
FOR SAVING ME.
YOU'RE VERY TALKATIVE FOR HAVING JUST WOKEN UP.
I-I DID NOTHING OF THE SORT.
COULD YOU LET GO OF ME?
YOU'RE PULLING ON MY ARM, AND IT HURTS.

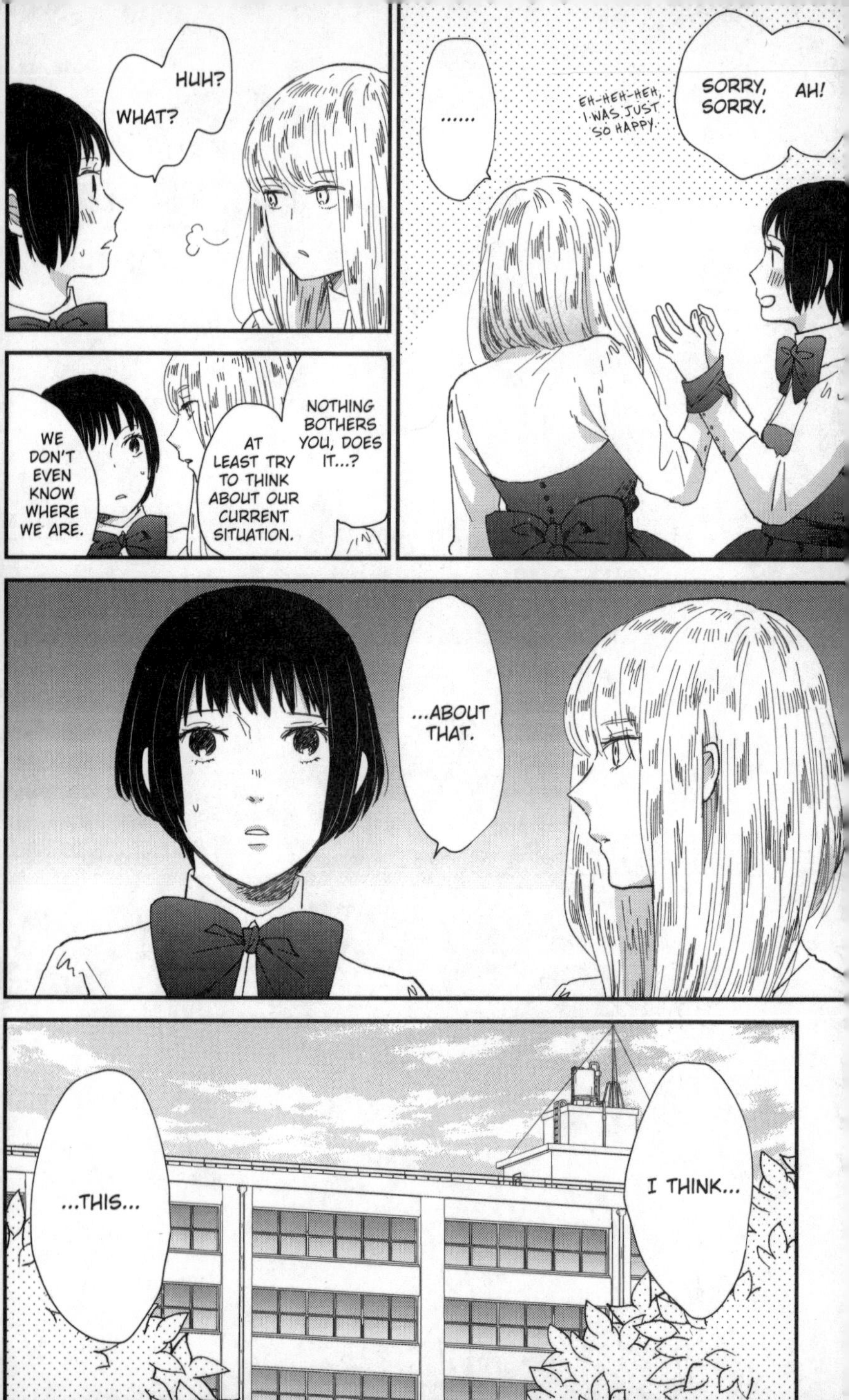
AH!
SORRY, SORRY.
EH-HEH-HEH, I WAS JUST SO HAPPY.
......
HUH?
WHAT?
NOTHING BOTHERS YOU, DOES IT...?
AT LEAST TRY TO THINK ABOUT OUR CURRENT SITUATION.
WE DON'T EVEN KNOW WHERE WE ARE.
...ABOUT THAT.
I THINK...
...THIS...

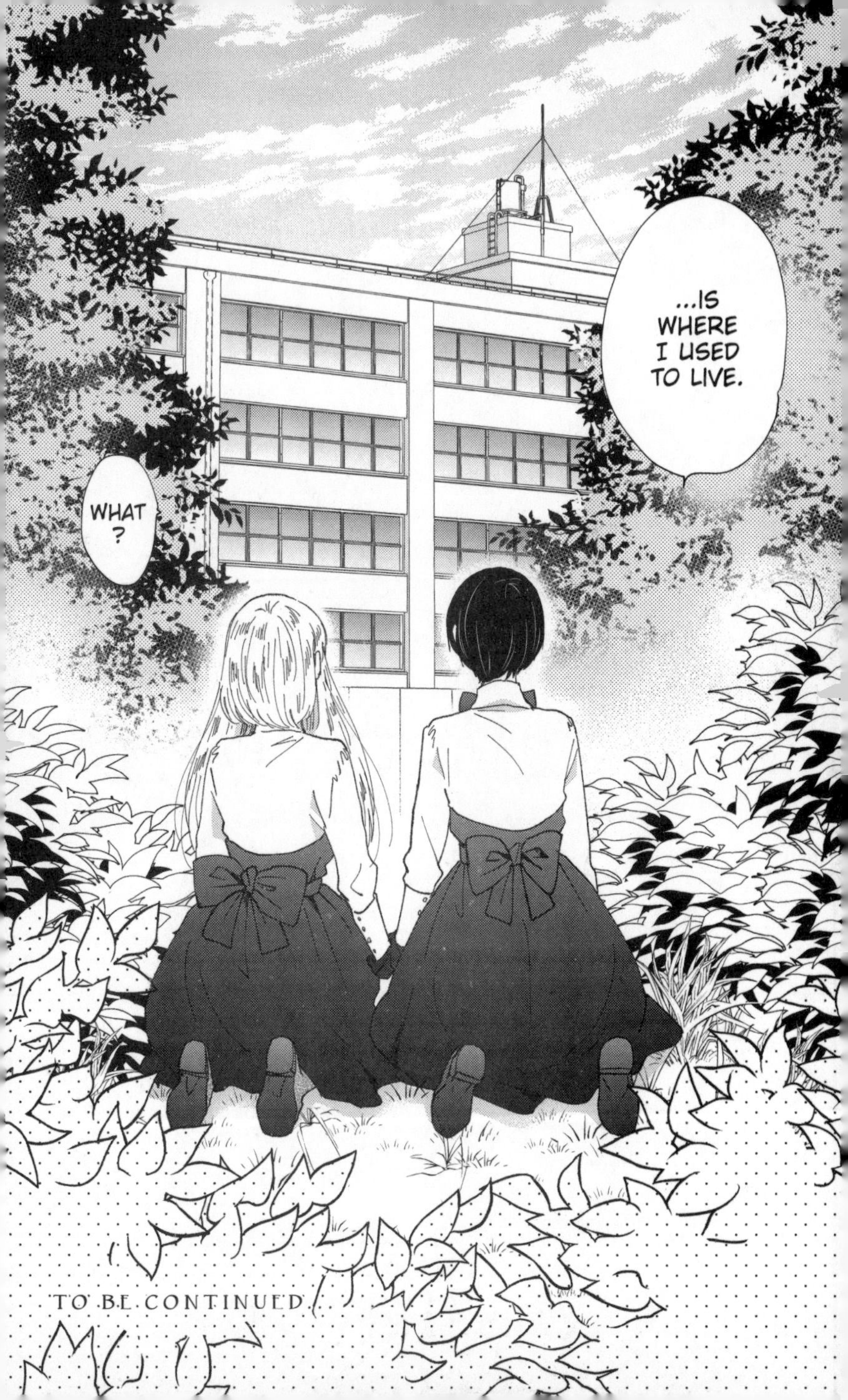
...IS WHERE I USED TO LIVE.
WHAT?
TO BE CONTINUED

A Witch's Love at the End of the World

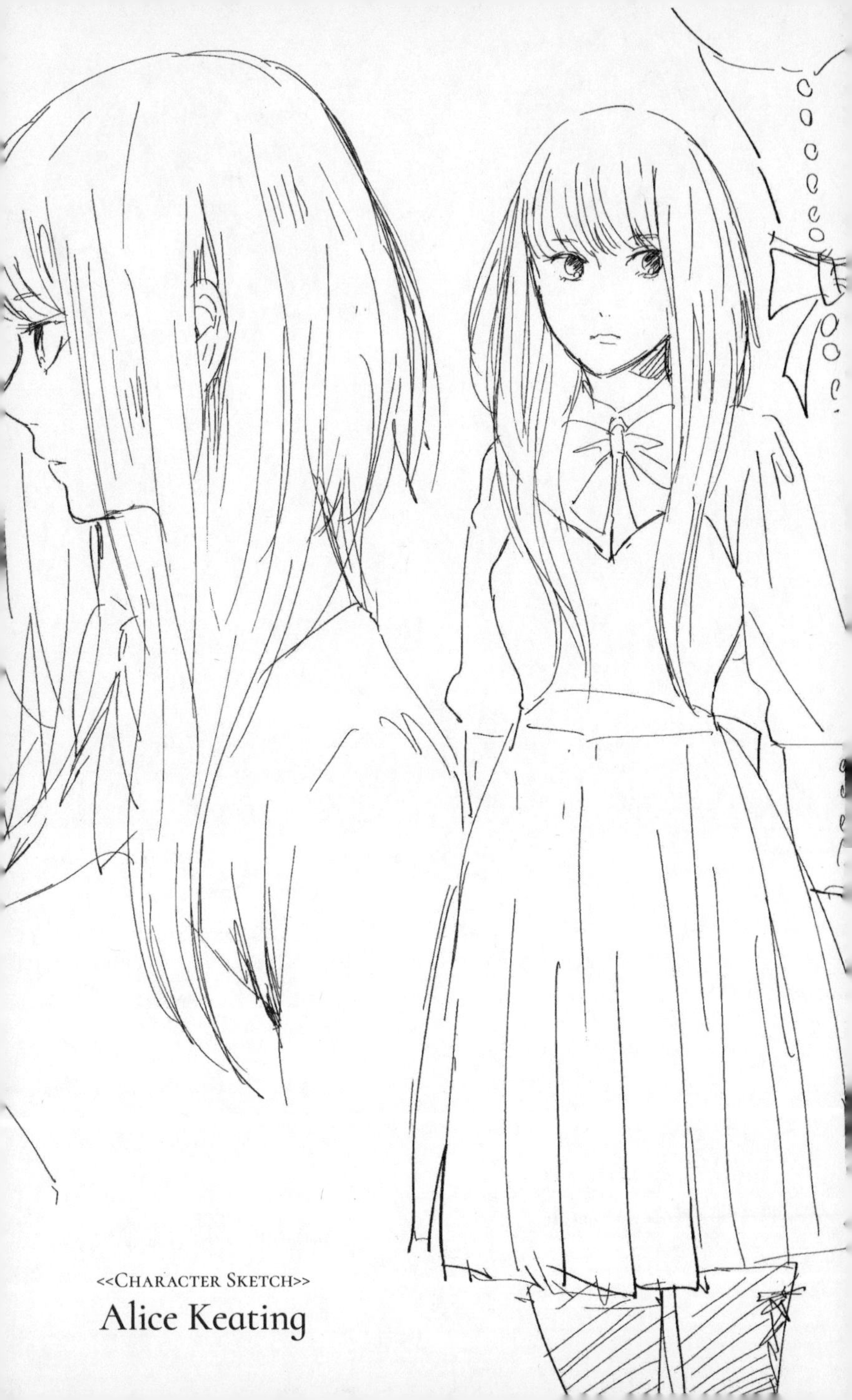

<<Character Sketch>>

Alice Keating

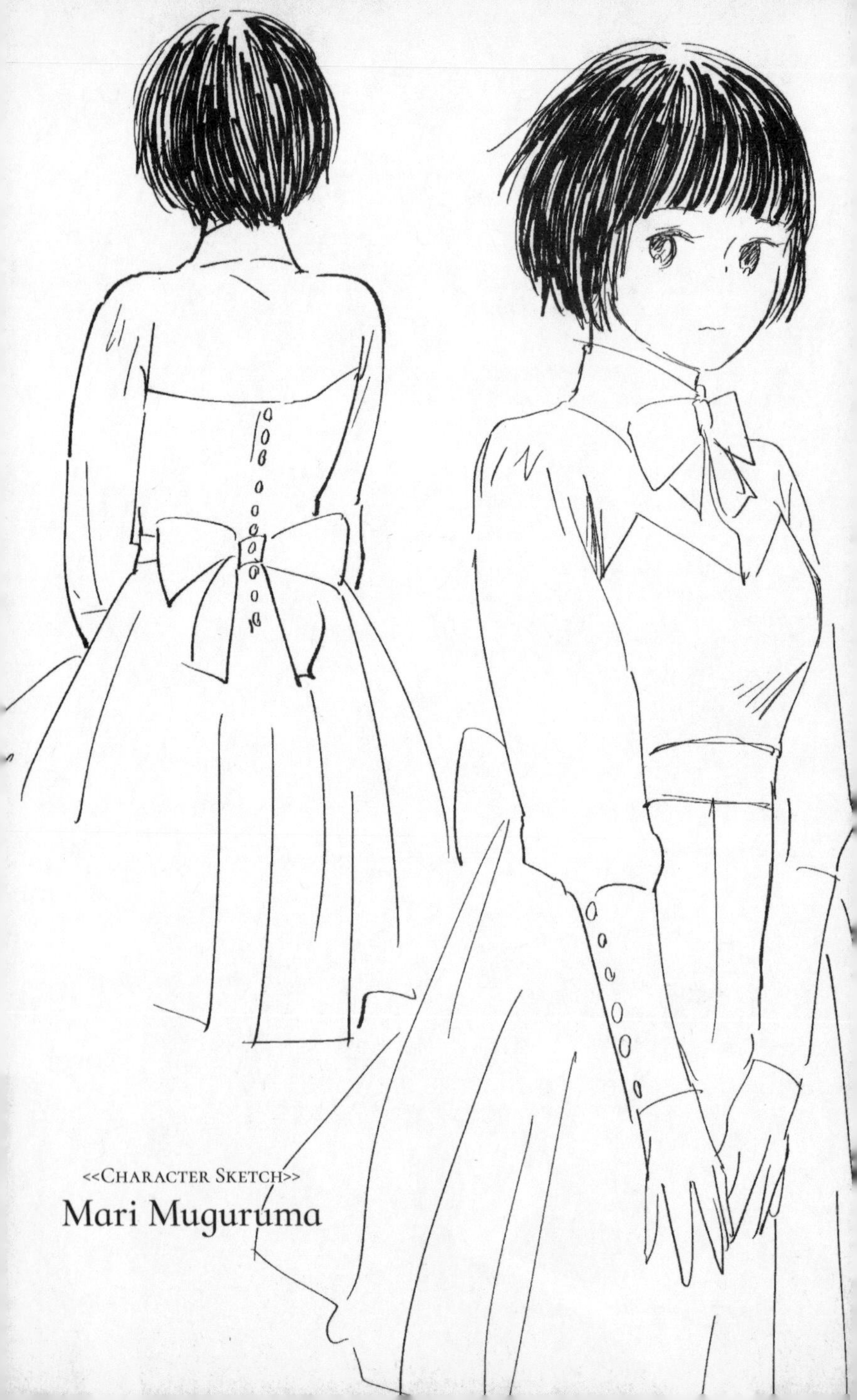

<<Character Sketch>>

Mari Muguruma

Afterword

Thank you for purchasing *A Witch's Love at the End of the World, Volume 1.*

It's a lot of fun getting to draw so many girls.

As a child, I loved witches, and I still like them even as an adult...

I dreamed of one day writing a manga about young witches.

I am very happy that dream came true.

I look forward to seeing you in Volume 2.

Kujira

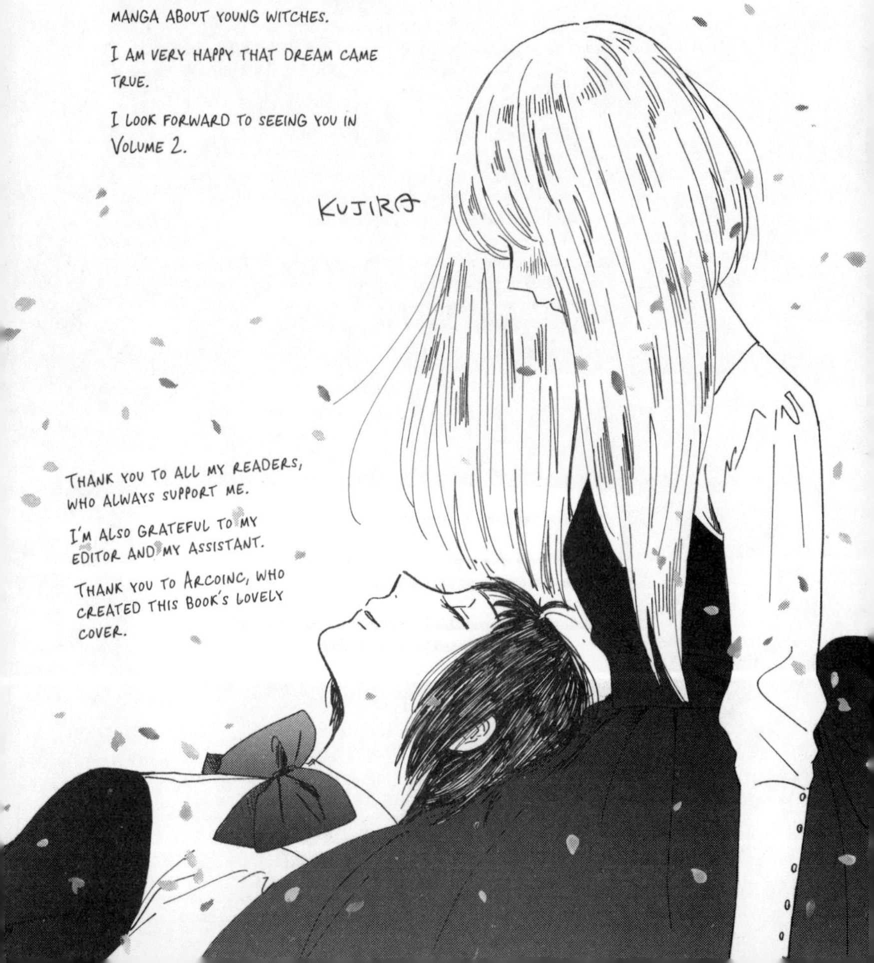

Thank you to all my readers, who always support me.

I'm also grateful to my editor and my assistant.

Thank you to Arcoinc, who created this book's lovely cover.

A Witch's Love at the End of the World

I

KUJIRA

TRANSLATION: **ELEANOR SUMMERS** ❧ LETTERING: **SARA LINSLEY**

SEKAI NO OWARI TO MAJO NO KOI, Vol. 1
©KUJIRA 2019
First published in Japan in 2019 by KADOKAWA CORPORATION, Tokyo. English translation rights arranged with KADOKAWA CORPORATION, Tokyo, through Tuttle-Mori Agency, Inc.

English translation © 2020 by Yen Press, LLC

Yen Press
150 West 30th Street, 19th Floor
New York, NY 10001

Visit us at yenpress.com • facebook.com/yenpress • twitter.com/yenpress • yenpress.tumblr.com • instagram.com/yenpress

The Y

The

Library of Congress Control Number: 2020944856

ISBNs: 978-1-9753-1803-1 (paperback)
978-1-9753-1804-8 (ebook)

10 9 8 7 6 5 4 3 2 1

WOR

Printed in the United States of America